KARL-MARX
VERLAG

A Collection of Scattered Articles and Letters of Proudhon
Author: Pierre-Joseph Proudhon
Editor: Lingkai Kong

✻ ✻ ✻ ✻ ✻ ✻ ✻ ✻ ✻ ✻ ✻ ✻ ✻ ✻ ✻
Copyright @ Karl-Marx Verlag 2024
This publication is in copyright. Subject to statutory exception and to the provision of relevant collective licensing agreements, no reproduction of any part may take place without the permission of Karl-Marx Verlag.
✻ ✻ ✻ ✻ ✻ ✻ ✻ ✻ ✻ ✻ ✻ ✻ ✻ ✻ ✻

ISBN: 978-3-9825536-2-7 (paperback)

Front cover image by Spotii Media
Type set in Palatino Linotype & Times New Roman
Printed in Paris, France / Potsdam, Germany
Published by **Karl-Marx Verlag**
Burgstraße 23
14467 Potsdam, Germany

A Collection of Scattered Articles and Letters of Proudhon

Pierre-Joseph Proudhon

Edited by
Lingkai Kong

KARL-MARX
VERLAG

[This page intentionally left blank.]

A Collection of Scattered Articles and Letters

of Proudhon

[This page intentionally left blank.]

Content

Content .... *I*
Acknowledgement .... *IV*

1837 1
   Application for the Suard Pension 2
1839 12
   The Celebration of Sunday 13
1840 101
   Letter to the Members of the Academy of Besançon 102
1842 106
   Explanations Presented to the Public Minister on the Right of Property 107
   Letter to Bergmann 137
1845 140
   My Testament: or, Society of Avengers 141
1846 150
   Proudhon To Marx 151
1847 154
   On the Jews 155
1848 157
   Letter to Jeanne Deroin 158
   The Malthusians, the Representatives of the People 161
   Toast to the Revolution 171
1849 186
   God is Evil, Man is Free 187
   In Connection with Louis Blanc: The Present Use and Future Possibility of the State 211
   Interest and Principal: A Loan is a Service 224

Interest and Principal: Arguments Drawn from the Operations of the Bank of France 234
Interest and Principal: The Origin of Ground Rent .243
Interest and Principle: The Circulation of Capital, Not Capital Itself, Gives Birth to Progress 249
Letter to Pierre Leroux 256
Parliamentary Isolation 267
The Coming Era of Mutualism 268
The Nature and Destination of Government 271
The State: Its Nature, Object, and Destiny 282
What is Government? What is God? 308

1850 319
Dilemma: Red or White 320

1851 326
Letter to A. M. Boutteville 327
Letter to Langlois 332

1852 336
The Extremes 337
The Social Revolution Demonstrated by the Coup d'Etat of December 2, 1851 340
Unanimity: Universal Consent 346

1855 350
New Propositions Demonstrated in the Practice of Revolutions 351
Propositions: To Leave Behind Abstractions, Utopias, Systems, Doctrines, Theories and Empiricisms of the Parties Schools and Sects 356

1857 363
Letter to Villiaumé 364

1861 366

Relation of the State and Liberty, According to Modern Right 367
The Theory of Taxation 374
1864 388
Letter to Several Workers in Paris and Rouen 389

Index 392

Acknowledgement

All articles in this collection are sourced from the list of Proudhon on the online forum: www.marxists.org. In the Proudhon list, Andy Carloff is credited with the role of "Transcription/Markup" for all articles. The editor expresses the highest respect and gratitude for his contributions.

Gratitude is extended to the anonymous discussants who contributed to the forum discussions, as well as to the translators who rendered these texts from French into English. For some works, translator information is available, and I have listed the translator's name alongside the titles of the works. For the majority of works, translator information is not available.

This collection consolidates these scattered works of Proudhon to provide researchers with citation sources in a paper format. The editing of this collection is a non-profit project. The price of the paper version will be set to the minimum, just enough to cover the printing costs. The editor pledges not to derive any profit from this book. After the publication of the book, the electronic version in PDF will be made public immediately.

Editor: Lingkai Kong
December, 2024. Istanbul, Turkey

1837

Application for the Suard Pension

Besançon, May 31, 1837.

Pierre-Joseph Proudhon, Candidate for the Suard Pension

To the Gentlemen of the Académie De Besancon.

Gentlemen, I am a compositor and proofreader, son of a poor craftsman who, as the father of three boys, could never bear the cost of three apprenticeships. I knew evil and trouble early; my youth, to use a very popular expression, was passed through a fine sieve. Just so Suard, Marmontel, and a host of writers and scholars struggled with fortune. May you, gentlemen, upon reading this memoir, have the thought that between so many men famous for the gifts of intelligence, and the one who now seeks your votes, the community of misfortune is perhaps not the only point of resemblance.

First destined to a mechanical profession, I was, on the advice of a friend of my father, placed as a free day student at the Collége de Besançon. But what was the delivery of 120 francs for a family where food and clothing was always a problem? I normally lacked the most necessary books; I did all my Latin studies without a dictionary; after having translated into Latin everything that my memory supplied, I left blank the words that I didn't know, and, at the door of the school, I filled the empty spaced. I was punished a hundred for having forgotten my books, but the fact was that I did not have them. All my off were filled by labor, either in the fields or in the house, in order to save a day of labor; on holidays, I went to the woods myself to seek the stock of hoops that would supply the shop of my father, a cooper by profession. What studies could I make with such a method? What meager success I was able to obtain!

At the end of my ninth year [quatrième], my prize was Fenelon's *Démonstration de l'existence de Dieu*. That book seemed to suddenly open my mind and illuminate my thought. I was heard to speak of materialists and atheists: I was anxious to learn how they went about denying God.

I will admit, however, that the philosophy of Descartes, embellished with the eloquence of Fénelon, did not entirely satisfy me. I sensed God, and my soul was permeated with him; captured from childhood by that great idea, it boiled over in me and dominated all my faculties. And in a book written to prove the existence of the Supreme Being, I only encountered a shaking metaphysics whose deductions had the appearance of a more practical hypothesis, but did not resemble a certain, scientific theory. Allow me, Gentlemen, to offer you an example. The soul cannot perish, say that Cartesians, because it is immaterial and simple. But why can something which has begun to be not cease to exist? What then? The soul, in its durations, would be infinite and eternal on one side, but limited on the other? That is inconceivable. — Matter, say the same philosophers, is not the necessary Being, because it is obviously contingent, dependent and passive. So it has been created. But how are we to conceive of the creation of matter by mind, rather than the production of mind by matter? One is a inconceivable as the other. So I remained what I was, a believer in God and the immortality of the soul, but, I ask the pardon of philosophy for it, that was less because of the evidence of its syllogisms than the weakness of the opposing arguments. It seemed to me that from then on it was necessary to follow another road to establish philosophy as science, and I never came back to that opinion of my youth.

I pursued my classics through the miseries of my family, and all the aversions with which a sensitive young man can be showered and the most *irritable* self-esteem. Apart from sickness and the bad state of his business, my father pursued a legal suit that completed his ruin. The very day when the judgment was to be pronounced, I was to be awarded with *excellence*. I came with a very sad heart to that formality where everything seemed to laugh at me; fathers and mothers embraced their laureate sons and applauded their triumphs, while my family was in court, awaiting the decision.

I will always remember it. — The rector asked me if I wanted to be presented to some relative or fried, in order to pour be crowned by their hand.

"I have no one here, Rector," I responded.

"Well!" he added, "I will crown and embrace you."

Never, Gentlemen, have I felt such a shock. I found my family distressed, my mother in tears: our trial was lost. That night, we all supped on bread and water.

1837: Application for the Suard Pension

I dragged myself along as far as rhetoric: it was my last year of secondary school. I had to provide for my own food and upkeep. — "Presently," my father said to me, "you must know your trade; at eighteen, I earned my bread, and I did not have such a long apprenticeship." — I found that he was right, and I joined a printing shop.

I hoped for some time that the trade of proofreader would allow me to resume my abandoned studies at the very moment when they demanded greater efforts and new activity. The works of Bossuet, the Bergiers, etc., would pass before my eyes; I learned the laws of reasoning and style with these great masters. Soon I believed that I was called to be an apologist for Christianity, and I read the books of its enemies and defenders. Must I tell you, Gentlemen? In the raging furnace of controversy, often being fascinated by imaginations and only hearing my inner feelings, I gradually saw my dear and precious beliefs disappear; I would successively profess all the heresies condemned by the Church and related by the dictionary of Abbot Pluquet; I detached from one only to sink into the opposite, until finally, from weariness, I stopped at the last and perhaps most unreasonable of all: I was Socinian. I fell into a deep despondency.

However, the political commotions and my private misery tore me from my solitary meditations, and I threw myself more and more into the whirlwind of active life. To live, I had to leave my city and homeland, take up costume and staff of the *compagnon* of the *tour de France,* and seek, from print shop to print shop, some lines to compose, some proofs to read. One day, I sold my school prize, the only library I had ever possessed. My mother cried; for me, there remained the manuscripts extracts from my readings. These extracts, which could not be sold, followed and consoled me everywhere. I wandered part of France in this way, sometimes exposed to lack of work and bread for having dared tell the truth to a boss who, in response, brutally dismissed me. That same year, employed at Paris as a proofreader, I was almost once again the victim of my provincial pride; and without the support of my coworkers, who defended me against the unjust accusations of a foreman, I would perhaps have seen myself, urged by hunger, obliged to hire myself out to some journalist. Despite all the privations and miseries that I had endured, that extremity appeared to me the most horrible of all.

The life of man is never so suffering and abandoned that it is not strewn with some consolations. I had encountered a friend in a young man that fortune tormented, as much as myself, by the moral conflicts and the sting of poverty. He was named Gustave Fallot.[1] In the depths of a workshop, I received a letter one day, inviting me to leave everything and go join my friend… — "You are unfortunate," he said to me, "and the life you lead does not suit you. Proudhon, we are brothers: as long as I have bread and I room, I will share it all with you. Come here, and we will or perish together." Then, Gentlemen, he himself addressed to you a memoir and present himself to you votes as a candidate for the Suard pension. Without saying anything about it to me, he proposed, if he obtained the preference over his friends, to abandon to me the enjoyment of that pension, reserving for himself the glory of the and the use of the

---

[1] M. Gustave Fallot was the first Suard resident.

1837: Application for the Suard Pension

precious advantages that are attached to it. — "If I am appointed in the month of August," he said to me, without explaining more, "our career will begin in the month of August." I flew to his call, and arrived to find him, stricken by cholera, consume his last resources for me, and arrive at death's door without it being possible for me to continue my care for him. The lack of money no longer permitted us to remain together; we had to separate, and I embraced him for the last time. Last January 25, I spent an hour meditating at his tomb.

Fifty francs in my pocket, a sack on my back, and my philosophy notebooks for provisions, I set out for the south of France... But, Gentlemen, it would be an abuse of your patience to detail for you here, in minute detail and in chronological order, all that I have suffered in my body and heart. What does it matter to you, after all, that I have been more or less shaken by fortune? It is not enough, to earn your choice, to have only poverty to offer, and your votes do not seek an adventurer. However, if I do not uncover my calamitous existence, who will recommend me to your attention? Who will speak for me? Such has been to this day, and such is still my life: living in the workshops, witness of the vises and virtues of the people, eating my bread earned each day by the sweat of my brow, obliged, with my modest wages, to assist my family and contribute to the education of my brothers; in the midst of all that, pondering, philosophizing, gathering the least of unexpected observations.

Fatigued by the precarious and miserable condition of being a workers, I wished in the end to attempt, together with one of my fellows, to organize a small printing business. The meager savings of the two friends were put in common and all the resources of their families cast in that lottery. The treacherous game of business deceived our hope: order, labo, economy, nothing served; the two partners, one went to the corner of a wood to die of exhaustion and despair, the other has no more to repent than having cut into the last piece of bread of his father.

Pardon me once more, Gentlemen, if, instead of exhibiting some real titles to your benevolence, I only show you my misfortune. Unknown to the majority of you, I must, it seems to me, tell you what I have been, what I am. It is not , moreover, without some repugnance that I have consented to recount to you some of the circumstances of my life, and to disclose to you the habitual state of my mind and character. Such confidences only appear to me well put between equals and friends. — "Well!" a man that I love and revere tells me, "Do you want to please the Gentlemen of the Academy? Speak to them as friend." — Would he be deceived, and would my confidence lead me to a bad end?

In 1836-1837, a long sickness having forced me to interrupt my labor in the workshop, I returned to study. Some fortunate enough attempts at criticism and sacred philosophy had given a new impetus to my literary and determined my penchant for philosophical speculations. In the insomnia of fever and the leisure of a laborious convalescence, I gave myself up to some researches on grammar that appeared important enough to merit your examination. Two copies of my work were addressed to you; but the immense labors of your learned company

1837: Application for the Suard Pension

alone have, until now, I at least dare to presume, delayed your judgment.

If, however, the weak composition that was submitted to you could answer for the one that I am preparing; if the presentation of my first glimpses sufficiently guarantee the accuracy of the ideas that I elaborate; if you would desire, Gentlemen, to see brought to the end new and fertile studies, would it be allowed to the one who already, since a year ago, has placed himself at your bench for trial, to count a bit more on your indulgent benevolence than on the doubtful hopes of his talent and the regard due to the extreme modesty of his fortune?

To see new regions in psychology, new ways in philosophy; to study the nature and mechanism of the human mind in the most obvious and most perceptible of his faculties, speech; to determine, according to the origin and processes of language, the source and line of descent of human beliefs; to apply, in short, grammar to metaphysics and morals, and to realize a thought that torments profound geniuses, that preoccupied Fallot, that our Pauthier pursued: such is, Gentlemen, the task that I would impose on myself if you would grant me the books and time; the books above all! The time will never be lacking to me.

After all the vicissitudes of my ideas and the long parturition of my soul, I had to finish, I have finished by creating for myself a complete, linked system of religious and philosophical beliefs, a system that I can reduce to this simple formula:

1837: Application for the Suard Pension

There exists, of superhuman origin, a primitive philosophy or religion, corrupted since before any of the historical eras, of which the cults of the different nations have preserved some authentic and homologues vestiges. The majority of the Christian dogmas themselves are only the summary expression of so many demonstrable propositions; and we can, by the comparative study of religious systems, by the attentive examination of the formation of languages, and independent of every other revelation, observe the reality of the truths that the Catholic faith imposes, truths inexplicable in themselves, but accessible to the understanding. From that principle can be deduced, by a series of strict consequences, a traditional philosophy the ensemble of which will constitute an exact science.

Such is today, Gentlemen, the compendium of my profession of faith.

Born and raised in the heart of the working classes, still belonging to it in my heart and affections, and especially through the sufferings and wishes, my greatest joy, if I gather your suffrages, would be, do not doubt it, Gentlemen, to be able to work from now on without rest, by science and philosophy, with all the energy of my will and all the powers of my mind, at the moral and intellectual improvement of those whom I am happy to call my brothers and companions; to be able to spread among them the seeds of a doctrine that I regard as the law of the moral world; and, while awaiting the success of my efforts, directed by your prudence, to already find myself, in some way, as their representative to you.

But, whatever your choice, Gentlemen, I submit to it in advance and applaud it; followig the example of an ancient, I would rejoice if you find one more worthy than me: Proudhon, accustomed from childhood to sharpen his courage against the adversity, would never had the pride to believe himself a disdained and unsung genius...

P.-J. Proudhon.

1839

The Celebration of Sunday

Preface

The celebrated Sir Francis Bacon was called the reformer of human reason for having replaced the syllogism with observation in the natural sciences; the philosophers, following his example, teach today that philosophy is a collection of observations and facts. But, certain thinkers have said to them, if truth and certainty exist in *philosophy*, they must also exist in the realm of *politics*: thus, there is a social science responsive to evidence, which is consequently the object of demonstration, not of art or authority, not, that is, of arbitrary will.

This conclusion, so profound in its simplicity, so innovative in its consequences, has been the signal for a vast intellectual movement, comparable with that which manifested itself in the Roman empire, at the time of the establishment of Christianity. We have set ourselves to seek the *new science*; and as the investigation cannot begin with anything but critique, we have arrived methodically at the negation of everything that makes up and sustains society.

Thus we have asked: What is royalty? And the response has been: A myth.

What is religion? — A dream of the mind.

What is God? — An eternal X.

What is property? — It is theft.

What is community? — It is death.

Christianity signaled its entry into the world in absolutely the same way; before positing its dogma, it said to itself:

What is Cesar? — Nothing.

What is the republic? — Nothing.

What is Jupiter? — Nothing.

What is nobility, philosophy, glory? — Nothing.

The negation that Christianity began against ancient society was then pursued against Christianity itself; and we told ourselves that the truth would appear to us only after we had demolished everything. When will this be accomplished? But, if the present and the past cannot give us truth in its essential form, they contain it substantially, since truth is eternal, and eternally manifests itself. It is thus as much in the institutions that have been destroyed, or are at the point of disappearing, as it is in the facts that spring up anew each day, that we should seek truth in itself, the face-to-face contemplation of the absolute, *siculi est, facie ad faciem*.

Among the monuments of antiquity, the laws of Moses are unquestionably those that have most occupied the meditations of the savants. For ourselves, the sublimity of the mosaic system would astonish us, perhaps, if we did not know that by virtue of the laws of human understanding, every primitive idea being necessarily universal, every primitive legislation must have been a summary of philosophy, a rudiment of knowledge. What we have taken for profundity and divine inspiration in Moses and the other legislators of antiquity was, at base, only a general intuition and aphoristic conception; as for its form, it was the living and spontaneous expression of the first apperceptions of consciousness.

But how did the Sabbath become, in the thought of Moses, the pivot and rallying symbol of Jewish society? Another law of the intelligence will explain it to us.

In the sphere of pure ideas, everything is connected, supported and demonstrated, not according to the order of filiation, or the principle of consequences, but according to the order of coexistence or coordination of relations. Here, as in the universe, the center is everywhere and the circumference nowhere; that is, everything is at once principle and consequence, axis and radius. Moses, having to formulate the totality of his laws by deduction, was free to choose for the culminating point of his system whatever economic or moral idea he wanted. He preferred the weekly division of time, because he needed a sensible and powerful symbol which constantly recalled to the hordes of semi-savage Israel the feelings of nationality, fraternity and unity, without which any subsequent development was impossible. The Sabbath was like the common meeting ground where all the Hebrews should gather themselves in spirit, at the beginning of each week; the monument that expressed their political existence, the link that held together all their institutions. Thus, public and civil right, municipal administration, education, government, worship, customs, hygiene, family and city relations, *liberty, public order*: the Sabbath supposed all these things, fortified them and created their harmony.

The author of this discourse has been reproved for lending to Moses views that could not have been his own, but this reproach is unreasonable. Today, it is much less a question of knowing what the individual who wrote them thought of these laws, than it is to know the very spirit of his legislation. Certainly Moses was not thinking of the Catholics or protestants; however, the vigor of the institution of the Sabbath was such, that the Jews passed it on to the Christians and the Mohammedans; that from them it extended around the globe; and that it will outlive all the religions, embracing within its vast reach prehistoric times and the most distant future ages.

We do not know who first imagined the division of time into weeks. It doubtless sprung from that spontaneous genius, a sort of magnetic vision, which discovered the first arts, developed language, invented writing, created systems of religion and philosophy: a marvelous faculty, the processes of which elude analysis, and that reflection, another rival and progressive faculty, weakens gradually without ever being able to make it disappear.

Today, when the questions of labor and wages, of industrial organization and national workshops, of political and social reform, occupy public attention to the highest degree, we believe a legislation based on a theory *of repose*, if we can put it this way, could be useful. Nothing comparable to the Sabbath, before or since the legislator of the Sinai, has been imagined and put into practice. Sunday, the Christian Sabbath, for which respect seems to have diminished, will be revived in all its splendor, when the guarantee of labor is won, with the well-being that is its prize. The working classes are too interested in the maintenance of the dominical holiday to ever let it perish. Thus all will celebrate the day, even though they don't attend the mass: and the people will see, by this example, how it is possible that a religion be false, and the contents of that religion be true at the same time; that to philosophize about dogma is to renounce faith; to transform a religion is to abolish it. The priests, with their scientific tendencies, march toward that inevitable conclusion: let them pardon us for having gone before them, and not refuse us the final benediction, because we have arrived first at the tomb of religion.

The Celebration of Sunday

"Remember the Sabbath day, to keep it holy.

"Six days shall thou labor, and do all thy work.

"But the seventh day is the rest of the Lord: in it thou shall not do any work, thou, nor thy son, nor thy daughter, thy manservant, nor thy maidservant, nor thy cattle, nor thy stranger that is within thy gates.

"For in six days the Lord made heaven and earth, the sea, and all that in them is, and rested the seventh day: That is why the Eternal has hallowed and blessed the day of rest."

Such is the literal text of the fourth paragraph of the first article of the Charter given to the Hebrews by Moses, and known under the name of the DECALOGUE.[2]

It is a question of penetrating the spirit, the motives and the aim of that law, or, to put it better, of that institution, that Moses and the prophets would always regard as fundamental, and to which we can find nothing comparable among any of the peoples who have had a written legislation; an institution the whole scope of which even the most celebrated critics—Grotius, Cunéus, Spencer, Dom Calmet, l'abbé de Vence, P. Berruyer, Bergier, etc.—have not grasped; of which Montesquieu has not even spoken, because he did not understand it; that J.-J. Rousseau seems to have sensed, however far his thought was from it; an institution, finally, which our modern genius, with all its theories of political and civil

---

[2] In our catechisms, the division of Decalogue is different from that which is presented here. According to the Hebrews, the first commandment teaches the *unity* of God; the second forbids the *fabrication of images*; it is an artificial, political. These two commandments have been merged into only one. The third forbids *taking the name of God in vain*; that prohibition is at once political and religious, completely within the customs of antiquity. We recognize here that *Punic faith*, to which imprecations and oaths cost nothing; Moses ordained that the oath by Jehovah would be inviolable. That precept is for us the second; it commands, it is said, to avoid *foul words and swearing*. The fourth commandment concerns the Sabbath. The tenth (for us the seventh), concerning covetousness, has been divided in two, in order to preserve the number 10. It is, on the one hand, the prohibition against desiring one's neighbor's wife; on the other, the prohibition against coveting his ox or his ass, etc. But in Moses this distinction does not exist.

right, with its niceties of constitutions and its vague desires for liberty and equality, has never measured up to. We know that, from the origins of Christianity, the weekly celebration of rest was transferred from Saturday, or the day of Saturn, to the following day, the day of the Sun; and that, in the thought of the Apostles, there should not exist, between the mosaic Sabbath and the Christian Sunday, any difference but a delay of twenty-four hours. The day of the observance was transferred for two reasons: to honor the resurrection of Christ, and to radically separate the two religions. Beyond that, neither the thing nor its spirit were changed; the obligation and the purpose of the precept remained the same. The intention of the reformers, as faithful disciples of their master, was never to abolish the ancient law, but to complete it. If then I should succeed in establishing that the object of the Jewish legislator, in that which concerns the holiday the seventh day, was quadruple; that that object, at once *civil*, *domestic*, *moral* and *hygienic*, was consequently the most vast, the most universal that the thought of a founder of a nation could embrace; if I could show according to what principles of a philosophy unknown to our age the fourth commandment was conceived, what its sanction was, what its consequences should be for the destiny of the people, I would have, I believe, satisfied all the conditions of the problem put forward; and by demonstrating the sublimity of the institutions Moses, I would have plumbed the depths of the question that I examine. It is nearly useless to caution that I contemplate all the facts relative to the Jewish religion, as well as those relating to Christianity, from a purely *human* point of view: today one is no longer suspected of religiosity, because they discover reasonable things in a religion.

I

It is rare that a law can be well understood and appreciated at its true value, if we limit ourselves to considering it separately, and independent of the system to which it is linked: that is a principle of legislative critique which no one contests, and suffers hardly any exceptions. How is it that this rule has been so badly followed with regard to the laws of Moses, that no one has yet thought to present them in their totality? I would not exempt from this criticism even Mr. Pastoret himself, whose work on the legislation of Moses seems to have been composed under the dictation of rabbis who wanted to mock their disciple. How is it, I say, that no publicist has even tried to sum up that governmental machine, to show its workings, to show the correlation of the parts with the whole, and the exact proportion between them? We have given ourselves up to minute researches on the laws of Lycurgus; for them, we have exhausted all the resources of erudition; by means of sagacity and critique, we have managed to give, if not a complete idea, at least an approximate, of the political state of the Lacedaemonians. The same work on Moses would be much easier; most of the materials exist; and, in order to reconstruct the edifice, it is a question only of arranging the scattered fragments.

We would hardly believe such an insufficiency on the part of the commentators, if the causes were not found recorded in their writings. According to the rabbis, it is not necessary to seek any reason in the Jewish laws other than the autocratic will of God, no other motive than the absolute, *sic volo, sic jubeo,* which allows neither examination nor verification. It is an impiety to probe the ways of the divinity. Obedience, in order to be meritorious, must be blind. Submission to the law loses all its prize, as soon as it is accompanied by science. That absurd opinion is ever so ancient and so profoundly established among them, that when a Pharisee, Saint Paul, came to proclaim before the nation that heretical aphorism, *Rationabile sit obsequium vestrum,* "Let your obedience be reasonable," a revolution was accomplished in religion.

On the other hand, Moses had not prepared himself to erect a dialectical monument; he did not want to make a theory. He never explained his principles. The needs of the people demanded a rule; Moses rendered an oracle. A question of right presented itself to be resolved; he dictated a law. But, despite that incoherence in the redaction, we need not imagine that his plan of legislation was as disordered as the collection of his decrees appears to us today, and that he had not had constantly in mind the archetypal idea of the simplest and most magnificent system. The Decalogue is the reduced expression and like the most general formula of that mass of detailed ordinances scattered in the Pentateuch. The very number of the commandments of the Decalogue and their sequence is not at all fortuitous: it is the genesis of moral phenomena, the scale of duties and crimes, based on a wise and marvelously developed analysis.

COMMANDMENTS	CRIMES AND MISDEMEANORS	VIRTUES AND DUTIES
1st, 2nd, 3rd, 4th	1. Impiety.	1. Religion, homeland.
5th	2. Parricide.	2. Filial piety, obedience, discipline.
6th	3. Homicides, assaults, etc.	3. Love of the neighbor, of humanity.
7th	4. Luxury.	4. Chastity, modesty.
8th	5. Theft, rapine.	5. Equality, justice.
9th	6. Lies, perjury.	6. Truth, good faith.
10th	7. Concupiscence.	7. Purity of heart.

What a magnificent creed! What philosopher, what legislator has there been but this one who has established such categories, and who has known how to fill out this cadre! Seek in all the duties of man and citizen something which does not boil down to this, but you will not find it. On the contrary, if you show me somewhere a single precept, a single obligation irreducible to that measure, I am justified in advance in declaring that obligation, that precept, outside of conscience, and consequently arbitrary, unjust, and immoral. We have exhausted all the forms of admiration and praise with regard to the categories Aristotle; we have not said a word of the categories of Moses. I will not do the same.

Supported by these certain foundations, the work of Moses was raised like a creation of God: unity and simplicity in the principles, variety and richness in the details. Each of the formulas of the Decalogue could become the subject of a long treatise: I will not explore even one of them in depth. The ordinance on the Sabbath is only one section of the first law, of which it forms the fourth paragraph.

"It is necessary," said J.-J. Rousseau (*The Social Contract*), "that there be fixed and periodic assemblies, that nothing can abolish or defer, so that on the indicated day the people will be legitimately called together by the law, without there being need for any other formal convocation."

What Rousseau asked, with the sole aim of forcing the people to show itself from time to time in all of their majesty, and thus to act as sovereign, Moses ordained, but not to gather a deliberative assembly:—about what would they deliberate? They have no right to claim, no privilege to destroy: all affairs, private or public, should be dealt with according to the constituent principles and by a sort of casuistic algebra. The marvel of modern times, the standing vote, taken on questions which could be resolved only by science and study, the preponderance of majorities, in a word, would then have appeared absolutely absurd. The laws like the institutions, founded on the observation of nature and deduced from moral phenomena in the same manner as the formulas in a treatise on physics are deduced from the phenomena of bodies, were immutable; and there was a penalty of death for whoever proposed to change or remove them. For extraordinary cases, the ancients gathered themselves in the public square: they did not wait for the Sabbath. The government of the Hebrews was not, as some imagine, a *democracy* in the manner of the *Social Contract*; neither was it a *theocracy*, in the sense of a *government by priests*. Moses, founding his republic by making the people swear to be faithful to the *Alliance*, had not submitted his work to the judgment of the multitude: that which is just in itself, the absolute truth, cannot be the object of an acceptance or a pact. Free, at his own risk, to obey the voice of his conscience, man has not be called to compromise with it: so the Jewish people were subject to the law. As for the priesthood, we will see what it was later.

Moses knew that man, rather than being born for society, is often dominated without knowing it by an unsociable instinct which leads him to isolation; he knew that reason, interest, even friendship, does not always suffice to vanquish his natural sloth; that suffering and labor, far from bringing him closer to his fellows, pushes him from them, and that his somber sadness is increased by the energy of his thought and his silent contemplations. Who should be more disposed than the preacher of Mount Horeb to absolve the reclusive man? For forty years, alone with his genius, always lost in the infinite, conversing only with the beasts, he had tasted all the delights and all the rancors of meditation. His soul, exalted by continual ecstasy, had made enthusiasm a habit. And suddenly the anchorite of the desert said to himself: Man is not made to live alone; he must have brothers. The interior life is not of this world. On this earth, action was required. And he was soon on his way: Israel had a liberator.

What Moses wanted then for his young nation, was not associations or musters, nor was it rallies and fairs. It was not only the unity of government, nor the community of usages. All of that is consequence, rather than principle; it is the sign, not the thing. What he desired to create in his people was a communion of love and faith, a fusion of intelligences and hearts, if I may put it that way. It was this invisible link, stronger than all material interests, that forms among souls the love of the same homeland, the worship of the same God, the same conditions of domestic happiness, the solidarity of destinies, the same memories, and the same aspirations. He wanted, in short, not an agglomeration of individuals, but a truly fraternal society.

But, in order to sustain the social sentiment that he desired to give rise to, something tangible was needed. For the symbol to be efficacious, it would be necessary to bring together consciences. On the day of the Sabbath, the children asked their fathers: "Why these celebrations, these ceremonies, these mysteries, that Jehovah our God has instituted?" And the fathers responded to their children: "We were slaves of an Egyptian Pharaoh, and Jehovah took us from Egypt by the strength of his arms! He led us to this land that he had sworn to give to our fathers. That is why he instituted all these solemnities, testimony to our gratitude and token of our future prosperity." Let us note these last words. While the common Jew saw in the Sabbath only a commemoration of his deliverance, the legislator made it the *palladium* to which the salvation of the republic was attached. And how is that? Because every system of laws and institutions needs to be protected by a special institution that encompasses and sums it up, which is its crown and its basis; because the Sabbath, suspending the rude labors of an almost entirely agricultural population, and connecting minds through the connection of persons, a day of public exaltation, national mourning, popular instruction and universal emulation, stopped the speculations of interest and directed the reason towards a more noble object. It softened manners by the charm of a rest that was not sterile, aroused a mutual goodwill, developed the national character, made the rich more liberal, evangelized the poor, and excited the love of the homeland in every heart. Let us examine some of these consequences.

Every man in Israel was required to read and meditate all his life, and copy with his own hand the text of the law. Some sentences drawn on the doors of houses and even on clothing, constantly recalled to memory that sacred law. Now, as there were no public schools, and as the entire week was filled by labor in the fields, it was during the rest of the Lord that the first writing lessons were given, and it was the BOOK which provided for this pious exercise. The first result, and the most important, of the sabbatical law, was instruction, and what instruction? That of religion, politics and morals. The teaching of the synagogue later developed the spirit of the letter that *kills*; the Levites and the prophets learned to sing it. "Such were," said Fleury, "the schools of the Israelists, where they taught not curious sciences, but religion and manners, and where on instructed, not children and some individual idlers, but all the people." Religion means, to express myself in our language, the science of government, political and civil right, the knowledge of duties, the principle of authority, obligation of discipline, the conditions of order and equilibrium, the guarantees of liberty, equality, or more accurately the original consanguinity. Our catechisms are, I cannot help noticing, a quite a ways from all that.

It is that spirit of religion that Saint Paul, so learned in the Hebraic traditions, tried hard to create among the Christians converted among the Gentiles. Already in his time, the pride of wealth and the luxury of sensual pleasures had crept in even among the *agapes*, or love feasts, which were taken in common. The wealthy did not want to eat with the poor, or eat the same food. "Each of you, St. Paul reproached them, brings home what pleases him: one gets drunk, the other dies of hunger." And he cried out indignantly: "Can you not stay in your houses to eat and drink? And do you come to the meeting (in *church*) only to insult those who have nothing?" How much these merchants of Corinth must have made the apostle miss the brothers of Palestine, so fervent, so disinterested, so pure! But they had been prepared by the Jewish religion, while the others had forsworn from paganism only the worship of multiple gods. The same social tendency shows itself in the famous Apology of Saint Justin. We see there that the principle exercises of Sunday were, after the catechesis, acts of charity and mercy, that part of religion which could then be reconciled with the secular power and with the obedience that one believed due to it.

A people, it is said, must have spectacles. I am far from contesting it; but since in everything we encounter evil alongside good, the question is to know what spectacles it is suitable to give to the people. For that, it is necessary to consult the times, the places, and the men. The representations of Aristophanes would have been an abomination to Orientals; the fierce Roman preferred the butchery of the circus to the pomp of the theaters; our fathers, in the Middle Ages, interrupted the offices of the church in order to perform the mysteries in the presence of the bishop and his clergy; and I would dare say that after two centuries of admiration, our Greek tragedies begin to seem a bit too distant from us. Besides, we don't even have spectacles: among us there exist only curiosities—more or less amusing, and more or less costly—in which nine-tenths of the people do not participate.

It has been said that the Sunday vespers were the comedy of servants: that disparaging phrase, cast on the ceremonies of worship, and a thousand times more insulting to the people than to religion, shows better than anything I could say how much the mania for distinction stifles the spirit of society, and how little we in France respect divine or human things. What's more, the priests, by a deplorable emulation, try to justify that mocking definition; the opera music introduced into the church, the theatrical effects, the taste for charms and incantations, the search for unknown devotions and new saints, all that, we must say, invented or foreseen by the priests, degrades the majesty of Christianity more and more, and manages to destroy the little bit of religious faith in the nation that escaped the libertinage of the eighteenth century.

What more beautiful spectacle than that of a whole people assembled for the rites of its religion, for the celebration of the great anniversaries? Such a spectacle suits the taste of all men; no nation ever did without it. "The feasts of the Israelites, says the same Fleury, were true feasts, real rejoicings. They were not profane spectacles, and contented themselves with some religious ceremonies and the mechanism of sacrifices. All men were obliged to be in Jerusalem at the three great solemnities of Passover, Pentecost and Tabernacles; and women were permitted to come. The assembly was thus very numerous: each appeared clothed in the best that they had. One had the pleasure of seeing parents and friends again; one attended the prayers and sacrifices, always accompanied by music.

After that, in the magnificent temple, followed the feasts where the peaceful victims were eaten. The same law commanded rejoicing, and united sensible with spiritual joy... It need not astonish us then that it was agreeable news that the festival approached, and that one would soon go to the house of the Lord; so, to go there, one traveled in great troupes, singing and playing instruments..."

These solemnities were rare, it is true; but each week brought their abbreviated image, and maintained their memory. The ceremonies of the synagogue finished, the fathers and elders gathered at the gates of the town; there they talked of labor, of the opening of the harvests, of the approach of the sheep-shearing, of the best methods for working the land and raising herds. There was also talk of the affairs of the country and of relations with the neighboring peoples. The young men, to the approving cheers of the women and girls, engaged in martial exercises: they held races, learned to draw a bow, tried to show strength and flexibility by lifting heavy loads, and by handling weights intended for that purpose. Sometimes they even competed in wit and subtlety, by riddles and apologues. We find traces of all these customs in the Old Testament; for we need not believe that prior to the migration in Babylon, the observation of the Sabbath was carried to that point of superstitious fastidiousness that Jesus Christ criticized in the Pharisees when he said to them: *The Sabbath was made for man, and not man for the Sabbath*. One of the most unfortunate effects of the sojourn of the Jews in Chaldea was to give them a taste for metaphysical reveries and a narrow, petty critique, a passion for disputes, a hunger for vain curiosities in speculation and refinement in practice. When we compare the Jews of the restoration of Cyrus with the Hebrews of the time of Samuel, Solomon and Hezekiah, we would think we see two different races. The greatness and simplicity of the Israelite genius has given place to the fault-finding, persnickety and false spirit of the rabbis; the good sense of the public seems eclipsed, and the nation has fallen. Between *Horace* and *Attila*, the distance is undoubtedly great; but between the Prophets and the Talmud, the contrast is monstrous. In general, we shouldn't seek the truth of the usages of the Hebrew people in the Talmudic traditions.

With regard to the government, the people should gather on the seventh day, not to make laws or vote on anything: I have already said that, according to Moses, all matters of legislation and politics are the object of science, not of opinion. The *legislative power* belongs only to that supreme reason that the Hebrews worshiped under the name of *Jehovah*: consequently all law, in order to be holy, should be marked with a character of necessity; all jurisprudence consisted of a simple exposition of principles, the knowledge of which was no one's privilege. To attribute to an official personage the right of *veto*, or of *sanction*, would have appeared to Moses as the height of absurdity and tyranny. Justice and legality are two things as independent of our consent as mathematical truth: to compel, it is enough for them to be known; to let themselves be seen, they demand only meditation and study. But,—and this will appear unprecedented,— the assembled people, whom Moses did not recognize as sovereign, in the sense that the will of the people makes law, formed the *executive power*. It was to the people,

1839: The Celebration of Sunday

gathered in its families and tribes that the charge of watching over the law was confided; it was for this great and sublime function that the legislator had wanted them to gather for a full week, judging that the people alone have a right to constrain the people, because they along can protect themselves.

What then was the legislator himself? A man inspired by God, which is to say a saint, a philosopher, a poet. Interpreter of that wisdom that founded the law, he was still, by his enthusiasm and his virtues, its herald and reflection. He commanded nature, conjured heaven and earth, ravished imaginations with the magic of his songs; but he spoke to the people in the name of God—in the name of *truth*. That is why he referred the guardianship of the law to the entire nation, why he allowed it that guarantee against the audacity of impostors and tyrants, the obligation to gather on a set day to oversee itself and its agents. Every citizen can affirm: This is true, this is just; but his conviction obliges no one but himself. The nation alone has the right to say: *We command and require...*

Such would be the institution of Sunday, if fatal circumstances, which did not exist for Moses and which time has not caused to disappear, had not stopped the development. In the cities, Sunday is hardly anything but a holiday without motive or aim, an occasion for parades for the women and children, for consumption for the restaurateurs and wine-merchants, of degrading idleness, and increased vise. On Sunday, the tribunals are closed, the public courts recessed, the schools vacant, the workshops idle, the army at rest: and why? So that the judge, casting off his robe and his gravity, can freely attend to concerns of ambition and pleasure, the scientist can cease to think, the student stroll, the worker stuff themselves, the grisette dance, and the soldier drink or just be bored. The trader alone never stops. If all of that was honest and useful, the aim of the institution would still be missed, and for two reasons: one, that all these amusements are without relation to the general good; the other, that they foment selfishness even in the connecting of persons.

In the countryside, where the people yield more easily to religious sentiment, the celebration of Sunday still preserves some of its social influence. The appearance of a rustic population, gathered as a single family to listen to their pastor, prostrate in silence contemplation before the invisible majesty of God, is touching and sublime. The charm works on the heart of the peasant: on Sunday, he is more gracious, more loving, more affable; he is sensible of the honor of his village, and he is proud of it; he identifies with the interests of his commune. Sadly, that happy instinct never produces its full effect, for lack of sufficient culture; for if religion has not lost all its influence on the heart, it has long since ceased to speak to the reason. And I do not intend this as a reproach: religion is immobile by its nature; it only modifies its discipline at long intervals and after endless delays. Moreover, the brusque changes that have occurred in our mores and social relations have, so to speak, taken it unawares. It has still not had time to adapt itself to the new order of things, or to harmonize itself with it. The people understand nothing of the ceremonies; the dogmas have no relation to their understanding. The prayers are not translated; and if sometimes they are recited in their language, the object of these prayers no longer interests them. Placed between the spiritual and the temporal, accustomed by their education to separate them, how would they grasp the connection? They believe that on entering the church they pass from one world to another, and rarely do they abstain, on that occasion, from sacrificing a present interest to some obscure and uncertain one. The priest teaches morals, but does he speak of the conditions of the social order, of the equality which should reign here below between the different classes of citizens, as it reigns among the orders of the blessed in the times that he heralds? Does he speak of the duties of the government, of the majesty of the sovereign nation, of the independence of reason, which alone can legitimate respect for the earthly powers and faith in God? Does he speak of progress, of the incessant transformation of religious dogmas and political institutions? No, the priest does not speak of these things. The mayor and the bishop forbid it; he could not do it without kindling revolt and incurring the blame for himself.

Incedo per ignes: I have touched on a revolutionary question, resolved in the eyes of all parties, but on which I dare to battle the common opinion, and defend the paradox which forms the basis of my discourse: *I mean the identity of religion and politics.*

The separation of powers, consummated in the era of Constantine and Theodosia, goes back to Jesus Christ himself, who did not make a dogma of it, but tolerated it: it is the result of certain metaphysical oppositions which should resolve themselves harmonically in a higher form, but which the routine of the legalists, as much as the fanaticism of the devout, has claimed to render eternal. Since the world has become Christian, paganism has always existed in the civil life: at the very center of Christianity, the state has not entered into the church, nor the church into the state. The monarch of Rome and the pope are two different things. Some attempts were made in the middle ages, sometimes by the sovereign pontiffs, and sometimes by the bishops, to reestablish the unity of government among the people, which is not the same thing as universal monarchy, to which the vulgar accuse Gregory VII of having dared to pretend. It is no longer priestly theocracy, for religion is no more the supremacy of the priest, than the law is the government of the judge; but it is necessary to believe that this idea of unity, or, to put it better, of synthesis, fair and true in itself, was premature, since it has ended by collapsing under a unanimous disapproval. The declaration of 1682, composed by Bossuet, sanctioned the distinction of powers, and nearly made it an article of faith. I will return to this question.

II

What I have said of the civil effects of the Sabbath sufficiently explains the importance that the legislator attached to it, when he made the stability of the State depend on it. But that institution itself had need of safeguards: it demanded to be defended against the negligence of some, against the ill will of others, and against the ignorance and barbarity of all. Now, it is from the guarantees with which Moses surrounded it that we have seen born the influence of the Sabbath on family relations. For such is the admirable economy of the Mosaic system, and the close connection of all its parts, that in studying it one seems to follow an exposition of physics rather than a combination of the human mind. It is of the legislation of Moses that we can truly say, that in it *all converges, all conspires, all consents.* Pull just one of its stitches, and the whole thing unravels.

Moses would not have believed in the solidity of his edifice, if it had not concerned all classes of people. Beyond the accomplishment of certain religious duties, such as attendance at the ceremonies, participation in the sacrifices, etc., he demanded that on the day of the Sabbath every sort of servile labor be suspended, and he accepted no pretext or excuse. *You shall not*, says Deuteronomy, *do any work, neither you, nor your son or daughter, nor your manservant or maidservant, nor your animals, nor the stranger within your gates.* That means: You will not labor, either by yourself or through another. The law allows no exceptions; it is the prerogative of all. The father of the family, representing in his person all those subordinated to him by birth, by natural domain, or by a consensual dependency, alone enjoyed certain civil privileges, such as those of sitting in council, to render justice, carry arms, etc. But there are some basic necessities that he cannot claim for himself alone, and rest after labor is among that number. Also Deuteronomy, or the second exposition of the law, adds: *So that your manservant and maidservant may rest, as you do. Remember that you have also been a slave.*

The laws of Moses, if we pay attention to them, are all, with regard to form, expressed in personal style, by the second person singular of the future tense. Now, as the expression always remains the same, whether it is a question of duties common to all individuals, or whether the law refers only to the heads of families, who alone were counted for some things, and as we might be able to quibble about the generality of the text, Moses added to the fourth commandment of the Decalogue, following the standard formula— *Thou shalt not work* — the commentary that we have just read, in order to remove all means of bickering from inhumanity and avarice.

Four-fifths of the population were thus interested in the rigorous observation of the Sabbath. The servants, recognizing for a day their dignity as men, put themselves back on the level of their masters; the women displayed the luxury of their households, the elderly the gravity of their lessons, their children, in their noisy joy, learned early some polite social habits. One saw the young girls sing and form dancing choruses, where they unfolded all the grace of their movements and the taste of their ensembles. Attractions formed and led to happy marriages. With such festivities once known, what father, what husband, what master would have thought to deprive their own of them? What domestic authority would have triumphed over an institution so sweet, transformed by the legislator into a religious precept? No, if paternal despotism had had the courage, it would not have succeeded.

What could I add to this quick description, that I have not already said? Sunday is the day of triumph for mothers and daughters. Bright with health and youth, beautiful from the expression of her conscience, accepted in the parish mass among all her companions, what village woman, once in her life, would not believe herself the kindest, most diligent or most wise? What wife, on a Sunday, does not give her household a certain air of celebration or even of luxury, and does not willingly receive, in a more affectionate mood, her husband's friends?... The joy of Sunday spreads over all: sorrows, more solemn, are less poignant; regrets, less bitter. The sick heart finds an sweetness unknown to its stinging troubles. Sentiments are uplifted and purified: husbands find a lively and respectful tenderness, maternal love its enchantments; the piety of sons gives in more docilely under the tender care of the mothers. The domestic, that furniture in human form, born enemy of the one who pays him, feels himself more devoted and faithful; the master more benevolent and less hard. The farmer and the worker, stirred by a vague sense of equality, are more content with their condition. In all conditions man regains his dignity, and in the boundlessness of his affections, he recognizes that his nobility is too great for the distinction of ranks to be able to degrade and damage it. In all these regards the spirit of Christianity gets the upper hand over the Jewish spirit, always marked with a coarse sensualism. The religion of Moses is scarcely contemplative. Much given to demonstration, it speaks to the senses rather than the soul, as its law was addressed more to the mind than to the heart. Christianity is more unctuous, more penetrating, more expansive: incomparable especially when you want to astonish crime, terrify the conscience, break the heart, temper pride, and console the unfortunate. Why has the effective virtue of its dogmas not yet triumphed, in the political order, over human obstinacy?

1839: The Celebration of Sunday

The most dangerous adversary that Moses could meet, in instituting a weekly holiday, was greed. How was he to tear the rich farmers from multiple and pressing labors, manufacturers from the demands of the practices, traders from their indispensable operations? What could the Levite, charged with announcing with this horn that the rest of the Lord had begun, respond to these sophisms of interest: "Will you add a day to the week, or will you take responsibility for loading the harvest and working the fields?... What compensation do you offer us if we withdraw this order, if we miss this investment?... Make your sacrifices anyway, and pray for us in the synagogue: we do not have the leisure to go there, our occupations do not permit it." What are we to say, once more, to people constantly alleging necessity, imminence, and unrecoverable occasions?

This is the stumbling block for all the adversaries of Sunday, ancient and modern. In order to give all possible strength to their reasons, I am going to quote the observations and calculations of a political man of the last century, of a man of the church, the abbot of Saint-Pierre, who, enjoying a fine abbey and having nothing to do, was perhaps not absolutely wrong to find the obligation to rest on Sunday unreasonable.

""It would be a great charity and a good work, more agreeable to God than a pure ceremony, to give to poor families the means to meet their needs and those of their children, by seven or eight hours of labor, and the means to instruct themselves and their children in the church, for three or four hours in the morning...

"To understand what a solace the continuation of their labor would be to the poor, we need only consider that of the five million families which are in France, there are at least a million who have almost no income except from their labor, who are poor; and I call poor those who do not have 30 Tours pounds of income, that is to say the value of 600 metric pounds of bread.

"These poor families could gain at least 5 sous each half-day of festival, one after another, during the 80 or so festivals and Sundays in the year. Each of these families would thus gain at least 20 francs per year more, which would make, for a million families, more than 20 millions of pounds. Now, wouldn't an annual charity of 20 millions be quite a hand-out, spread proportionally among the poorest?

"If, when the first canons on the cessation of labor had been made, the bishops had seen some of the cabarets and games established, if they had foreseen all the disorders that idleness can cause, they would have limited themselves to the hearing of the mass and the instructions of the matins." (Tome VII, page 73).

All these speculations are very nice, and the principle of this charity is very commendable; it only lacks a little good sense. For, as Bergier remarked, it is absurd to recognize, on one hand, that Sunday is instituted to give rest to the people, and to pretend on the other that this rest is itself harmful to them. In wanting to provide for the subsistence of the poor, we must have regard for the measure of their strength as well as their moral and intellectual needs. Our philanthropist is a cassock wanted to make the poor work seven to eight hours each Sunday, plus three a four hours of mass and sermon, which makes in all eleven to twelve hours of exercise on the day when others rest. And that five sous piece earned on Sunday, that fruit of an excessive labor, that wage of a people at bay, he charitably calls *alms*! Moses meant things in a rather different manner; his legislation had provided for all, and if the modern nations have not followed its windings, that was not the fault of the councils, which we would defend against the reproach of lack of foresight leveled against them by the abbot of Saint-Pierre. [3]

The Israelites, Fleury remarked, could not change place, nor enrich or ruin themselves excessively. The reason is easy to discover: among them the fortunes in real estate were equal, at least as much as the division flowing from successions and unforeseen accidents could allow. A law, called *levirate,* had even been made to prevent the goods of one family from passing to another; and it was subject to various applications, as we see from the example of

---

[3] Here is the portrait that J.-J. Rousseau has drawn of the Abbot of Saint-Pierre: "A famous author of this century, whose books are full of grand projects and small views, had, like all the priests of his communion, desired to have no wife of his own; but, finding himself more scrupulous that the others with regard to adultery, it is said that he opted to have pretty servants, with which he repaired as best he could the affront to his species made by that bold commitment. He regards it as a duty of a citizen to give others to the homeland, and with the tribute he paid of this sort, he peopled the class of artisans..." If the Abbot of Saint-Pierre had the population so much at heart, why didn't he go, like another Vincent de Paul, to the Hospital for Foundlings? For, according to the same Rousseau, in order to have men, it is less a question of procreating than of providing for those children who exist.

Ruth and of the daughters of Salphaad. From the beginning, the lands had been subject to an equal partition: a sort of general cadaster had been executed by Joshua, in order that in certain cantons the natural sterility of the soil was compensated by a greater extent of territory or by other equivalents. According to the law, no immovable good could be alienated in perpetuity; the legislator exempted from that measure only houses in towns surround by walls. And the motive for that restriction is blindingly obvious; while promoting the growth of the people, he wanted them to spread uniformly over the territory, instead of crowding and corrupting themselves in large cities. He found there as well a guarantee of independence and security for the nation: we know that the lure of the wealth of Jerusalem was the perpetual cause of the invasions of the kings of Egypt and Babylon, and, in the end, of the ruin of the whole people.

Every child of Abraham was thus obliged to preserve his patrimony. Each should be able, in the general prosperity, to eat beneath his own vine and fig tree. There were no large farms, no great domains. The unfortunate or insolvent Israelite could stake his inheritance, the legacy of his father, as he could hire out his person and his strength, but in the year of the Jubilee all the properties were freed of debt and returned to their masters, all the servitors were freed. It followed from this that property sales, being subject to repurchase, were negotiated with an eye to the greater or lesser proximity of the year of Jubilee; that debts were difficult for the same reason, which made lenders cautious; that the passion to acquire was arrested at its source, and that labor, activity, diligence, were inevitably maintained among the citizens. It also resulted from it, relative to the Sabbath, that the exploitable materials, or the patrimonial soil, not being able to be extended, could not be increased for anyone; consequently, that no one could add a surcharge to his own fatigues, and hence, that it was easy to rule in advance the distribution of the labors of the week and even of the whole year, setting aside the Sabbaths and other feasts. And in cases of necessity, such as the approach of an enemy tribe, a fire or a storm, we must believe, in honor of the human spirit and of the Jewish nation, that the high priest who successor of Aaron was no more embarrassed to grant exemptions than the least curate in our villages.[4]

As for the merchants, artisans and foremen, the effect of the suspension was such for individuals of all conditions, that a delay caused by the Sabbath was not a delay, because that day no longer counted. No debt, no delivery of merchandise, no repayment of labor was due on that day. It is thus that, according to our laws and commercial practices, every commercial paper whose maturity took place on Saturday evening was only protestable on Monday.

Equality of conditions and fortunes was so much in the thought of Moses, that the majority of his civil laws and reforms were made with that aim. The right of the eldest had existed under the patriarchs: Moses abolished it, and

---

[4] During the war of the Maccabees, a troop of Jews having been attacked on the Sabbath day, they thought it better to let themselves be massacred than to defend themselves, for fear of breaking the law. Mathathias then made an ordinance that allowed the people to defend themselves on the Sabbath if they were attacked.

only granted a bonus to the eldest. Among the Hebrews, it was the husband who made up the dowry, and not the parents of the wife, because the goods could never leave the family. Mr. Pastoret calls that *buying a wife*; today, it is the fathers who *buy the husbands* for their daughters. Which of the two is preferable? If a daughter found herself sole inheritor, without male children, she could only marry within her tribe, and, as much as possible, in her bloodline; and in that case, the goods that she brought were not dowry, but paraphernalia. The language itself enshrined that principle of all good society, the equality of fortunes: the words *charity, humanity,* and *alms* are unknown in Hebrew; all of that was designated by the name of JUSTICE.

But here an objection presents itself. Could Moses legitimately, and without injuring the right of free development of individual fortune, limit the right of property? In other words, is the equality conditions a natural institution? Is it equitable? Is it possible? On each of these points, I dare to answer in the affirmative.

Let me reassure you; I have no desire to warm over the theories from the famous discourse on *the inequality of conditions*; God forbid that I should here reclaim as an underpinning the ill-conceived thesis of the philosopher of Geneva! Rousseau has always appeared to me to have not understood the cause that he wanted to defend, and to have embarrassed himself in some of his baseless à priori arguments, when it was necessary to reason according to the relations of things. His principles of civil organization were like those of his politics, they were flawed at base: by founding right on human conventions, by making the law the expression of wills,—in short, by submitting justice and morals to the decision of the greatest number and the opinion of the majority,—he turned in a vicious circle: he sunk more and more into the abyss from which he thought to depart, and absolved the society that he accused. Not being able, at this moment, without leaving the scope of my discourse, to give myself to a deep discussion of this matter, I will content myself with submitting to the judgment of the reader the following propositions, urged solely by fraternity and solidarity, and whose necessary conclusion will be the same as Moses derived. Moreover, if I do not disavow the agrarian law, neither do I cast myself as its defender; I only want to prove to all the monopolizers of labor, exploiters of the proletariat, autocrats or feudal lords of industry, hoarders and triple-armored proprietors, that the right to work and live, given to a crowd of men who do not enjoy it, whatever one says, will be on the part of the beneficiaries not a bonus, but a restitution.

1. The man who comes into the world is not a usurper and intruder; a member of the great human family, he is seated at the common table: society is not a master to accept or reject him. If the fact of his birth does not give him any right over his fellows, neither does it make him their slave.

2. The right to live belongs to all: existence is the taking of possession of it; labor is its condition and means.

3. It is a crime to monopolize livelihoods; it is a crime to monopolize labor.

4. When a child is born, none of its brothers have a right to contest the newcomer's equal participation in the father's goods. Similarly, there are no junior members of a nation.

5. All the brothers have an equal duty to support the family: the same thing is true between the citizens.

6. After the death of the father, none can demand a share of the estate proportional to his age, to his strength, to the talent that he has been given, or to the services he says he has rendered: unequal division is essentially contrary to the spirit of the family. To accommodate one is to deny the other. — Just as the city recognizes neither preeminence, nor privileges of duties and employments: it accords to all the same favor and reward.

7. Man is a transient on the earth: the same soil which feeds him has fed his father and will feed his children. The domain of man, no matter is object, is not absolute: the enjoyment of goods must be ruled by the law.

8. We punish the man who burns down his house or puts fire to his crops; in this we do not have in view only the security of the neighbor and guest, but we also want to make it understood that, the man always receiving more from society than he could give back to it, what he produces no longer belongs to him. The artisan, the writer, and the artist, each in that which concerns his work, must be subject to that law.

A moment will suffice to appreciate what distance there is between such a doctrine and that of Jean-Jacques: the one established the respective rights of the citizens on the familial regime; the other on conventions and contracts, which always carry a germ of the arbitrary, and give rise to all sorts of despotism.

What pity they inspire in me, these makers of tear-stained homilies, these *friends of the people*, these *friends of the working class*, these *friends of the human race*, these *philanthropists* of every sort, meditating at their ease on the evils of their fellows, who suffer, in a feeble idleness, because the poor have only six days of toil, and never conclude anything from the insufficiency of their wages, except: "You must work! You must save!" Like that doctor who, treating a patient with scrofula, constantly applied a new patch to a new ulcer, and only neglected to try to purify the mass of the blood, these doctors always have on hand some topical of recent invention and rare effectiveness: nothing is forgotten by them, except one thing with which they hardly troubled themselves, which is to turn to the source of the evil. But let us not fear that they will engage in that search, which would infallibly lead them where they never want to look, at themselves. With their capital, their machines, their privileges, they invade all, and then they become indignant that one takes labor from the laborer. As much as they can, they leave nothing for anyone to do, and they cry that the people waste their time; all magnificent in their flourishing idleness, they say to the journeyman without work: "Work!" And then, when the canker of pauperism comes to trouble their sleep with its hideous visions, when the exhausted sufferer writhes on his pallet, when the starving proletarian howls in the street, then they propose some prize for the extinction of begging, they give dances for the poor, they got to the show, they throw parties, they hold lotteries for the indigent, they take pleasure in giving alms, and they applaud themselves! Ah! If the wisdom of modern times is exhausted for such lovely results, such was not the spirit of all of antiquity, nor the teaching of Jesus Christ.

We know the parable related in Matthew, Chapter 20, in which Jesus Christ proposes as a model the head of a family who had risen early in the morning to send out laborers to his vineyard. He paid one denier per day. As he had occasion to pass through the place several times during the day, each time that he saw some daylaborers without work, he brought them to his vineyard. When night came, he gave everyone one denier. There were murmurs and protestations: We have carried the burden of the day and heat, said some, while those have done almost nothing, and they are treated like us! — My friend, said the householder to one of the malcontents, I have done you no wrong: didn't you agree with me on one denier? Take then what is due to you, and go your way: if it pleases me to give to one as to another; can't I do what seems good to me, and must I cease to be human because you are envious? With me the last are like the first, and the first like the last.

This is the moral tale which has so revolted the equitable reason of the philosophers, and of which I have not always thought without outrage, though I ask pardon for it from the divine wisdom of the author of the Gospels. What truth is taught to us in that lesson of the householder? The very same truth of which I have just presented, in the form of a proposition, the principal corollaries: that every inequality of birth, of age, of strength or ability, vanishes before the right of the individual to produce their subsistence, which is expressed by the equality of conditions and goods; that the differences of aptitude or skill in the workers, and of quantity or quality in the execution of the work, disappear in the social labor, when all the members have done their best, because then they have done their duty; in short, that the disproportion of power in individuals is neutralized by the general effort. Here again is the condemnation of all those theories of division in proportion to merit or capacity, increasing or decreasing according to capital, labor or talent, theories whose immorality is flagrant, since they are diametrically opposed to the familial right, basis of the civil right, and since they violate the liberty of the laborer and ignore the fact of collective production, the unique safeguard against the exaggeration of every relative superiority; theories founded on the bases of sentiments and the vilest of the passions, since they only turn on selfishness; theories, finally, which, to the shame of their magnificent authors, contain, after all, only the rejuvenation and rehabilitation, under perhaps more regular forms, of the same civilization that they denigrate while imitating it, a civilization which is worth nothing, but which they resuscitate. Nature, said these sectarians, shows us inequality everywhere: let us follow its indications. — Yes, responds Jesus Christ, but inequality is the law of the beasts, not of men. — Harmony is the daughter of inequality. — Lying sophist, harmony is equilibrium in diversity. — Remove this balance, you will destroy the harmony.

I halt myself, for I would not dare pursue this sacrilegious colloquy further. When Jesus Christ, explaining to the people the different articles of the Decalogue, taught them that polygamy had been permitted to the ancients because of the rudeness of their intelligence, but that it had not been thus in the beginning; that a bad desire is equal to a fornication consummated; that insult and affront are as reprehensible as murder and blows; that he is a parricide who says to his poor father: "This morning I have prayed to God for you; that will benefit you." He said nothing of the 8th commandment, which concerned theft, judging the hardness of heart of his audience still too great for the truth that he had to speak. After eighteen centuries, are we worthy to hear it?

Equality of conditions is in conformity with reason and it is an irrefutable right. It is in the spirit of Christianity, and it is the aim of society. The legislation of Moses demonstrates that it can be attained. That sublime dogma, so frightening in our time, has its roots in the most intimate depths of the conscience, where it is mixed up with the very notion of justice and right. Thou shalt not steal, says the Decalogue, which is to say, with the vigor of the original term, *lo thignob*, you will divert nothing, you will put nothing aside for yourself.[5] The expression is general, like the idea itself: it forbids not only theft committed with violence and by ruse, fraud and brigandage, but also every sort of gain acquired from others without their full agreement. It implies, in short, that every violation of equality of division, every

---

[5] The verb gandb means literally *to put aside, to hide, to retain, to divert*.

premium arbitrarily demanded, and tyrannically collected, either in exchange, or from the labor of others, is a violation of communicative justice, it is a misappropriation. It is that depth of meaning that Jesus Christ had in mind in his parable of the workers in the vineyard, veiling by design some truths that it would have been dangerous to leave too uncovered, but that he did not want his disciples to be unaware of. Yes, he would have told them in his sublime language, if he had thought it useful to express himself without veils, he would have said to the ancients: "Thou shalt not steal. And I say unto you: Whoever imposes a tax on the field, the bullock, the ass or the coat of his brother, is a robber." Did he foresee that, despite the feeble attempts that have been made after his death, his doctrine would be unable to find its application for so long, and did he only want to entrust to his church a seed of salvation, which would be discovered again under more opportune circumstances? This is a possibility to which we cannot refuse our support, when we relate his thought to the anxious times in which we live.

Indeed, what do we see all around us? Here are some men, bored and discontented in the midst of opulence, and poor despite their wealth; there are some maneuvers which destitution prevents their reason and their soul from even dreaming of,—so that they are happy even when they find themselves working on Sunday! The excess of selfishness provokes general horror, some sophists indoctrinate the multitude, but a providential instinct still preserves us from their unintelligible systems, and, in the midst of all that, Christianity, finger resting on the Decalogue, and without explaining more, upholds the celebration of the day which renders us all equals by making us all brothers. Does it not tell us clearly enough: there is a time to work and a time to rest.. If some among you have no rest, it is because others have too much leisure. Mortals, seek truth and justice; return to yourselves, repent, and reform...

Thanks should be given to the councils which, better advised than the abbots of the eighteenth century, have ruled inflexibly on the observation of Sunday: and may it please God that the respect for that day should still be as sacred for us as it has been for our fathers! The evil that gnaws at us would be more keenly felt, and the remedy perhaps more promptly perceived. It is up to the priests in particular to awaken spirits from their sleep: let them courageously grasp the noble mission which is offered to them, before others grasp it. Property has not yet made its martyrs: it is the last of the false gods. The question of the equality of conditions and fortunes has already been raised, but as a theory without principles: we must take it up again and go into it in all its truth. Preached in the name of God, and consecrated by the voice of the priest, it would spread like lightning: one would believe in the coming of the son of man. For it will be with that doctrine as with so many others: first it will be booed and loathed, then it will be taken into consideration, and discussion will be established; then it will be recognized as just at base, but ill-timed; then finally, despite all the oppositions, it will triumph. But straight away a problem will present itself: *To find a state of social equality which would be neither community, nor despotism, nor allotment, nor anarchy, but liberty in order and independence in unity.* And this first problem being resolved, there remains a second: *to indicate the best method of transition.* That is the whole problem of humanity.

The equality of goods is a condition of liberty. Like liberty, the right of association, and the *republic,* are conditions of every civil and religious celebration: I need, in order to treat my subject thoroughly, to dwell on all the considerations which came before.

The firmest rampart of the institution of the Sabbath, and its most vigilant guardian, was the priesthood. The Levites did not form a congregation placed apart from the republic and completely foreign to civil society. On the contrary, they were the grand spring, the king-pin of the State. Their Hebrew name, *cohanim,* means ministers or functionaries. Thus, besides the multiplying duties they fulfilled at the sacrifices, in the synagogues, the majority of the civil employments were entrusted to them. "Justice," says Fleury, whom I always cite because I can think or speak no better, "was administered by two sorts of officers, *sophetim* (judges), *soterim* (bailiffs, sergeants, archers, executioners). These charges were given, there was no distinction between the tribunals; the same judges decided case of conscience and closed civil or criminal trials. Thus, only a few different offices were needed, and few officers, in comparison with what we see today. For it is shameful for us to be a simple individual... everyone wants to be a public figure."

The Levites, like the *fetials* among the Romans,[6] made the declarations of war and called the people to arms. In the army, they marched in the first rank, sounded the trumpet, and led the combatants. It was good that the same men who in times of peace served as counsels and teachers, led the citizens into combat. Thus we have seen in the most heroic century of our history, when the armies of the kings invaded the homeland, more than one schoolmaster armed with a rifle, harangue his students, and, all together, singing the hymn of war, rush off to the field of batter, and conquer or die for liberty. Why shouldn't our priests emulate them?

The Levites alone administered nearly all the medicine, which was nearly limited to dietetics and hygiene. They were charged with the policing of lepers and all the legal impurities, which necessitated on their part some rather extended theoretical studies, and a painstaking diagnose. We can see in Leviticus the details of the prohibited foods, and the precautions taken to recognize the appearance of that formidable malady, leprosy.

After all that, one could believe that the preponderance of Levites in the body of the State was immense, and that it would constantly threaten the independence of the tribes: this was not the case at all. Among the Hebrews, there were no castes; or if you prefer, each tribe was the caste within the range of its territory. The Levites were the only cosmopolitans in the country and spread all through the

---

[6] *Fetials*, that is *denuntiatores*, heralds. This word comes from the verb *facere*, taken in the sense *to speak*, just as the Hebrew *dabar* means at once *to do* and *to say*, *speech* and *action*.

nation according to the needs of their service. Having had no share in the division of the lands, they possessed no land of their own; they were only allowed to raise some herds on the margins of the towns where they lived. Their whole subsistence came from the people, by way of sacrifices and offering; these were the salaries that Moses had assigned to his public servants in a time and place where money was little used. The accuracy of their payment was only guaranteed by the Sabbath. Such was also the origin of the casuel paid to our own village priests. "The legislator, by entrusting the Levite to the generosity of the other families, wanted to increase the union of all. On his part, the child of Levi naturally clung to the law by which he held his means of living, to the peace and public abundance which brought abundance and peace to him. Even from self-interest, he had to respect that law in order for others to respect it; from self-interest, he had to publish it, so that no one forgot the precepts which sanctioned his right; finally, from self-interest, he had to oversee its full execution." (SALVADOR, *Institutions de Moses*.) But, since Moses did not permit castes or privileges, why assign one entire tribe to public functions, and exclude all the others? Why, introducing a necessary order into the State, did he not leave it to that order to recruit for itself from among all the people? First, it is not true that the priests were the only public functionaries: there existed in each town a communal council composed of all the heads of families, which chose from its own ranks a large number of public officers. There was besides a sort of senate or elected national representatives for each tribe. Finally, the nation had at its head a supreme assembly, called the Sanhedrin, formed of the deputies of all the people. But by giving guardianship of the laws and such a great part of the executive power to the priesthood, Moses acted in conformity with the usages and opinions of his times. Everywhere, the priesthood was the privilege of certain families: India and Egypt are famous examples of this. Another reason for this conduct is that Moses desired the preservation of his work. After dividing the land between the eleven tribes, he had ordained that the Levites, salaried by the State, would have no place in Israel, because the principle of equality which was the basis of the constitution was incompatible with the accumulation of properties and places. To admit into the priestly order an individual capable of inheriting, would be to introduce property into public service public and to destroy the national equilibrium.—But, it is said, could Moses ordain that anyone who becomes a priest loses the ability to be an heir? I do not believe that this objection would be made by a jurist. The forethought of a legislator aims to make absolute laws and to avoid all qualification.

I believe that these quick reflections will not be regarded as beyond the scope of the work, since, taken in the context of our Sunday celebration, they encourage reflection, much more than a special discourse would, on the close affinity which unites the occupation of the priest with the happiness of the families. I will dispense then with making any comparison between the ancient and modern priesthood, and emphasize the common links, which we all know. It is on Sunday that the character of the priest, in its conciliatory and apostolic aspects, shines in all its brightness. The visit of the parish priest is the joy of the rural family. Sickness relieved, the poor rescued, the unfortunate soothed, hatred quelled, enemies reconciled, spouses reunited, and all through the work of the parish priest!... Now the priest, especially in the country, does not have much time at his disposal. He must seize the moments as they pass, and it is on Sunday that his duties multiply, his works bear the most beautiful fruits; it is on Sunday that he discovers all the good that he can do.

III

I approach what is perhaps the most difficult part of my subject, because of the pitfall that it seems to cover: moral utility. What is the influence, on the morals of individuals and of society, of the observation of Sunday considered in itself, independent of the force that religion lends to it, and setting aside faith in dogmas and mysteries? Such is, at least, the manner in which I take up the question, and I do not think, I admit, that one could understand it otherwise. It is not a question of launching oneself into the vast field of religious opinions, to demonstrate the utility of public worship by the benefits of religion. All these questions are pointless and even, with regard to truth, trivial. It is not a homily on the effectiveness of Sunday as a source of divine favors that is called for, it is the indication of the relations that can exist between a conspicuous, public ceremony and the affections of the soul. Thus, it is necessary to separate the material from the spiritual, the nominal from the abstract, the human from the revealed, and say that what one practices apart from society, isolated, still preserves some moral utility; for the thought of the founder had to have been that every religious observance has its natural as well as its theological reason.

Another distinction is still necessary. The moral effects of Sunday are either *mediate* or *immediate*. By mediate effects, I mean those which rise from the circumstances which accompany the Sunday celebration; such are the relations of family and city, with which I will not concern myself further; and by immediate effects I understand those that Sunday produces by its own special action, independent of every social or domestic influence. This distinction, relatively unimportant in practice, has the advantage of better specifying my point of view, and sparing me repetitions.

"Nature has placed within man the feelings of pleasure and sadness, which force him to avoid the physical objects that seem harmful to him, and to seek those that suit him. The chief work of society will be to create in him a rapid instinct for moral affairs, which, without the tardy aid of reasoning, would lead him to do good and avoid evil. For the individual reason of man, lead astray by his passions, is often only a sophist who pleads their cause, and the authority of the man can always be attacked by his love of self. Now, what produces or replaces that precious instinct, what makes up for the insufficiency of human authority, is the sentiment that nourishes and develops the compulsory exercise of worship; it is this respect mixed with fear that inspires for the moral precepts the full spectacle and majesty of the solemnities which consecrate and celebrate them."[7]

---

[7] Session of the National Convention for 18 Floréal, Year II, Carnot presiding. Report of Robespierre in the name of the Committee of Public Safety.

The thought expressed in this passage is ingenious and beautiful; what's more, it is perfectly true. That quick instinct, that second conscience, if I dare put it thus, has been created in the heart of the Israelite by the Sabbath, and Sunday lifts it to a higher degree than it does the soul of the Christian. Moses spared nothing to deeply instill respect for the Sabbath: ablutions, purifications, expiations, abstinences, absolute prohibitions, and strict injunctions. He multiplied, almost to excess, anything that could inspire the idea of the highest sanctity, and carry the veneration almost to the point of terror. On imaginations more impassioned because they are less cultured, the opinion of a more present divinity is all-powerful. The majesty of the sanctuary seems to forbid the approach of crime, and more than once we have seen great culprits, seized by a divine panic, flee frantic and shaking from a refuge where their crimes would no longer find themselves safe. Moses transported that horror of sacrilege from space to time: he rendered certain days inviolable, as he had consecrated certain objects and certain places. And vise, surrounded on all sides by the forces of religion, had no rest, no longer knowing where to hide itself.

But this charm that Moses had cast on the Sabbath, this new sort of scarecrow by which he warded off evil spirits, took all its virtue from a rather vulgar accessory, scarcely worthy of respect or fear: it was, if I dare make use of this withering word, (which is, thank heavens, not from our language,) it was the far niente, doing nothing. A philosopher would not have been aware of it, but Moses seized it.

The ancients, greater observers than we like to believe, perhaps because we don't observe the same things, had remarked very well the effects of solitude on the morals of man. In solitude, the feeling of the infinite touches us, the passions fall silent; reason, clearer and more active, deploys all its strength and gives birth to miracles: character is strengthened and developed, imagination increases, the moral sense responds to the urgings of Divinity. The temples and oracles were placed by preference in remote places, planted thickly with trees, whose shadows invited meditation and contemplation. The wise, returned from the world and the passions, the lovers of the muses and nature, the legislators themselves, as well as the seers and poets, fled, sometimes in agreeable retreats, sometimes in frightening solitude, the indiscreet regard of the profane, who believed them to be in commerce with the gods. Solitude, when it is not the effect of a savage humor or a proud misanthropy, appeared to them the purest image of heavenly beatitude, and the fondest wish of a great soul would have been that all mortals know how to enjoy it and make themselves worthy of it. But if such is truly the highest destiny of man on the earth, in what sense is it sociable? How will its narrow residence suffice for a multitude of anchorites?

If Moses had had the power, he would never have had the thought to transform his farmers into effective hermits; he only wanted to make them men, to accustom them, by reflection, to seek the just and the true in everything. Thus he strove to create around them a solitude which would not destroy the greatest affluence, and which preserved all the prestige of a true isolation: that was the solitude of the Sabbath and the feasts. Constrained, under terrible penalties, to cease their labors for these solemn days, the Israelites submitted to the yoke of an unavoidable meditation; but, incapable by themselves of directing their attention and occupying their thought, they found themselves delivered up to the mercy of circumstances and the first comer: it was there that their teacher awaited them. I have already said what occupations had been assigned by Moses to the Sabbath day. That great and holy man had wanted all the Hebrews, from the children to the elderly, to be able to walk, by his example, with the Lord, and to live in a permanent communication with him. That is demonstrated, indisputably, by a passage in the book of *Numbers*, where it is related that Moses having chosen seventy men to aid him in the details of government, these men were animated with the same spirit as him and prophesied. And when Joshua came to say: "Master, there are still two men who prophesy in the camp; stop them.—"May it please God," he responded, "that all the people should prophesy!" Let us say, in a slightly more human language, that nothing seemed more desirable to him than to maintain in the intelligence that tempered enthusiasm which produces knowledge of the good, the contemplation of ourselves and of the spectacle of nature.

The last night of the week is passed; the sun begins again its daily course; all the vegetation blooms and salutes the father of the day. Faithful to their instinct, the animals do not stop any more than the plants: the dormouse digs its burrow, the bird builds its nest, the bee collects pollen from the flowers. Nothing that lives suspends its labor: man alone stops for one day. What will he make of his long and drifting thoughts? He will hardly have roused himself from slumber, and already his inactivity will weigh on him: the evening arrives, and the day appears to him to have lasted for two days.

For frivolous spirits, Sunday is a day of unbearable rest, of frightening emptiness: they complain of the ennui which weighs them down. They blame the slowness of these unproductive hours, which they do not know how to spend. If they flee, in polite visits and worldly conversations, from the emptiness of their thoughts, they only add the void of the thoughts of others. From that arise the inventions of debauchery and the monstrous joys of the orgy.—Let those blame only themselves for the numbness that makes them stupid, the inconstancy of heart and understanding that exhausts them, and the dull paralyzes that gnaws at them. When its partner lies idle, the spirit only goes more quickly: be careful, if you don't know how to feed its all-consuming activity, that it does not consume itself.

Happy is the man who knows how to shut himself us in the solitude of his heart! There he keeps company with himself; his imagination, his memories, and his reflections respond to him. Let him promenade then along the crowded streets, let him stop in the public squares, let him visit the monuments; or, more happily, let him wander across the fields and meadows, and breathe the air of the forests; it matters little. He meditates, and he dreams. Everywhere his heart, happy or sad, elegant or sublime, belongs to him. It is thus that he judges everything soundly, that his heart is detached, that his conscience is invigorated, that his will is sharpened, and that he feels virtue bound up in his chest. It is thus that he begins with

God himself, and that he learns from him, in conversations that none will repeat, what it is to LIVE, and what it is to DIE. Oh! Then, as all things are reduced to their just value, how little worthy it appears that for their sake we hold onto life, or that for them we would seek death! We ask fearfully what the best remedy would be for the epidemic of suicide which multiplies its victims every day. That remedy, which we have sought everywhere except where it was to be found, was furnished by homeopathy. Make life contemptible, and we will no longer want to leave it; we only esteem it if we find it to be a burden. The stoic who, in prosperity, knows how to sacrifice his existence, also knows how to bear pain; he even denies that it is an evil. The disciple of Epicurus, lazily in love with life, curses it as soon as it no longer offers him pleasure. It is among the tombs, a skull in his hand, that he must preach against suicide.

What heroic self-sacrifices and heart-rending sacrifices were consummated internally in these inexpressible monologues of the holy days! What high thoughts, magnificent conceptions, descend into the soul of the philosopher and the poet! What generous resolutions were made! Hercules, at the end of adolescence, offered a sacrifice to Minerva. Standing before the altar, after having made some libations and singing hymns to the goddess, he waited, immobile and silent, until the flame had consumed the offering. Suddenly he saw two women appear, two immortals, Pleasure and Virtue, who, displaying their charms, demanded his homage. Pleasure flaunted all her seductions. Virtue offered labors and perils with an incorruptible glory. The young hero chose Virtue. Woe unto those who do not have the same vision!

1839: The Celebration of Sunday

Great woe unto those who do not choose as did the son of Jupiter!

According to the preceding observations, the same cause suffices to explain both the energy that the moral sense can acquire, and the excesses where libertinism is plunged as a result of the observation of Sunday: that cause is the increase of activity given to the mind by the rest of the body. It is up to those charged with the protection of the customs, the education of the young and the direction of the public amusements, to turn to the advantage of morals an institution which, after religion itself, is the most precious remainder that we have preserved of the ancient wisdom, and the excellence of which is demonstrated by the very debaucheries for which it furnishes the occasion.

Among the upper classes, Sunday is no longer recognized; the days of the week all resemble one another. For those only occupied with speculations, intrigues and pleasures, it hardly matters what day it is; the intervals marked for rest no longer mean anything. The people sometimes holds back its passions for a week; the vises of the great are not deferred. Is the impiousness of the rich, established in their habits, incurable? The people, more faithful to its traditions and less open to attack in their character, are always under the hand of religion. I would even dare to suggest that with respect to Sunday the last glimmer of poetic fire is extinguished in the souls of our rhymers. It has been said: without religion, no poetry. It is necessary to add: without worship and without holidays, no religion. But since poetry, becoming *rationalist*, has raised the veils that covered the Christian *myths*, since it has left the *allegories* and *symbols* to raise itself up to the *absolute*, it is true to say that it has killed its foster-mother, and with the same blow committed suicide. Among the people, on the contrary, the lack of devotion does not exclude every religious idea. They can detest the priest, but never hate religion. They blaspheme against the dogmas and mysteries, and they prays at the graves and kneel at the blessings. And when faith no longer resonates for them, the poetry of Sunday still thrills.

Blond Marie was loved by the young Maxime; Marie was a simple working woman, and in the naïveté of a first love; Maxime, a hard-working artisan, combined reason with youth. Nature seemed to have predestined these lovers to happiness, by blessing both with simplicity and modesty. Diligent at work every day of the week, Maxime tried hard to increase his savings; Marie braided in silence her wedding crown. They only saw each other on Sundays; but it was beautiful, it was solemn for them, this day when it was sung in heaven: *Love is stronger than death!* It spread the influence of religion and innocence over their mutual affection! True lovers are never sacrilegious: full of a loving respect, what would the young man have dared? What would the girl have allowed, beautiful in her modesty and the joy of the Sabbath? Alone with their love, they were under the protection of God. The revolution of July came suddenly to destroy such bliss. Maxime was told to provide for himself: no more work, no more joy. He resolved to move away for awhile and make for the capital. On the eve of his departure, a Sunday evening, he took Marie's hand, and, without speaking to her, led her to the church.—"If I remain faithful, how shall I find you, Marie?"—"Do as you say, and you may count on my faithfulness."— "Will you promise me before God?" She promised. They went out; the night was fine; Maxime, according to the custom of lovers who part ways, showed Marie the polar star and taught her to recognize its position.—"Your eyes will no longer meet mine," he said to her; "but every Sunday, at the same hour, I will look in that direction. Do the same, so that at a single instant, as our hearts are united, our thoughts will merge. That is all that I ask, until I see you again." He left. Paris did not always give him work; his days of unemployment became fatal to him. At the instigations of some friends, Maxime joined a republican society. An invincible melancholy took hold of his soul and altered his character. "Do you know," he wrote to Marie, "why you are so poor, when so many shameless sorts live in luxury? Why I can't marry you, when so many men throw themselves into debauchery?... Do you know why I sometimes work on Sunday, when others play or indulge their boredom all week long?... God has allowed the good to be the first to suffer from the vises of the wicked, to teach them that it is up to them to prune society and make virtue flower again. If the just were never to complain, the wicked would never mend their ways; the contagion would always spread, and the world, soon all infected, would perish... Pray to God for me, Marie; that is all that a weak woman can do. But there are a million young men, virtuous and strong, all ready to rise up, who have sworn to save the nation... We will triumph or we will know how to die." Maxime was killed behind a barricade during the June days. From that time, his lover wore mourning. Orphaned from a young age and no longer having a mother, she attached herself to the aged mother of her fiancé. Her days were passed in labor and in the cares of a tender devotion. Every Sunday she was seen, in the dark chapel where she promised Maxime her heart and faith, assisting in the divine office. It is there that her heart, calm and resigned, was strengthened and purified in an ineffable love. And at night, after her prayers, heart full of the last words of Maxime,— *until I see you again,*— the sad Marie gazed sighing at the polar star.

IV

It remains to examine the importance of the Sunday celebration with regard to public hygiene. This text will perhaps appear rather petty after the serious subjects that I have treated; and I do not know if, by reversing the order of the question proposed, I could reasonably flatter myself that I had fulfilled the law of progression so recommended by the rhetoricians. However, I do not despair of succeeding: the reader will decide if my boldness has been felicitous.

There is no doubt that Moses, in establishing the law of the Sabbath, had in mind the health of the people and the healthiness of their homes; and if he did not invoke this motive in the Decalogue, it is because he avoided with the most extreme circumspection allowing human motives to appear in his laws. He had observed that where the mysterious and impenetrable did not exist, reason, too soon satisfied, is uncontrollable, faith vanishes, and obedience slackens. Moses thus prescribe nothing in particular for the Sabbath with regard to hygiene, judiciously awaiting the effects of his institutions and of the numberless guarantees with which he surrounded them, which he would certainly have had more trouble obtaining by a rule regarding property. If he was not mistaken in his predictions, things should develop by themselves; he had only to command that which would produce by itself the zeal for religion and competition in propriety. Don't we see every day the most laudable efforts of authority fail before the indifference and idleness of individuals? The walls are covered with immense placards on the public roads, the cleaning of the sewers, the removal of refuse, the care of trees, etc.; what effect results from all this prefectorial eloquence? The people allow themselves to be eaten away at by gangrenous humors and infected by miasmas, rather than remove what poisons them. The insects eat them and they do not stir. But let opinion, the point of honor or passion be mixed in, and the people will work miracles: they will drain lakes, move mountains, exterminate swarming breeds; after which, not being able to believe in the prodigies that its strength gives birth to, they will glorify heroes and geniuses for it. That contradiction of the human mind, which accuses in such a conclusive manner the preponderance of sentiment over reason, and which the makers of passional theories have explained so little, Moses made the most powerful spring of his policy, and it is to that fact that we are still indebted for the only hygienic habits which triumph over popular apathy. I will linger no more on this section; for, if I exhausted all the reflections that the metamorphosis of the malign Sunday would suggest, if I countered in a thousand ways that vulgar thesis, I would not depart from this same idea. I would fatigue the attention without enlightening the mind. We must see the thing from higher up. Let us eliminate all pointless discussion.

Rest is necessary to health;

1839: The Celebration of Sunday

Now, Sunday commands rest;

Thus Sunday is beneficial to health.

Thus would an inattentive observer reason, concluding too quickly from coexistence to likeness. This syllogism lacks precision, because rest is not linked to the celebration of Sunday in such a way that, the latter being suppressed, the former would be irrevocably lost. Where Sunday is no longer respected, it is clear that one does not labor more—and perhaps one will labor less. In the second place, the argument misses the question; for it is not here a question of rest in itself, an excellent thing, which has few detractors. Rest is the father of movement, generator of strength and companion of labor. Rest, taken moderately and at useful times, sustains courage, enlivens thought, fortifies the will, and makes virtue invincible. But all that has nothing to do with our subject: it is not as the sanction of rest that Sunday exerts an influence on hygiene.

What matters is this fixed and regular periodicity, which cuts, at equal intervals, into the succession of works and days. Why this constant symmetry? Why six days of labor, rather than five or seven? Why the week, rather than a period of ten days? What statistician first observed that in ordinary times the period of labor should be to the period of rest in a ration of 6 to 1, and according to what law? That the two periods should alternate, and why?

Doubtless no one expects me to respond to these questions: they are the despair of all science and modern erudition, and I pity whoever, facing this same matter, does not perceive that abyss. The origin of the week is unknown: as for the law of proportion between the duration of labor and that of relaxation, we don't even suspect the reason, and I do not believe that it has excited the attention of the economists and physiologists. Our ignorance is complete on all these things. Excuse me, then, if, lacking positive documents, I find myself reduced to giving some reports on that ancient philosophy, which, in the times of Moses, already bore the same fruits.

"Going back to the first days of humanity, we see the men who cultivated wisdom occupied particularly with three principal objects, directly relative to the perfecting of human faculties, of morals, and of happiness. 1) They studied man, healthy and ill, in order to know the laws which rule him, and to learn to preserve him and bring him health. 2) They tried to draw up some rules to direct their minds in the search for useful truths, and laid out their lessons, either on the particular methods of the arts or on philosophy, whose more general methods embrace them all. 3) Finally, they observed the mutual relations of men, but in that determination they included as necessary data some more mobile circumstances, such as time, place, governments, and religions; and from them arose for them all the precepts of conduct and all the principles of morals."

I would observe in passing that it is this linking of the moral and physical in the mind of the ancient legislators which has contributed everywhere to the assumption of a primitive pantheism, or worship of the soul of the world.

Pythagoras was the first who applied mathematical calculation to the study of man. He wanted to subject the phenomena of life to mechanical formulas; he perceived between these periods of feverish activity, of development or decline in animals, and certain regular combinations or recurrences of numbers, relations that the experience of the centuries seems to have confirmed, and the systematic exposition of which constituted what we call the *doctrine of crises*. From that doctrine followed not only several indications useful in the treatment of illness, but also some important considerations on hygiene and the physical education of children. It would perhaps not be impossible to still draw from it some views on the manner of regulating the labors of the mind, of seizing the moments when the disposition gives it the most strength and lucidity, to conserve all its freshness, by wearying it inappropriately, when the state of remission commands it to rest. Everyone can observe in themselves these alternations of activity and languor in the exercise of thought: but what would be truly useful would be to restore its periods to fixed laws, taken in nature, and from which one could draw some rules of conduct applicable, by means of certain individual modifications, to the diverse circumstances of climate, temperament, age, in short, to all the cases where men can be found…

"Such is the data from which the different founders of religious orders began, who, by hygienic practices more or less happily combined, strove to adapt minds and character to the sort of life of which they had conceived the plan." (Cabanis, *Relations of the Physical and the Moral*.)

It is through an error of memory or attention that Cabanis proclaims Pythagoras *the first who applied mathematical calculation to the study of man*. Long before that philosopher, the secrets of numbers were known. What he knew of it himself was very little, and came to him from elsewhere. His glory is to have been their initiator and promoter in Magna Graecia. Nearly a thousand years before Pythagoras, Moses made use, in his legislation, of all the science of the Egyptians; and that science, already old in that period, appears to have consisted above all in a sort of metaphysics of rhythm and number, of which it is perhaps easier to conceive the general reason than to find the principles and facts. The Greeks retained something of it, which they expressed by the name of mousiki, which included aesthetics, moral science, poetry, oratory, and grammar, and which we properly call music. But the relations of the physical and the moral, those of religion and politics, the multitude of relations between all the parts of intelligent, living and animated nature, the analogies between the various branches of human knowledge, that the numerical operations served to calculate and formulate, all of that was excluded from their music, and philosophy itself has retained hardly any of it. Some have sought, in our own times, to recall attention to these objects of antique curiosity; but up to the time in which I write, they have only succeeded in giving caricatures or puerile allegories. It is not with the imagination, but with observation and fact, that we will create such a science. It will not be guessed. We must infer it from phenomena. Moreover, what renders it so difficult for us is the unequal development of the sciences: in order for a synthesis to be able to occur, there must be one single intelligence which embraces all the parts, which presumes either all the infinite sciences, or their parallel progress.

But were the sciences more advanced in Egypt, four thousand years ago, than they are in France in the nineteenth century? I will not speak about matters whose nature is foreign to me: perhaps the Egyptians had discovered methods and sciences of which we are unaware, as they were necessarily unaware of ours. In any event, according to Chainpollion, the arts and sciences appear to have been in decadence in Egypt from the reign of Senusret, 2,000 years before Christ. And I will add that, to judge by all of the propositions that one could extract from the most ancient Hebrew books, modern philosophy still lags behind its inspiration.

It was by a sort of methodical materialism analogous to the doubt of Descartes, that the ancient sages theoretically raised themselves to the knowledge of God and the soul, and let them deduce the persistence of the self beyond the tomb, and the eternally active and conservative personality of the Great Being. Very different in this regard are the modern spiritualists, who, always alarmed by the progress of a pretentious physiology, want to isolate it from psychology, and, to insure the subjective reality of thought, reduce all the phenomena of organic life, and even the determinations of the sensibility, to a crude mechanics,. They knew, these first observers of nature, that the notion of God and of a future existence had been revealed in the beginning to the conscience of man by a mysterious utterance, and that it is still by an immediate transmission from person to person that this notion is preserved in society. But they also thought that, reason having been given to us to contemplate the ineffable ways of the Divinity, no less than to admire his works, that reason extends his domain over that which is above him and that which is below; that he is within his rights to reduce the study of God and the world to one unique point of view, to subject that double study to a single mode of development, and to imitate the cosmogonic succession of beings in the synthesis that they exhibit. The universe, in their eyes, was an immense pyramid of which the visible substance formed the base, the phenomena that this substance proved made up its various tiers, and at the summit of which appeared the Spirit.

"Matter, said the Hierophant, is extended and impenetrable. These two properties, which signify for us only indestructibility, are essential to matter; without them we could not conceive of it. Considered with regard to solidity and surface, it gives rise to the *science of number and measures,* an infinite science, capable of absorbing the life of the man. The dimensions of matter will be sufficient for the exercise of the created intelligence.

"It is a fact that mass will rush towards a center; bodies seek one another, and matter is drawn towards matter: why is this? But while this tendency is general and constant, it does not appear essential to bodies; for we can conceive of them perfectly without gravitation, something that we cannot say of extension or impenetrability. What is more, there is, in this propensity of bodies to join, a circumstance quite contrary to their nature: they are limited and circumscribed, while their sphere of attraction is infinite. The intensity of that attraction is increased or diminished in certain proportions; it is never extinguished. If there had existed only two molecules of matter, they would have been drawn towards one another across all possible space: the subject is without proportion to the attribute. Bodies finally according to the relations of their masses, and by their resilience or expandability, halt, transmit or reproduce movement; they do not create it. There is an external force, distinct from the bodies, that moves and directs them. The science of quantities can calculate the apparent proportions formulate the laws of that force, but it is unable to explain the principle. The knowledge of the effects of bodies, considered as acting on one another by their mechanical power, namely, their movement and their weights, gives rise to a new science, *physics*.

"You think you know something already: enter into the laboratory of nature, and all that you know will vanish like a dream, and leave you only the feeling of your ignorance. What produces between this inert masses this mutual penetration, these sudden metamorphoses, these aversions and preferences, these loves and hates? This is the second incorporation of force. An uncontrollable and certain power presides over all the combinations, and, varying its laws according to the variety and quantity, awaits before acting only contact or repose. See these products so different from their elements; admire the complex geometry of this precipitation. The snow, like a crystallization of transparent flowers, floods with its symmetrical flakes the heights of Mount Lebanon and the Caucasus, father of rivers: what paintbrush has ever drawn figures more regular, and more elegantly varied? But here, the more the intelligence sparkles, the more illusive the cause becomes: science is nothing but a series of names and phenomena. Each fact recorded by the observer blurs his classifications; each discovery is a refutation of his systems; and the deeper you penetrate into this labyrinth, the more its detours increase and entwine. There is still *no chemistry*.

"Who has examined the sources of life? Who has discovered the principle of the sensibilities? Who has seen the lighting of the torch of instinct? Tell me by what virtue plants and animals assimilate their nourishment; from whence comes the autonomy that preserves and guides them?... Oh, mystery! All living beings are armed for reproduction; individuals die, but species are indestructible. Before these marvels, what is the science of the chemist or the physician? What is it that gross matter can teach you about living matter? Gravitation, the attraction of cohesion, the elective affinities, soon find the end of their action. The elementary combinations, once carried out, remain fixed. The spring released, the machine stops and everything returns to rest. There is no resurgence, no internal development, no perpetuity, and no center of operations. You will never explain life by weights and resistances, by molecular attractions or atomic combinations. We need, for this new order of phenomena, a new mathematics, a new physics, and a new chemistry. You may, if you like, call that science *physiology*.[8]

---

[8] "[A]ll the efforts of philosophers have not yet been able to discover matter in the act of organization, either of itself or by any extrinsic cause. In fact, life exercising upon the elements which at every instant form part of the living body, and upon those which it

"But, Fate! What can physiology do for the theory of intelligence? Are ideas acquired as the organs grow? Are judgments formed by a digestion of the brain! Is it the nervous system or the vascular system that produces metaphysicians and geometers? You speak of organic predispositions, natural appetites, temperaments, etc.; that is to say that an organism is necessary as a *substratum*, or place of exercise, for thought, but not that it engenders the thought, just as matter is necessary to the production of force, and is not force; to the development of life, but is not life. No one knows the genesis of the soul. No one has sounded the abyss of his faculties.

"What use will man make of that light which illuminates his instinct? Isn't it to be feared that he will put it in the service of his selfishness, at the expense of all those around him?... A brake is imposed on his fierce greed; an inner voice warns him of what is allowed, of the rights he must respect, and of the punishments that await if he disobeys. Well! You will succeed in knowing this invisible legislator, whose dictates arrest the appetites of the nature, this reason to act independent of speculative reason, no better by reducing it physiology, than you have by attempting to reduce it to sensibility, to reduce sensibility to attraction, or weight to expanse. We require *morals*: who will give them to us?

---

attracts to it, an action contrary to that which would be produced without it by the usual chemical affinities, it is inconsistent to suppose that it can itself be produced by these affinities." G. Cuvier. *Introduction to the Animal Kingdom*

"The sciences we have just enumerated form so many systems, which are distinct but do not contradict one another. The facts proper to each being varied, but not opposed, can only give rise to different laws: the expression of one of these laws is not the negation of the other. On the contrary, the object of the second and the third of these sciences being the object of the first, plus a new element, *force*; the object of the fourth being the object of the first three, plus another element, *life*; the object of the fifth being the same as that of the previous ones, plus a third element, *reason*; the object of the sixth, finally, being the object of five others, plus a last element, *justice*, it follows that they form an ascending gradation, along the whole extent of which the mathematical formulas must find their application. There is thus a science of sciences, a philosophy of the universe, of which *number*, which is to say *rhythm*, series, is the object.

"Thus, all the sciences demonstrate one another, and serve reciprocally as cross-check and criterion. If, for example, the succession of days of rest, instead of corresponding to the arithmetic progression 1, 8, 15, 22, 29, 36, etc., had the relation: 1, 6, 14, 25, 29, 39, 47, you could conclude, with no other demonstration, and by that fact alone, that the numbers 1, 6, 14, 25, 29, 39, 47, did not form a regular period, that such a distribution of holidays is contrary to hygiene, morals, and liberty.

"A living, intelligent and moral creature, a creature of both mind and matter, man is subject to the laws of life, thought and science; shape, force and number are the bases of his intelligence as was as his being. To understand something of this microcosm, you must have observed all of nature; to aspire to direct it, you must know all the orders of phenomena and the secret of their balance. Of all the studies, the study of man is the largest; of all the arts, that of governing him is the most difficult.

"When you raise a building, you use the plumb and lever to assure that the centers of gravity of all the stones meet in a single perpendicular plane; for you know by statistics that by neglecting that precaution you compromise the solidity of the structure. Likewise, you have observed that, to farm successfully, it is necessary to observe the times of grafting, germination, flowering and maturity, the advantages of the season and the soil, and all the rules of vegetable life. You can accelerate and multiply the development of that life, but you can only do it by virtue of its own laws: to act on it, you need a pressure point, and it is in that pressure that you will find it. Thus, the eagle that plane in the sky triumphs over gravity by the use of gravity itself.

"What! Man is order and beauty, and you will abandon his education to chance! His will is free, and, instead of directing him, you will impose chains on him! His conscience raises him towards his maker, and you will render that conscience impious! Under the pretext of emancipating reason, you will proclaim your republic without God! To build up the flesh and blood, you will recommend passion and deny duty! Legislator of swine, your barn will not stand: the conscience, the will and the intelligence will react against a blind tyranny, and since you have not been able to rule them, and you have been afraid to destroy them, you will see them burst out in a frightful confusion, until finally, exhausted by their excesses and obeying their nature, they return to their legitimate ordination and harmonize themselves in an eternal society."

I would like now to be able to say how, with that powerful method of induction, the ancient philosophy escaped the reef, so common today in a certain kind of shipwreck, of speculative and practical pantheism; how it resolved the subsequent problems of the destiny of man, of the origin of evil, of the principle of our knowledge and of the foundations of certitude. But I have not been initiated in the sanctuaries of Heliopolis and Jerusalem, and I have not inherited the mantle of Elijah. Moreover, such a reconstruction, not being made of special fragments, but only inferred from the general spirit of the beliefs and institutions, would always preserve an arbitrary character, and however plausible one makes the ensemble and the details, they will attest less to the exactitude of the doctrine than the spirit of the critique.

Moses, having thus to rule in a nation the works and day, the feasts and holidays, the labors of the body and the exercises of the soul, the interests of hygiene and morals, political economy and the subsistence of persons, had recourse to a science of sciences, to a *transcendent harmonic*, if he will permit me to give it a name, that embraces everything: space, duration, movement, minds and bodies, the sacred and the profane. The certainty of that science is demonstrated by the very fact with which we concern ourselves. Reduce the week by a single day, labor is insufficient in comparison with rest; add the same quantity, and it becomes excessive. Establish a half-day of rest every three days, and the fragmentation multiplies the loss of time, and by splitting the natural unity of the day, you break the numerical balance of things. Grant, on the contrary, forty-eight hours of rest after twelve consecutive days of effort, you kill the man with inertia after having exhausted him with fatigue. I omit, for the sake of brevity, the mass of similar considerations that might suggest the inversion of relations in the family and city, and which would bring to light other disadvantages. How then did Moses calculate so well? He did not invent the week, but it was, he believed, the first and only thing that would serve for such a great purpose. Would he have adopted that proportion, if he had not calculated in advance its whole impact? And if it was not the effect of a theory he held, how are we to explain such a prodigious intuition! Moreover, as for supposing that chance alone had thus favored it, I would rather belief in a special revelation that had been made to him about it, or the fable of a sow writing the Iliad with its snout.

We rightly mock the foolish mania of those people who exalt the ancients beyond measure, and who discover the vestiges of the most sublime knowledge where the judicious observer only perceives the mark of good sense. But when the facts are multiplied and clarified by each other, when several monuments render a common testimony, the probability increases as the doubt diminishes. We have seen at the beginning of this memoir the septenary number figure in the categories of duty; the same number is present in the cosmogony of Moses and in a multitude of other circumstances, for example, in the symptomatology of the leper; finally, we have cited the reflections of Cabanis on the relations of numbers: were all these laws recorded by the ancients, or just dreamed up at random? The response would presume the very science of which I have spoken—and spoken too long, since I don't even know the name it bears.

V

If I have accomplished the task that I imposed on myself in beginning these researches, it remains certain and proven:

> 1. That the institution of the Sabbath was conceived on the principles of a higher politics, the greatest secret of which consisted in making the means arise from the end;

> 2. That this institution, analyzed in the circumstances of its origin and its reform, supposes liberty, equality, supremacy of religion and the laws, executive power in the people, absolute dependence of the functionaries, means of subsistence the same for all;

> 3. That its effects, mediate and immediate, is summed up in the following: highly developed sociability, perfect morality, health of the body and mind, constant happiness, always capable of increase and variety, according to ages and characters;

> 4. That it was eminently conservative of the social order, which conserved it in its turn.

It remains for me to clarify some difficulties.

If it is true that the plan of Moses was such as I have tried to describe, how did he let nothing of that plan appear? Why do we not find a word of it in the motives that he alleged, and he cited everywhere only to the absolute will of God? Why, instead of these fine political teachings, did he always resort to promises and threats?

Moses spoke to his century so that he could be understood by it; he explained himself as he had to. The law of the Sabbath was not the only one in which the name of Jehovah took the place, outwardly, of every motive and every sanction: the other laws, whether political, civil or criminal, as well as the detailed ordinances, were in the same position. It is always the same formula—*I am the Lord*— which is the supreme reason. Sometimes the benefit of deliverance is recalled, in order to add the sweeter bond of gratitude to the motive of fear. But everywhere the true spirit of the law is concealed: Moses seems to have wanted that knowledge to be reserved for the faithful, for it to become the prize of perseverance and meditation. Sometime he only half expressed it, and sometimes he wrapped his thought in a symbolic and figurative style, leaving to the attentive reader the task of penetrating the sense of his words. Never, however, did he deign to anticipate a *why* or a *how*, or to forestall a single objection.

Moses instituted a *Sabbath year*, that is he forbade the cultivation of the soil each seventh year, declaring that the Lord wanted it thus, and promising on his part a triple harvest for the sixth. Mr. Pastoret finds that it is not easy to justify that law. He even remarks that the triple harvest was always lacking. However, that law is nothing but an agricultural precept, and the abundance promised for the sixth year is the natural result of a renewed fertility. With more knowledge, the Israelites would have glimpsed the aim of the legislator, and they would have ordained that the Sabbath of the land would have taken place each year in one-seventh of the lands, so that at the end of seven year the whole territory would be rested. The law dictated that they content themselves, during the seventh year, with the products of the herds: it was an invitation to convert the fields into artificial prairies. Don't we know today that his mode of farming rests the earth and enriches the laborer?

Bestiality was punished with death; among us, that infamy would hardly be judged worthy of the whip. The wretch who soiled himself with it would excite more disgust than blame from the tribunals. But that crime, in the time of Moses, was part of idolatrous ceremonies; in Egypt, women prostituted themselves in public to the Goat of Mendes and to crocodiles, and similar customs were to be seen elsewhere. It is that execrable superstition that motivated the severity of Moses: none of that, however is reflected in the law itself.

He declares abominable anyone who exchanges their clothing for that of the opposite sex. Is it a question of simple disguise? That would be to be a slave of the text. Moses designated under an innocent surface the sort of infamy for which Sappho was famous, which the Greeks deified in Ganymede.

He forbade mixing any foreign seed in the vineyards, *lest*, he said, *the two plants harm one another and are ruined.* This is another law of public morality disguised under a rustic image. Moses, in prohibiting a custom honored since Sparta, which Plato wanted to introduce into his republic, taught the people to care more for conjugal inviolability than for the production of children.

It is a capital crime to imitate the composition of the holy oil, *because,* said Moses, *such a counterfeit is sacrilege.* What made that oil so precious? It is because the mark of the clergy and royalty consisted in consecration; and what Moses called *counterfeiting the holy oil* was nothing less that aspiring to *tyranny.* It was primarily the crime of national lèse-majesté.

Pythagoras said in the same style: "Don't stir the fire with the sword. Don't sit on the bushel." He meant: "Don't provoke an angry man. Avoid idleness."

When Moses instituted a clergy, he did not go out of his way to explain to the people its nature and attributions; he told them nothing of the functions of that order, or of its prerogatives. He did not allow even a glimpse of the reason why no property was allowed to the Levites, while in Egypt the priests possessed a third of the land. He made God say: *I have chosen the children of Le vi to serve in my tabernacle; every intruder will be put to death.* And that was done to Core and Dathan.

The successors of Moses acted in exactly the same way.

Under the judicature of Samuel, the people demanded a king. What was the prophet's answer? Did he reason with the deputies of the tribes? Did he consider whether royalty is in itself a just and moral thing; if it is in the spirit of the constitution; if it did not wound the rights of the people; if it would not lead to a revolution in the State? No; he said to them:

"This will be the right of the king who will command you:

"He will take your sons and make them man his chariots; he will make them horsemen, runners, tribunes and centurions, laborers for his lands, harvesters for his wheat, makers of arms and chariots." Samuel seemed to threaten the Hebrews with conscription.

"He will make your daughters his perfumers, his cooks and his bakers.

"He will take hold of your fields, your vineyards, your olive orchards, and give them to his servants.

"He will take a tenth of your harvests, to pay his eunuchs and his domestics.

"He will take your menservants and your maidservants, the strongest of your young men, and your asses, and put them to work at his chores; he will take a tenth of your livestock, and you will be his slaves."

Samuel did not enter into a discussion with the people; he did not return to principles; he invoked neither rights, nor morals, nor the constitution. Like the democrats of 93, he showed royalty with all its extravagances, its usurpations, its vises and its tyranny; he reviewed its odious cortege, and he cried: *There is your king*!

Thus, when Moses, establishing the Sabbath, said to the people: *Thou shalt sanctify the seventh day, because it is the rest of the Lord who has brought you out of Egypt*, it is not necessary to believe, with the Anglican Spencer and the Calvinist Benjamin Constant, that behind these words are not hidden other motives, more direct, more human, and more capable of satisfying the scruples of a formalist and positive politics. But we must recognize in that language the necessities of the age. Moses, forced to proportion his message to the intelligence of his freemen, chose, from among all the reasons he could have given to his commandments, the most impressive and formidable, and let us say it boldly, in the last analysis, the most true, the only true one.

But I sense that my paradoxes become more and more appalling.

What! Some indignant philosopher will doubtless cry: You dare to say that God rests, that he is concerned with our feasts, that he must observe the Sabbath because he gives the example for it! to set up some rules, useful if you like, on revelations and oracles, when one claims to have better reasons! To make Divinity intervene where only reasoning is admissible! To lead men astray, instead of instructing them, that is what will be called truth! What is your philosophy? What do you profess?

Unfortunate one, how will you understand me, if you refuse to see the trend of my thought? My profession is this: that Moses believed in his own God; that he believed in his soul and conscience, and that he was imbued with that faith which alone established his authority and his strength. He adored foremost, in spirit and in truth, that Jehovah whose prophet he was. But his worship was not of the common sort.

God, as Moses conceived him, is living Force, effective Will, infinite Reason.

He is, he creates, and he commands.

As supreme being, he is the principle of all existence; as action and life, he moves, animates and preserves; as intelligence, he regulates all creation.

The extraordinary revolutions of the world, which are always destroyed and always restored, announce the eternity and immutability of his being; the constancy of physical laws, the permanence of forms, and the recurrence of movements attest to his inflexible will; the sequence of causes and effects, the exact disposition of each thing for a single end, demonstrates his wisdom.

The existence of God is not proven a priori, nor a posteriori, because he has no before or after. We see that existence and feel it. We think, speak, reflect and reason about it. God is necessity; the alpha and omega, the principle and complement of all. He is the Unique and the Universal, embracing all truths in an infinite chain. We grasp some links here and there, some more or less extensive fragments of that chain, but the immensity of its ensemble escapes us. Whoever expresses a thought,by that alone names God; all our sciences are only partial or unfinished expositions of the absolute science, which is the *scitum* and *fatum* of God himself.

The organisms that God has created are predisposed by him in such a way that, coming from his hands, they accomplish their destinies by themselves. Thus, the celestial orbs have each been weighted for the route that they will travel. Thus the atoms find themselves formed for all combinations. In the vegetable realm, the assimilating power is never deceived: we have yet to see the grapevine produce melons.

The animals are endowed with memory and imagination, and capable of some experience: they enjoy nearly from birth an entirely developed and innate intelligence, which we call instinct. Their movements are spontaneous, and their will is free; but that liberty only acts under a lawful order, and only obeys a sort of impulse, that of physical and sensible nature.

Compared with the animals, man has, with regard to thought, more intelligence, which reflects, counts, judges, reasons, combines, generalizes, classes and distinguishes; with regard to sentiment, more conscience, which dictates new laws to him, often contrary to the appetites of his sensibility. The field of human liberty is double: enlightened by reason, the masterwork of that liberty is to harmonize all his acts; its greatest effort, to sacrifice passion to duty.

The will of man, obeying two different impulses, has a composite movement. It is thus prone to going astray. In that case, man is at fault and always unhappy. The direction of the will demands the most attentive monitoring and the most discriminating temperament. It is in the study of the relations between the physical, the intellectual and the moral, that the best of mode education for the will is to be discovered.

But man is born into society: it is thus also necessary to study the relations between men, in order to determine their rights and sketch out some rules for them. What complications! There is a science of quantities which forces assent, excludes willful objections, and rejects every utopia; a science of physical phenomena, which rests only on the observation of the facts; a grammar and a poetics based on the essence of language, etc. There must also exist a science of society, absolute and rigorous, based on the nature of man and his faculties, and on their relations, a science that he will not *invent*, but *discover*.

Now, admit that the principles of that science have been fixed, with every application made by means of the principles of deduction and causation, and we will understand how Moses, starting from the absolute, found as the ultimate reason for his laws only the commands of God.

5 multiplied by 5 gives a product of 25. Why? It is impossible to give any reason for it, if not that this is a fact, that this is the logic of numbers, that our intelligence, whose laws are the same as those of nature—or God—make us understand the fact in this way.—Bodies weigh on the earth. Why? Because of gravitation. And what is gravitation? The order of God, said Newton.—Nitric acid shows a stronger attraction to iron

than to copper. Why? That is perhaps the result of the shape, the density, and the different arrangement of their atoms. Why don't the atoms of all bodies resemble one another? It is because God wills it. — The elements of verse, in Latin, consist of prosody and measure; in French, in rhyme or measure. Why this difference? Because of the diversity of idioms. But, while the intelligence and organs of man remain the same, where can this diversity come from? From a multitude of causes which all amount to the decree of destiny.

To govern men, it is also only a question of seeking God's order. Everything that enters into that order is good and just; everything that strays from it is false, tyrannical and bad.

It is just to make, or to speak more precisely, to discover and ascertain the economic laws, restrictive of property and distributive of labor; Why? In order to maintain equality in conditions. But why should conditions be equal? Because the right to live and develop completely is equal for all, and the inequality of conditions is an obstacle to the exercise of that right. How is the equality of rights proven? By the parity of penchants and faculties; because God, in giving them to all, did not want them to be stifled or subjugated in one for the benefit of another. The equality of fortunes is the expression of the divine will, which has reserved for rebellious societies a terrible punishment, destitution. It is a question of knowing how that equality will be realized: for it is not for us the object of a restoration, but of an institution.

The command of an individual will only be counted for something to the extent that it conforms to reason: in this case, it is no longer the man who commands, it is reason. It is the law. It is God. Nobody has the privilege of interposing his will in the legal exercise of right, to suspend the law or sanction it. Thus all royalty is contrary to order; it is a negation of God. Everywhere royalty exists, even when subjected to some rules, even if it is beneficial and protective, it will only be an abuse that nothing can legitimate, a usurpation that no one can dictate. Its origin is always blameworthy. It is, if one will allow me this scholastic jargon, *ex ordine ordinando*, never *ex ordine ordinato*. —We must say as much of all aristocracy and democracy. The authority of some over all is nothing. The authority of the greatest number over the least is nothing. The authority of all against one is nothing, without the authority of the law, which alone cannot be contradicted.

It is good that some men be specially charged with instructing the others, with recalling them to their rights, warning them of their duties, teaching manners and religion, bringing up the young, settling contentions and disputes, cultivating the sciences and practicing medicine. These men are not masters, but teachers of the people, *demagogues*.[9] They command no one; they say what should be done, and the people carry it out. They do not impose belief, but show the truth. They neither give nor sell religion, philosophy and the sciences, for they are not their property. They are only their physicians and

---

[9] *Demagogue*, conductor or tutor of the people; as *pedagogue*, tutor of children; *mystagogue*, master of sacred ceremonies.

guardians. Their doctrine is true: all that they announce is the word of God.

It is necessary from time to time for men to rest, that they even rejoice: the soul must be nourished and the body repaired. What should the duration of labor be? What will the intervals of rest be? Will the holidays be observed simultaneously by all the citizens? How will hygiene, morals, the family and the republic profit by them? Search the will of God.

It is thus that, in their political foundations, all the legislators and philosophers of antiquity would proceed. Never would they enter into the spirit of separating the rights from the man, of placing some under the protection of a justice armed with a sword, and abandon the others to the tutelage of religion. For them every moral proscription was civil law, and all civil law was sacred. With regard to religious rites, as those rights had for principle a reasonable and useful object, the greatest men submitted to them, conceiving no virtue and propriety without a rule, as they did not conceive justification without works.

From the unity of the law followed the unity of power: so it happened that Jeroboam erected a temple in Samaria, that Ozias wanted to award himself the censer, in Rome the consuls were at the same time soothsayers and supreme pontiffs, that the further one goes back into antiquity, the more one finds that the chiefs of the peoples brought together the three positions of king, priest and prophet. But soon all those notions would be obscured. The usurpations entered like a mob into the sanctuary and the temple of the law. The kings and priests, each on their side, would make a patrimony of the government and the church, and sometimes quarreling, sometimes associating their interests, too often made the yoke of fanaticism and tyranny weigh on the people.

Moses wanted to spare the Israelites these fatal drawbacks. He founded a police which, confided to a more faithful race, would certainly have led to the highest degree of domestic felicity and national strength. But the people, not knowing how to be free, wanted a king. Now, the establishment of a royalty was something so contrary to all the ideas of the legislator, so eccentric to his plan, that the Jewish monarchs never believed that they could consolidate their power beside a law that they had not made and which troubled them in all their movements. That is what explains that dogged idolatry, that long apostasy into which the kings of Judah strove to lead the nation. And, indeed, to return to my subject, (which I have never abandoned, even when I seem to be diverting ever more from it,) what could have been more dreadful and odious for the sultans of Jerusalem, than these feasts and Sabbaths when the people were obliged by their religion to gather and to read the law, that law that taught them who they were and who was their sovereign? How could they bear those great solemnities of Passover and Tabernacles, which, gathering the whole nation as a single family, made them reflect on their strength and on the weakness of the corrupting and liberticidal tyrant? The schism of the ten tribes was accomplished in one of these great gatherings. Athaliah was cast down from the thrown during the feast of Pentecost. The Maccabees would use a Passover to rouse the people against the king of Syria, and this was also the occasion when the revolt of the Jews under Vespasian took place. According to the prescriptions of Moses, the king could only be a president of the republic. This was clearly the sense of the instructions given to the king in Deuteronomy, of which, until the time of Josiah, no one had been aware. To be king, truly king, as the Hebrew melks understood it, and as one always expects it to be, it is necessary to corrupt the people and separate them from the institutions: that was, it is true, what led to its loss and prepared the ruin of the throne. No matter, the kings would not hesitate. The seduction was accomplished, and it was total. It will last as long as the monarchy itself, since, in the words of the fourth book of Kings, it was an unheard of novelty that the Passover was celebrated under Josiah and, according to Ezra, the captivity had lasted seventy years, in order that the earth had the time to *rest and celebrate its Sabbaths*. As soon as a nation has right, even if granted [from above], it is ungovernable by any will that wants to be the equal, if not the ruler of the law; because, sooner or later, the Charter, whether awarded or consented to, rebels against the will which is not its own, and opposes it.

In it origins, religion was politics and science; the priesthood were thus also magistracy and teachers. Every social organization is contained in that trilogy. But it is necessary that the priest becomes dogmatic and intolerant, that the judge becomes violent and despotic, that the philosopher, contemptuous of priests and kings, makes himself their persecutor and curse; it is necessary that all mankind should bear the penalty of their follies, to teach us that the division of functions does not entail the separation of powers, and that if there is a contradiction between reason and conscience, between conscience and the law, that contradiction comes from us. Today, peace is on the verge of being concluded: the civil law recognizes its insufficiency, and calls for the support of religion; philosophy touches on the demonstration of the mysteries; faith, without abandoning any of its doctrine and traditions, offers rational explications. Who would dare to say that something greater than the code, philosophy and religion will not spring from these reciprocal concessions?

There was always, within the homeland, an elite of citizens, the first in science and virtue. Let their functions be to instruct, counsel and resolve. Let them form the greatest and most glorious university. Let them give to the people a perpetual example of equality and disinterestedness. Let their reward be to hear themselves called *prudent as well as wise and fathers of the nation*.

Let us abolish royalty without hatred and vengeance, because with royalty we are all guilty. Let us reject it, not only as vicious, extravagant, corrupting and unworthy, but as illegitimate. We dispute endlessly: *The king reigns and govern, the king reigns and does not govern*. Let us begin by saying: He *governs and does not reign*; and if we are not still in the realm of truth, at least we have made a step towards it; for it is the people who are the *executive* power, and it is the law that inaugurates them.

And let us preserve, let us restore the solemnity of Sunday, so eminently social and popular, not as an object of ecclesiastic discipline, but as an institution that conserves mores, a source of public spirit, a meeting place inaccessible to the cops, and a guarantee of order and liberty. In the celebration of Sunday is lodged the most fruitful principle of our future progress; it is by taking advantage of Sunday that the reform will be achieved.

Let there rise in the midst of his brothers, with all the authority of virtue and genius, the reformer that some await. Let him come, powerful in words and deeds, to convert and to punish. Let him see the horror of our vises, and hear the tale of our follies. Let him lament our miseries and let him cry out: The cause of the evil is in the ideas. To heal the heart, you must correct the brain. Can you remake your understanding? Can you change your opinions, condemn what pleases you, hate what makes you laugh, love and respect what hardly concerns you? Do you believe these truths that you no longer understand?

Crime is imputable, satisfaction necessary, and punishment just and legitimate.

Labor is obligatory, property only usufruct, and inheritance a mode of conservation of shares; liberty is balance ; the inequality of nature is weakened by education, and effaced by the equality of fortunes. Marriage is exclusive and holy: fornication is an offense against nature, against persons and against society.

Reason oversees the senses; the conscience imposes a brake on the animal passions. Man's end is not to enjoy, but to cultivate his soul and contemplate the works of God.

Falsehood is the murder of the intelligence; the oath is inviolable.

The law is not the expression of a single will, nor of a general will; it is the natural relation of things , discovered and applied by reason .

The sanction of the law is in God, who gives it.

Oh citizens! If you can't handle that medication, if you find this brew too bitter, stop complaining, ask for no medicine and rot in your own corruption. But listen to what will happen.

The sun will shine neither more nor less on the soil where you live. The dew and gentle breezes will refresh your fields and meadows in the same way. Your trees will not be less productive, your vines less fertile. You will not see hail, floods or fire desolate your towns or countryside more often. The elements will not be more murderous.

But opulence and misery, inseparable companions, will increase in an endless progression; large properties will invade everywhere. The bankrupt peasant will sell his inheritance; and when there are only landlords and tenants, lords and serfs, the first will give to the second a few clothes, lodging and some bread, and they will say to them: See how happy your are? What is liberty and equality? Long live harmony!

In those times, trivial talents and arts of luxury will be rewarded lavishly. We will see singers more wealthy than large villages are now. The wage of a comedienne will be more than the cost of a hundred bushels of wheat in a famine. The poor worker, the laborer's wife and the artisan will be humiliated.

The merit of women will no longer be anything but an evaluation of their beauty, their most sacred right, to be surrendered to the highest bidder. The wealthy will possess them all, because they alone can pay; the poor will be left with the disgraced and the castoffs of luxury.

The ignorance and exhaustion of the proletarians will be at its height. They will not be prevented from learning, but they will not be able to live without working, and when they are not working, they will eat nothing. If someone among them shows talent, he will be encouraged, rewarded, and *enriched*; he will enter into the upper class and be lost to his own.

The people, who always follow the example of the rich and powerful, having lost respect and faith in the old religion, which at least taught them the equality of men before God, and could make them suspect that they are also equals on earth, will traverse all the degrees of a materialist and pantheist superstition; and when they have been persuaded that God is All and that all is God, then they will return to fetishes and manitous. They will worship, as they once did, the trees and stones; they will believe in the power or relics, and carry amulets; and the wealthy, under the pretext of utility and tolerance, will protect the new devotion, saying: There must be a religion for the people.

However, they will sometimes encounter some proud souls, men who refuse to bow down before the golden calf. Those will want to compare accounts with the favorites of fortune. — Why are you so rich and we are so poor? — We have labored, respond the rich; we have saved, and we have acquired.—We labor as much as you, how is it that we never acquire anything?—We have inherited from our fathers.—Ah! You invoke possession, transmission, prescription. Well! We call on force. Proprietors, defend yourselves!

And there will be combats and massacres; and when force will again be established as law, when the *rebels* have been destroyed, they will write on their tombs ASSASSINS, while their victims will be glorified as martyrs.

And that will endure until God takes pity on us.

But who today will dare to speak in such language? Let us save ourselves from all illusions. Certain people imagine that a great personage must soon appear in the midst of humanity, one of those *providential beings*, as we call them, who will summarize all ideas, disengage truth from error, strike down the old prejudices, put all opinions on a new level, and with his strong hand launch the present generation down a new road—or a new rut. The nineteenth century will not pass, they say, before our prediction comes to pass. Some go further: the great man has already come; Elias has walked the earth; but the world has not understood. The Turk says: God is God, and Mohammed is his prophet. These modern believers make a similar profession of faith. But the time of the great reformers, like that of the founders of religions, is gone forever. It is up to societies to fend for themselves. Let them await their salvation only at their own hands. Men never lack truth, but they often lack the good faith and courage to recognize and follow it.

1839: The Celebration of Sunday

As for myself, I have not placed my confidence in anything new under the sun: I have faith in some ideas as old as the human race. All the elements of order and happiness, preserved by imperishable traditions, exist. It is only a question of recognizing the synthesis, the method of application and development. How has humanity still not succeeded in this? It is up to history to teach us. I could say something of it as well as anyone; but, in my opinion, the philosophy of history will exist only when the social problem is resolved. Truth is necessary to give the definitive reason for error. But can that truth itself be found other than in unity? It is when the most furious antagonism has been succeeded by general equilibrium, when the struggle of all the doctrines has given birth to the one and indivisible science, when the religions and philosophies have been joined at the altar of truth, that we will be able to shout: The times of testing are over; the golden age is before us! Yes, humanity will know that it has entered its legitimate path, when, looking upon itself, it can say: One sole god, one sole faith, one sole government, *Unus Deus, una fides, unum imperium*.

1840

Letter to the Members of the Academy of Besançon

Besançon, August 3, 1840

To the Members of the Academy of Besançon

Gentlemen, I have learned through the confidences of some of my friends that the publication of my Memoir on *Propriété*, and especially the preface addressed to the Academy of Besançon, which appears at the beginning of that Memoir, have roused your displeasure, not to mention you indignation, against me. That is the motive that enlists me to explain to you here, in few words and in all their simplicity, my conduct and my intentions.

First of all, what has been taken for a dedication is only a simple report, which my condition as the Suard *pensionnaire* and the obligation imposed on me to make known each year the progress of my studies seemed to me to explain sufficiently. I knew that a dedication is a certification of patronage of the person or the body to which one has dedicated it, so that it must be agreed to or even planned between the parties involved; I did not wish to free myself from that rule of decorum. On the other hand, a report is necessarily determined in form and content by the work on which one reports; that, Gentlemen, is what explains the silence that I have kept with regard to you, concerning the work, and concerning the address that precedes it.

As for the book itself, I would not argue here the cause that I have embraced; I had no desire to place myself before you as an adversary, no than as an accused; my conviction, what I am saying? my certainty concerning the truths that I have elaborated is invincible, and I respect your opinion to much, Gentlemen, to ever combat it directly. But, if I advance some unheard of paradoxes concerning Property, that basis of our present political state, does it follow that I am an implacable revolutionary, a secret conspirator, an enemy of society? No, Gentlemen; in admitting my doctrines without reservation, all that you could conclude from it, and all that I conclude myself, is that there exists a natural, inalienable right of *possession* and labor, for the enjoyment of which the proletarian must be prepared, just like the black of the colonies, before receiving the liberty of which no one today contests the right, must be prepared for liberty. That education of the proletarian is the mission confided today to all the men powerful in intelligence and fortune, under pain of being sooner or later crushed under an deluge of those barbarians to whom we are accustomed to give the name of *proletarians*.

Should I respond to another sort of accusation? Some have seen in my conduct toward my academic tutor, to whom I have never made any communication, a sort of ingratitude.

My conduct with regard to Mr. Droz has been dictate to me by a sentiment of decorum; could I enter with that venerable writer into some conferences on moral science and political economy, when those conferences must have, in my opinion, the result of calling into doubt the value of the moral and economic writings of Mr. Droz? Should I put myself in a state of argumentativeness and, so to speak, permanent disobedience with him? No one loves and admires the talent of Mr. Droz more than me; no one can ever demonstrate a more profound veneration for his character. Now, these sentiments were precisely so many reasons that that forbade a polemic that would have been awkward and too perilous for me.

Gentlemen, the publication of that work was commanded of me by the order of my philosophical studies. This is what the future will demonstrate to you. One last Memoir remains for me to compose on the question of Property; that work accomplished, I would pursue, without turning aside from my path, my studies in philology, metaphysics and moral science.

Gentlemen, I belong to no party, to no coterie; I am without advocates, without partners, without associates. I make no sect, and I would reject the role of tribune, were it ever offered to me, for the simple reason that I do not wish to enthralled myself! I have only you, Gentlemen. I only have hope in you. I await favor and a solid reputation only from you. I know that you propose to condemn what you call my *opinions,* and to reject all solidarity with my ideas. I will nonetheless persist in believing that the time will come when you will give me as much praise as I have caused you irritation. Your first emotion will pass, the distress born among you by the bold expression of a still unperceived physical and economic truth will ease, and with time and reflection, I am sure, you will arrive at the enlightened consciousness of your own sentiments, which you do not known, which you combat and I defend.

I am, Gentlemen, with the most perfect confidence in your understanding and in your justice, your very humble and devoted *pensionnaire*.

P.-J. Proudhon

1842

Explanations Presented to the Public Minister on the Right of Property

Court of Assize of the Department of Doubs

(Session of February 3, 1842.)

Last February 3, there appeared before the jury of Besançon, the author of a brochure entitled *Warning to the Proprietors, or Letter to M. Considerant, editor of* la Phalange, *on a defense of property*, on the charge: 1) of attacking property; 2) of provoking various classes of citizens to hatred; 3) of inciting hatred and contempt of the government and king; 4) of offense against the catholic religion.

It is not our intention to give a detailed relation of that trial, which had in common with so many others of the same type only the form of the proceedings and the jurisdiction. The public minister invoked the *written law*, the accused spoke in the name of a science, and, by the form and content of his responses, seemed less to await a verdict of acquittal than a declaration of the court's incompetence. Thus, let no one accuse us of unfaithfulness, if we limit our account to that purely explanatory part of the defense which was intended by the accused as a sort of program of his researches on political and industrial organization, and the constitution of equality.

The advocate general, M. Jobard, defended the charges with all with all the skill of a consummate jurist, but was

1842: Explanations Presented to the Public Minister on the Right of Property

obliged to limit himself to the text of the law. After him, the accused read a written defense, from which we extract the following passages:

I have only written one thing in my life, gentlemen jurors, and I will tell you that thing right away, so there is no question: *Property is robbery*. And do you know what I have concluded from that? In order to abolish that species of robbery, it is necessary to universalize it. I am, you see, gentlemen, as conservative as you; and whoever would tell you the contrary, would prove by that alone that they have understood nothing of my books, and, I would say, nothing of the things of this world.

It is up to the legislator, according to Justinian, to interpret the law; it is also up to the writer to explain his writings. Now, although I do not wish to make my defense a lesson in political economy, it is important to my justification that I explain how that *universalization* of property should be understood: that will be the best response to the charges of the advocate general. For if I prove that in order to render properties equal, it is necessary to preserve the existing rights, it follows that the thought of expropriation would be a contradiction in my own doctrine and, consequently, that it is logically impossible that I could be guilty of the act of which I am accused, and which is imputed to me only because the idea of dispossession, which I reject, has been confused with that of the abolition of the domain of property, which I proclaim.

Let us speak of labor. Labor, gentlemen, is, after God and religion, doubtless what you love and esteem most, and what you recommend every day to your children. It is though labor that you have become what you are; and whoever would try to prove to you—to you who have labored all your life, who have inherited legitimately from your fathers, who feel you have clean hands and pure conscience—whoever would try, I say, to prove to you that your possession could be, without your knowledge, vicious and founded on an illegitimate title, would not be heard. You would dismiss him as a sophist.

Thus, let us leave the metaphysics of right; it is not within the competence of the court of assize.

For you, gentlemen jurors, nothing is more justly acquired than that which you have gained by the sweat of your brow; nothing is more formally condemned by the catechism than holding back the wages of the workers.

Religion has made that crime one of the four sins which cry to the heavens for vengeance. That posited, I asked myself one day how many ways one can retain the wages of the worker; and that examination showed me some very curious things—things that you, gentlemen, do not suspect.

If a laborer made three francs worth of products in a day, he is right to ask three francs for it. All deduction is a crime which cries vengeance, and do not forget it. Now, the world is full of people from whose daily wage a quarter, a third, or a half is retained every day, and that without the Code Napoleon, which certain people admire as the equal of the Decalogue, even anticipating the case.

A pair of shoes is worth, I suppose, five francs. Estimating at two francs and fifty centimes the supplies which enter into the fabrication of a pair of shoes, the rest makes up the wage of the worker, the price of his day of labor. And allowing that the worker is free, that he receives his wage entirely, and that every day he makes a pair of shoes, we would say of his that he gains two francs and fifty centimes per day. But it frequently occurs that a worker is not known in the business, or else that he lacks the means to form an establishment; besides, it is with a clientele as with a piece of land; it is attached to individuals, transmitted from father to son, and not obtained by just anyone. The public has its habits. It gives itself to a boutique, to a sign; nothing is more capricious than its favor. In this case, the worker who is without work offers his services to another worker who is established, and who is called *bourgeois*.

Like the other worker, the bourgeois sells his shoes for five francs. There is competition on one side, which prevents the indefinite increase of the price of merchandise; from the other, the value of supplies and the necessity to live, which prevents the lowering of prices below a certain level. If then, the bourgeois has work, it is probable that he will make his fellow labor, but on the condition that that fellow renounces a part of his wage, for it is necessary that *the master gain from the worker*. And so the worker will not receive all that is coming to him, every day he will see with his own eyes his product selling at a price higher than he has received, and all this without any right to reclaim the deduction.

1842: Explanations Presented to the Public Minister on the Right of Property

Soon, gentlemen jurors, I will show that this *bourgeois*, on whom you perhaps believe that I call all the fury of the populace, is in general a very honest man, who cannot do otherwise, and who is often more to be pitied than the one that he despoils.

But let us see what results from the deduction made from the daily labor of the workers.

When you buy a pair of shoes, you buy the day of a shoemaker. When a cobbler buy shoes, he buys back his own day. Thus if his day is worth fifty sous on the market, and he gains only forty at the workshop, how do you want him to pay his own goods? In that case, you say, he must make his shoes himself. He will have them at cost price, and escape the deduction.

The observation is fair, but we are not finished. The shoemaker cannot procure by himself all the things he needs, since he has only one profession; it is necessary, in order to survive, that he buy, by turns, the day of a tailor, the day of a baker, the day of a vintner, etc. And as he can buy all these days only by offering his own in return; as on the other hand, assuming equal pay for all the trades, and also an equal deduction, the price of all these days surpasses what the purchaser can offer for them. It follows that a worker who needs to buy three hundred sixty-five days of others' labor, at three francs, in order to live, and who receives only two francs and fifty centimes per day, finds himself at the end of the year damaged a sum of one hundred eighty-two francs and fifty centimes according to Barrême.

You will perhaps say that wages not being everywhere the same the worker at two francs fifty centimes makes up for the worker at two francs and below. But, gentlemen jurors, it is precisely that which makes the inequality of conditions; it because of this that there are *poor states*, as one says, although the ancient wisdom had declared that there were no *foolish trades*, but only *foolish people*. Society is like a pyramid: the lower courses support the upper, and sink under the weight. In addition, it suffices for a rule of proportion in order to find the mean of the deductions, and consequently the arithmetic reason for the impoverishment of certain classes of laborers. That is calculated exactly like the tables of mortality.

And that is what explains to us the hopeless profundity of the popular proverb: *The cobblers are always the most poorly shod*; that is also why the masons find themselves the most poorly housed, why the vintners often drink only water, and rarely of the best sort; why the bakers cry famine in the very heart of abundance. It is because there are some bourgeois, some masters, placed over the workers, who make a deduction from their wages, because they are themselves robbed by others, until finally we come to a privileged few who, raised above all the others, profit from all the deductions, but do not suffer any, for the excellent reason that they work for no one.

Now, gentlemen jurors, political economy, a science of recent date, but which already promises marvels, gives the means of escaping that impasse, without harming anyone's lifestyle, without detracting from any interest, without taking anything from the rich, without asking anything of them but the permission to work more and better than one has done up to this day.

Like geometry, political economy has its axioms, its definitions, its laws and its formulas; like geometry it proceeds methodically from the known to the unknown, and starting from the most trivial truths, it raises itself to the intelligence of divine and human laws.

What say the geometers?

The straight line is the shortest route between one point and another.

All the radii of the circle are equal.

Every straight line which falls on another straight line, forms with it two adjacent angles, which are equivalent to two right angles.

It is with this that the geometers measure the circumference of the globe and the height of mountains, calculate the course of the celestial bodies, predict eclipses, weigh the moon and planets, and find the distance and diameter of the sun.

The economists, in another order of ideas, proceed in absolutely the same way. Here are what principles they rely on.

Man produces nothing except by labor.

Wages must be equal to product.

1842: Explanations Presented to the Public Minister on the Right of Property

The productive force of labor is in direct relation to its division.

With the aide of these simple principles, and of some others which follow from them, the economists propose to abolish robbery and property without dispossessing anyone. To organize labor, to explain the causes and the accidents of revolutions. To plumb the secrets of God and to calculate the future. And they will come to the end of it, do not doubt it, gentlemen of the jury, for every question that the human mind can address, it can also resolve.

According to this new species of levelers, of which I count myself a member, who hardly resemble those who terrified France fifty years ago, according to these reformists who are so slandered and so little understood, it is absurd to give six thousand francs to a rector and fifteen hundred francs to a judge, and we know why; according to them, property is a monopoly the temporary existence of which entered into the views of Providence, and we explain what those views have been. But also, according to them, it is necessary to always increase the income of the proprietors, in order to make possible the equality of conditions. I will, gentlemen of the jury, give you an idea of their theories in this regard, theories that the government, which will soon be as egalitarian as I am, has already begun to put into practice.

Let us speak of finance.

We call a *rentier* every capitalist who loans to the State, in perpetuity, a sum of money, at 3, 4, or 5 percent interest. Now, the smallest sum the State accepts in loan being, I believe, 100 francs, and the share of the loan limiting to a small number of persons the advantage of the rent, it follows that the constitution of that rent, always much sought after, creates a true privilege. That creation dates from the National Convention.

But all the French, according to the Charter, are equal before the law; as a consequence, the government, not being able to abolish the privilege of the rent, has occupied itself in recent years with making all the French privileged on the same basis, but how much better it is to interest them in order and public peace. Hence the savings banks, where one receives from 1 franc up to 200, and where interest is paid from 2 up to 4 percent.

Now, gentlemen of the jury, let the worker who does not receive from his bourgeois all the wages from his labor, come in the end, by dint of economies, to create a little income, and you will understand, on the one hand, that this income will form the supplement of the wages that he was expecting to gain, and that he had not received completely; on the other hand, that this rent paid by the State to the thrifty workers being taken from the revenues of the State, and these revenues being deducted in the form of a tax on the proprietors, the State would have to make a part of the revenues pass from the latter into the pockets of the former, an operation which, in the long run and with a bit of consistency, would lead to the equality of all the revenues.

Thus the whole secret consists in making the deduction take place in a circular manner from the one to the others and come back to its point of departure, that is to say that the citizens all work for one another, and, by turns robbed and reimbursed, receive a profit equal to the loss they suffer. At first glance, it seems much simpler that each wage be equal to each individual product; but things could not happen in this way at first, and the organic reason for *this rotation of profit*, if I dare put it that way, is perhaps the most admirable secret of political economy.

Thus, profit, interest, the right of increase, property or suzerainty, is a usurpation, a theft, as Diderot said, more than a century ago, and yet society could live only with the aid of that theft, which will no longer be one, as soon as by the irresistible force of institutions it will become general, and which will cease completely when an integral education has rendered all the citizens equal in merit and in dignity.

In order not to prolong this audience, I will spare you, gentlemen of the jury, some detailed means and processes by the aid of which the egalitarian economists propose to accelerate the realization of that future. Nothing is more curious than to see them transform by circulating money houses, lands, furniture and even tools; to constantly increase everyone's income, by decreasing the fatigues of labor, and gradually enriching the workers, by making greater and greater deductions from their wages.

Those are some trade secrets that I do not have to teach you.

You see, gentlemen, why the true egalitarian is necessarily a conservative; it remains for me to show you how the adversaries of property are necessarily friends of order and government.

The Code Civil, article 556, states:

"The deposits and increases which form successively and imperceptibly on the banks of a river or a stream are called *alluvium*. Alluvium profits the riparian proprietors.

Art. 557. "It is the same with the relays formed by the current, which insensibly remove material from one of its banks and carry it to the other: the proprietor of the increasing bank profits from the alluvium, without the resident on the opposite side being able to come to demand the land that he has lost.

Art. 559. "If a river or a stream, navigable or not, carries away by sudden violence a considerable and identifiable part of a field on its banks, and bears it to a lower field, or on its opposite bank, the owner of the part carried away may reclaim his property, etc."

It is useless to add that on this point there exist as many customs as countries, as many opinions as doctors; this much jurisprudence has known how to work in matters of economy!

Such is the spirit of the Code: if the water takes from me a chunk of the field that I possess, I can reclaim it, provided that I make my demand within a year; if it takes it from me grain of sand after grain of sand, then I lose my property. Too bad for me if my field is found too close to the stream: the legislator will do nothing for me. We see that the spirit of conquest has passed this way.

The economist, on the contrary, maintains that the property must be restored; he demonstrates, by a mathematics of his own, that all the riparian proprietors are connected with one another; that none of them can ever be dispossessed; that all are responsible for the property of each, and each interested in the property of all; that it falls to the municipal authorities ensure the maintenance of the possessions, and to their perfect development. Now which of these two appears the better friend of order and society, gentlemen of the jury, the conquering legislator or the egalitarian economist?

The economist also proves, by analogous principles, that the worker without clientele is like the proprietor dispossessed by a flood; that the homeless proletarian falls under the charge of those housed; that it is among the duties of the administrative authorities to see to it that the laborers are housed according to their nature and the demands of their position in life; that a mayor, a prefect, can and should in some cases require, in return for rent, the rich citizen to house the poor one; to order the restoration of a property, at the expense of the selfish proprietor who has let it degrade and become ugly, as well as the demolition of a shack that disrupts the alignment of a road; to ensure finally that each uses his goods as prescribed and for the greatest advantage of industry, architecture, commerce, morals and hygiene.

1842: Explanations Presented to the Public Minister on the Right of Property

That is what the egalitarian economists call *disciplining possession*, or, in other words, *abolishing property*. What is so frightening about that abolition?

But they add, these economists, that to succeed in that enterprise, it is necessary above all to abstain from dividing goods and establishing an agrarian law; it is necessary to teach, with the national spirit, the spirit of family, and instead of changing the systems of institutions, to develop all the institutions.

The economists, gentlemen, may be wrong, and I doubt that you will give the least bit of faith to the things that I announce. But in the end, their errors are at least very innocent, since instead of tending to destroy, they tend to preserve.

And what I say here is not a subterfuge devised to support my cause; nor is it a tactic of opposition. Might it please God that the radicals had pursued a similar tactic! We would have long since ended our disputes, the government would be tranquil, and the royals would be secure. What I have just said in my defense, for two years I have not ceased to repeat it: I will, among other proofs, read a letter addressed by myself to the Minister of the Interior, a few days before the seizure of the work which is remanded to you. You will see how, after having destroyed the right of property by critique, I propose to transform it by means of organic and industrial development, and you will ask yourself if the author of such a program is a despoiler and anarchist.[10]

---

[10] The public minister, in response to these words of the accused,

To M. Duchâtel, Minister of the Interior

"If we want to spare society new upheavals, we must shake up jurisprudence; we must reconstitute it with the help of a new administrative right, and by imbuing it with the economic element.

"Such is the opinion today of the most learned jurists. According to the Attorney General of the Court of Cassation, our Civil Code needs to be rewritten from one end to the other. We can say as much for the other codes, and for the Charter itself. But, in order to accomplish that great work, we must associate three powers, until this time lamentably enemies, civil jurisprudence, the administration, and political economy: that is the aim of the memoirs that I have published.

"Property, basis of our social order, is also, by the transformation of its principle into that of sovereignty, the basis of our government. But what is that property? it is quiritaire property, jealous, invasive and antisocial property; property which gives all to the citizen to the detriment of the State, which consecrates individual monopoly to the detriment of the general interest. Now,

---

has cited a passage fro the First Memoir, in which the author declares himself *anarchist*. The public minister has not understood that the word *anarchy* was meant in this place in the sense of the *negation of sovereignty*, that is, a substitution of pure reason for caprice in the government. In a word, the author believes in science and recognized the sovereignty of no one. But, in his defense, in conformity with received language, he declares himself non-anarchist, by which he means "a friend of order."

that property, as it was established by Roman law and preserved by the Code Napoleon, is no longer sufficient, in its ancient form and determination, to the needs of civilization: all persons, finally—philosophers, jurists, economists, and men of State—and all doctrines—theories about centralization, industrial solidarity, the organization of labor, the systematization of rights, mortgage reform, the progressive abolition of commercial duties, the allocation of taxes, etc., etc.—conspire to restrain, modify, and transform the ancient right of property.

"It is in consideration of that movement of the public spirit that I dared to describe property as *theft*, expressing in this way a sort of anticipation of future views, and not intending to formulate an accusation against the proprietors. And allow me to say, Monsieur Minister, that the nation's repose, the strength of its powers, the grandeur of France, will only date from the day when that proposition has become an article of faith and principle of government.

"In the past, victories and conquests were the sole source of the legitimacy of the sovereign; Voltaire, hardly more than a century ago, still celebrated that barbarous right. Today the king holds his powers as a result of elections and the law: that is certainly progress, but the constitutional monarchy is not the last word of the political creed, nor the last expression of sovereignty. As for the sovereignty of the people, constantly alleged by those who know nothing more, I regard it simply as an abstraction of words, an ideological generality, but not as a principle, much less as a formula.

1842: Explanations Presented to the Public Minister on the Right of Property

"Now, just as the royalty constituted by the Charter is a middle term between divine right, or conquest, and the ideal of government, just so, between brutal force and association there is, in relation to civil right and political order, a legal intermediary that all existing institutions, all tendencies of opinion, and all the acts of the government work to eliminate; that middle term between barbarity and civilization is property.

"But, Monsieur Minister, it is with these political elements as with simple bodies: combined in certain proportions, they produce chemical compounds with properties totally different from those of the principle components. Thirty-three parts oxygen and sixty-seven of hydrogen give water, a liquid body, stifling, and anti-phlogistic, formed from the combination of two gases, the one breathable by itself, and the other highly combustible.

"Thus, in the political order, the institutions change by the addition of new elements. Sadly, society is not always conscious of the metamorphosis that happens to it. Hence, there is an extraordinary effervescence, and sometimes dangerous resistances in the heart of the nations. If the new idea comes from an individual, it raises general disapproval against it; if it comes from the reigning powers, it excites the trembling of the people and long agitations among the masses. The minister has proven it quite recently in the matter of the census.

"Mixed with pure democracy, the absolute monarchy has produced, according to the differences in the doses, the varieties of constitutional government that we have seen in England and France. Granted by turns to the prince or

1842: Explanations Presented to the Public Minister on the Right of Property

the nation, the election of a Senate, a body aristocratic by its nature, gives either a house of peers or a house of deputies, assembled sovereigns in which nothing oligarchic or feudal will any longer be found. Similarly, introduce into diplomacy and the parliamentary cabals the elements and methods of science, and you will soon arrive at a system of true government, rid of all the wars of parties, and all the intrigues of the opposition.

"Property, according to Mr. Rossi, is a monopoly, but a necessary monopoly. Now, this is the gloss that I have made on that definition of the learned author. Mix the general interest, up to the point of saturation, into monopoly property, and you will have a new principle, analogous, but not identical, to the right of possession and use, known to the old jurists.

"The phenomenon of political composition is precisely that which has passed before our eyes and which, stopped by various obstacles, causes all the anxieties of society and all the confusions of government. There, monsieur, is the fact of social progress that I have labored to record for eighteen months, and of which I hope to determine the laws and calculate the consequences. Society advances, without hardly sensing it, toward a political organization that is absolutely and divinely true, legitimate, perfect, and eternal. It is no longer a question here of ontological aphorisms on equality, fraternity, the rights of man and the citizen, the sovereignty of the people, etc. The metaphysics of the *Social Contract* and *The Spirit of the Laws* is worn out; in the place of these hollow theories rises a new science, exact and mathematical, before which the uncertainties of journalism and the tempests of the gallery must cease forever. Already the people begin to reason and reflect. Now, when the people reflect and reason, we no longer need to fear that they will revolt. For it is in the nature of science to stop the enthusiasm of the mind by the contemplation of its problems and mysteries; the difficulties show themselves more formidable as the intellectual develops, the imagination disciplines itself to the extent that the reason is enlightened, and consequently the furor of revolutions fades before the conditions of reform.

"But what are these conditions? Do they exist apart from active society and the power that directs it? Must we, finally, destroy in order to build?

"Here, Monsieur Minister, is my thought in that regard, a thought expressed more and more energetically in the series of my publications, and which I am about to demonstrate by the deepest and most certain proofs that economic science can offer.

"Society, like every organized and living being, develops continuously, without leaps or jolts, without interruption or substitution. *Interruption*, I said somewhere, *for society as for men, is death*. Thus we must not think to replace the present government and the institutions which serve as its cortège for others; but we must make it produce, by natural means, the government and the institutions that it contains potentially, as the animal and plant are contained in the germ. After that, a revolution would only be a grievous upheaval and a time of suffering for society, that the prudence of the men of state must seek to forestall.

1842: Explanations Presented to the Public Minister on the Right of Property

"You sense now, Monsieur Minister, without me needing to press the argument further with a man as perceptive as you, how vain all these theories of equality, abolition of property, community, and phalanstery are, if the authors do not prove that the reforms they propose and the systems of which they demand the application arise necessarily from accomplished facts and existing institutions; and, on the contrary, how advantageous they are to society if that correlation is true. Finally, you must see how easy it will be to turn them to the profit of the government, if, taking the radicals at their own principles, we knew how to make the form of government under which they live precious to them, and lead them to forcefully declare themselves conservatives,—I mean conservative in the sense implied by progress. Indeed, break the egg before the day fixed by nature for the hatching of the animal, and you will obtain only a miscarriage; kill the bird before the eggs are laid, and you will have no clutch; give the child ideas and tastes which are not for its age, and you will make it a depraved subject. Thus every social doctrine which cannot prove its direct and legitimate descent from the system in force, is by that fact alone a false doctrine, condemned in advance; every premature attempt at reform is an assassination. It was according to this principle, implicitly or explicitly accepted by all reformists, that I propose to develop this thesis soon, which seems so eminently paradoxical today: *The interest of the people, like the duty of every radical writer, is to attach themselves to the charter, and, provisionally, to the government of July.* That will be one of the most curious elements and, I hope, the most conclusive of my next work.

"What I have just outlined for Your Excellence, Monsieur Minister, explains sufficiently, it seems to me, the sometimes heated critiques that I have made of men and things, and the always increasing fear that I have helped, perhaps more than any other, to spread among the proprietors. Starting from an essentially different principle of property, since property is only one of its elements, and reasoning with an inexorable rigor, I should appear, and have been called, *demolisher*. All critique, by itself, is alarming, especially in matters of society; but also, in matters of society, it is far from critique to destruction. Moreover, how do we correct and heal ourselves, how do we know ourselves, without critique? On the other hand, the more the insights increase and spread, the more the disorder becomes apparent and grows in the imagination; the more the feeling of unease penetrates us, the more the vices of power seem to increase with the years: the more, consequently, the complaints and invectives become vehement. I have followed, like all the others, the universal practice: am I less excusable?

"I said on page 7 of my last book: *Is the government the most hypocritical, the most perverse, the most voracious, and the most anti-national that has ever been*?

"I must make more intelligible to you, or if you like, monsieur, more *tolerable* each of these epithets.

"The present government, with regard to its tendency (what in the individual we call *intention*), is better than those that came before; as to its present effects, it is still all that I just described. The uncertainty and the fear of the future; the shouts and the bad faith of the factions; the ambition, venality, and flagrant corruption of several of those who hold the tiller of affairs; a mass of general and particular causes make the government what it is today, and justify all the charges I make against it. If there is one that I regret, though, and in which I have only just perceived the ambiguity, it is that of being *perverse*, which marks the depravity of the reason, reflected in crime: I meant to say *perverted*.

"In short, I regard the vices of the government as engendered by its precarious and false position, not as the result of an abominable calculation.

"Yes, the government is *hypocrite*, because it is forced to use deception and cunning every day; to respect certain prejudices, whether aristocratic or popular; to yield before the errors of opinion, and transform itself by means of intrigues. And it becomes more hypocritical, as those who rise within it become more clever and more dishonest.

"The government is *voracious*: you know better than me, Monsieur Minister, what certain accessions cost it, and all the shameful necessities to which survival forces it to submit.

"The government is *perverted* by the bad passions of its adversaries, by the incomplete knowledge and the false prudence of its partisans, by the concessions that one rips from it, by its own distrusts, by the overwrought stubbornness inspired in it by the injustices and calumnies of the press, etc.

"The government is *anti-national*, because nothing suits the French character less than that rigmarole of ambition and cupidity, but especially because the present parliamentary form is the silliest, I mean the least French of all.[11]

"The government, finally, does not know itself, because it does not know where it comes from, nor where it is going, nor what it should do, nor how it should defend itself.

"From all that results a system of uncertain legislation, a hesitant and confused administration; an antagonistic magistracy and endless pains which make the poor patients cry and swear.

"For why, I ask, do we have a town hall, an institution from the Middle Ages, rivaled by a prefecture, a creation of the empire? Why a double parliament? Why one administrative jurisprudence and one civil; one procedure for the criminal, another for the civil, a third for commerce, a fourth, which will soon come, for the administration? Why these institutions placed side by side as enemies, these jurisdictions and these great bodies which have no common principle and do not understand one another, these incoherent, inharmonic judiciary formalities, when they should be unified, centralized, coordinated?"

That, gentlemen of the jury, is the series of my ideas on property.

---

[11] And what government in France was never called a *foreign government*?

1842: Explanations Presented to the Public Minister on the Right of Property

Metaphysics, right, economy, concluding with the equality of fortunes.

Then comes history, which shows us society subject to the metaphysical, jurisprudential and economic laws, even when it has neither metaphysics, nor jurisprudence, nor economy, and advancing instinctively for centuries towards the realization of that equality.

Finally the constitutional charter itself implies equality; equality is at the base of the representative system, it is the consequence and result of all our institutions.

So it must be said with certainty:

Those who do not want the charter do not want equality.

Those who want more or less than the charter, want more or less than equality

Those who want something other than the charter do not want equality with the shortest delay. The charter! There are people who believe that the charter is the work of one Abbe Montesquieu, reviewed and corrected by a Mr. Bérard: this is to attribute large effects to very small causes.

The charter is the ensemble of the principles elaborated n French society since the establishment of the communes under Louis the Fat, and successively brought to light by the transient forms of feudalism, despotism, the republic and the empire.

1842: Explanations Presented to the Public Minister on the Right of Property

The charter is the symbol of the spirit of liberty and equality which has tormented us for twelve centuries.

Doubtless the charter is incomplete and unfortunate in its expression, in its composition, and it is the work of Bérard and Montesquieu; but the core of the ideas belongs to the nation, and it is that core that I am interpreting.

And because it seems to me that the men of power brushed aside the charter, I have, as an egalitarian and friend of the charter, opposed those ignorant governors. Will they dare to claim that he who does not love them does not love the charter? I await that aphorism from them.

How then can the attorney general reproach me for *having appealed to the passions?* I have criticized violence, murder, riots, secret societies, and revolutions in twenty places in my brochure, in the very passages which serve as the basis for the accusation, so that I at first believed that it was a recording error on the part of the clerk. So much for the proletarians. As for those who, having the mission to instruct the people and see to their interests, only know how to insult and corrupt them, to cry out against the socialists and the theoreticians, I have not been able to stop myself from making reprisals towards them, and I boast of it. I would never hear a French citizen say in cold blood that all those who possess nothing are the enemies of the government; or a president of the parliament declare that the chambers do not have a mission to organize labor and to provide bread to the workers, but to make law; or some deputies and some journalists, maintain that whoever only pays two hundred francs in taxes is stupid and unfit.

But what am I saying? Yes, gentlemen jurors, I have appealed to the passions; I have excited the passion for liberty against the passion for privilege; the passion for science against the passion for obscurantism; the passion for labor against the passion for idleness. I have done like the preachers, who excite the love of penitence against the love of pleasure; but they are hardly heard.

You will soon judge, gentlemen, if, in arousing all these passions against one another, I have acted like a good citizen, or if I have given in to an evil inspiration, to a detestable instinct for disparagement.

The accused then discussed the last three charges. We omit all that part of his defense, which keenly interested the audience, but which only connected in a distant manner to the great economic and social questions, alone worthy, in our opinion, of the honors of publicity.

The floor was turned over to the defender of the accused.

M. Tripard began by recalling that Franche-Comté is the region which, in our time, has produced the boldest thinkers and most innovative minds. Thus, in the order of the sciences, Cuvier; in the realm of letters, Victor Hugo; in the social sciences, Fourier. It is to that family of free thinkers that Proudhon seems to belong. The defense attorney recalled the first two booklets on property, so energetic in form, so bold in content, and remarks that in each of them we see a maxim established: *Property is theft*.

1842: Explanations Presented to the Public Minister on the Right of Property

However, no proceedings had been directed against them, and the Minister of Justice himself, M. Vivien, had decided that there was no cause for proceedings. Thus, M. Proudhon had reason to hope for the same freedom for this last booklet as for the first two. M. Tripard recalled the movements that, in 1834 and 1835, soaked Paris and Lyon in blood: the workers, armed and in the street, demanded labor or death. In that era, all the dynastic journals called serious minds toward that great question, which so strongly interested the proletarians, the organization of labor. Mr. Proudhon felt obliged to respond to this call, and today when he announced the results of his painstaking research, he is conveyed to the assizes! The lawyer showed Proudhon researching in history the principle of property and discovering beside quiritary domain a world of slaves; beside fief, serfdom; beside the *cens* or quitrent, the *censitaire* or sharecropper and the trades; and free people nowhere. It is only in 1789, when a transformation takes place in property, and notably in the property in money, the loan at interest, that liberty, and human equality are consecrated. Since that time, the laboring classes have fallen again into the malaise, ands M. Proudhon attributes this malaise to property. *Property is robbery*, Mr. Proudhon has said: but that is not the first time that property was attacked by men of the highest merit. The lawyer cited Vattel and Burlamaqui, who only considered property as *temporary* and *incidental*; Beccaria, who called it a *terrible right, though that right is necessary*; Pascal, who called it *usurpation*, but usurpation that should be hidden from the people, *if one does not want it to end soon*; finally Considérant, who calls it a *fundamental spoliation*. Usurpation, spoliation, these words have a great affinity with robbery, and M. Proudhon has not even the credit of the invention. M. Proudhon could be mistaken, but there are some eminent men to cover his responsibility. In addition, he asked, what does Mr. Proudhon mean by property? He distinguishes *domain* from *possession*, the right of use from the right of abuse. Property is distinguished then from *possession* by the *domain* of the man over the thing. And, he says, possession is according to right, but property is against right. Possession, it is the right to use; but the right to abuse, that privilege of the right of property, he wants to destroy it by making of property a vicegerency whose source is in the government. According to this theory, property, it is robbery, because property is the sum of the abuses or the right to abuse. If the proprietor of a field which conceals ore does not want to exploit it, or to sell it, said Mr. Tripard, the law considers that this proprietor abuses his right to the detriment of the public good, and constrains him to allow the exploitation of the mine in exchange for an indemnity. Well! Mr. Proudhon wants to generalize this principle of the law, and make property an *administrative* matter. In this way, the abuses of selfishness will disappear and public utility will profit. The lawyer strove to point out that, seen in that sense, the expression, *Property is robbery*, loses its aggravating character and returns within the conditions of the discussion permitted by the law. He showed that the author always himself distinguishes between property and the proprietor; that he is without hatred against the proprietors, and, in support, he cited this passage from the author: *Me, hate anyone, Good God! You might as well say that the doctor hates the illness, because he describes it!* As to the means of realizing his theory, the advocate demonstrated, by numerous passages from the brochure, that he wants neither riots, nor revolutions; that everywhere, on the contrary, he considers *time, progress and the government* itself as the necessary agents of his reform.

The advocate recalled that in his brochure Mr. Proudhon has created a large overview, and that one could not split or divide it up, and grasp its true character. He set out to respond to the offending passages with others passages from the same brochure, in order to restore them to their true sense. He then discussed successively the four offenses of which the author is accused. In closing, he said that in a similar time, ten years ago, a young man, a Saint-Simonian, appeared in the Assizes of Paris, accused of attacks against property and the family; he was acquitted by the jury, and today he renders eminent services to the country as a professor at the College de France, as a member of the Council of State and editor of the *Journal des Débats*.[12]

---

[12] Did Mr. Chevalier become conservative only in order to better serve equality? When we recall the old opinions of this famous publicist, opinions that he has never retracted; when we read the recent discourse of the College de France, and we think of the terrors he inspires, on the one hand, the retrograde movement of the men of power, on the other, the rapid disclosure of certain economic truths, we cannot help regarding Mr. Chevalier, egalitarian conservative, as a secret martyr to the reformist cause. Instead of listening foolishly, as we do, to these itinerant politickers who cry: *Democracy! democracy!* we would do better to inquire after the men who, among the auxiliaries of power, work, without encouragement or witness, to make the true principles of order and liberty penetrate into the highest social regions.

The president, Mr. Béchet summarized the debates, and discharged this difficult task with a concision and an impartiality that everyone admired.

After an hour of deliberation, the jury pronounced a verdict of "not guilty."

Conclusion

From this judgment and from the explanations that have just been read, and which seem to have motivated it, we can infer the following theoretical and practical consequences, which we will summarily express:

1. Every scientifically demonstrated proposition is outside the jurisdiction of the tribunals, and arises only for science itself. If the office of the magistrate is to watch over the novelties that threaten the established order, and to seek their authors, the duty of the jury, when the offending doctrine takes on a scientific character, is to abstain.

2. Every political reform, intended or unintended, being an inevitable result of the law of progress, and for that very reason always based on the system in force, taking from it its principle and it point of departure, the critique of institutions is a right, and their conservation with an eye to the future a duty.

3. The equality of conditions and of fortunes, final end of progress, resulting from the organic movement of institutions, as well as from the economic theories and the evidence of history, from now on radical writers must place themselves on legal terrain, taking hold of the charter, strengthening themselves within the representative system, and, from that unassailable position, putting outside the bounds of legality and conventional right the adversaries of progress, however highly placed they may be found to be.

Let us hope that the author of the *Memoirs on Property*, understanding the full extent of his work, will not be slow to give to you, in an organized form, that "official" (so to speak) demonstration of his doctrine. Misfortune then, three times misfortune to the mad fools who want to stop the revolutionary coach by lying down across the rails!...

Letter to Bergmann

Besançon, February 8, 1842.

To Frédéric-Guillaume Bergmann

My dear Bergmann, I have just been judged, and have been absolved by the jury, on the four charges formulated against me. I have presented a written defense, the reading of which lasted more than an hour. As I intend to print it, you will judge its worth. It is a sort of general prospectus of my studies, by past and to come, and of their object. I win and I lose all at once, as a result of this trial. I *win* a small moment of celebrity, which does not even extend very far, for, as you know, I don't have the sympathies of the press; I win, which is more important to me, and which no one realizes, the advantage of being able to innovate, to analyze and reestablish at my leisure principles, rights, beliefs and institutions. For that judgment, acknowledging that I am a *man of meditation, not of revolution*, aneconomist, not an anarchist, and that I wish, according to the president's expression, *to convert the government and the proprietors*, it follows that I can say everything, like a teach or a friend, and I am declared outside the ranks of the conspirators. It is up to me to preserve that magnificent position.

But I *lose*, in the sense that, in order to defend myself, I have been forced to expose views and ideas that I only wanted to give at an appropriate time; for example, that as equality and non-property from the legislative metaphysics, from economy and history, all the same that are a necessary consequence of the Charter, and of all the institutions that *accompany* it; so much, as I declared elsewhere, that it is today only a question of *developing*, not of *destroying*. That is magnificent for those who are sympathetic and are in the habit of linking together their ideas; but for the multitude of sots who make and unmake reputations in an instant, it is excessively dangerous: for several of them have already concluded that I have won over power and that I have made so much noise only in order to be paid more. To begin with *equality* and *the abolition of Property*, in order to end with the acceptance and development of the Charter, that routs all our democrats, as in the audience it defeated the public minister.

Yet is it as beautiful, as fruitful, as true; you will understand it, I hope.

It remains for me to ask you for some news of a Mr. *Ferrari*, a professor of political economy at your Strasbourg Academy, who has just, I am told, been suspended by order of the minister. I would like to know who the man is, what he thinks, and what you think of him. Write to me as soon as possible.

I remain at Besançon; I believe that I have written that our mayor and his municipal council think to accommodate me in order to assure me the rest and independence necessary for study; I can do no better, I believe, than to go along with these good arrangements. I have a hard year to get through; but, I repeat, I think that it will be the last, *as to needs of the first order*. I gain friends every day; I nearly have them in the public prosecutor's office; I hope that soon the powers-that-be, without accepting me, will tolerate me. I know that they already respect and honor me.

Farewell, my friend; I have just passed a phantasmagoric day, as vain as all the others. *All is vanity*, said Salomon, *except to love God*; let us add, *and to understand him*.

Would it be an indiscretion to beg you to offer my respectful regards to your young wife? You shall do it, or not, at your pleasure.

All my best,

P.-J. Proudhon.

1845

My Testament: or, Society of Avengers

Summary of principles, facts, and complaints, against the exploiting caste.

Exhortation to the proletariat to organize and take action against their oppressors, by any sort of means, until the avengers take a hand, and justice is done.

To write slowly and in my own hand, 25 copies, to be distributed and disseminated after my death.

To write down clearly the principles of economic right.—Bring out above all those that make up the right of the masses and guarantee leveling;--collective force, gratuity of public services, determination of values;--assurances ;--corporations; marriage; family; land-rent; state; taxation; general disarmament.—

Right of revendication, by secret judgment; and of execution.—

Recall the principles concerning war, penal law, regicide, and insurrection.

Such acts are never good in themselves: on the contrary, they are only rendered excusable in certain cases. The political offense, so casually dealt with, is an offense: but it can be the case that the provocation being such, the greatest part of the fault is with the prince, or [ ], and the right is with the rebel, or tyrannicide.

So repeat this phrase often: What you will do, by acting as I recommend to you, will not be pleasant; but yours will be a case of legitimate defense, legitimate vengeance; you can be excused.

This:

> 1. Exposition of the facts: situation of the laborer and the privileged; social iniquity in economics, politics, taxation, etc., etc.

> 2. Exposition of the rights: what may be. Forms of redress to be carried out, reforms indicated, practical, simple, and forbidden.

> 3. Theory of revendication by force: war, insurrection, tyrannicide, and secret vengeance.

The time has come to organize those things.

By the fact of the publication of this Testament, the Society of Avengers exists. Never gather. No need of secret meetings, rolls, papers, or offices. You have principles, a law, a faith, a hope, wrongs to avenge, the world to save, and your dignity to safeguard.

Your right, invincibly established, clearer than the precepts of the Decalogue, is confirmed by the refusal of discussion, la proscription directed against the writer who, for twenty, 30, or 50 years, has wanted to proclaim it.

Today, all politics tends to the glorification of immorality, to impunity for theft.

There is no more remedy; it is necessary to strike.

To distinguish the innocents from the guilty...

To limit oneself to a single sort of communication between supporters: that the principles are true, that the right is certain, that the oppression is flagrant, and the vengeance excusable.—Certain that these ideas exist, the strong and heroic man, who feels he has the power to cut down an enemy, has only to seek some endorsers, some accomplices: when he has them, let him act.

Never strike any but public, notorious crooks; principal agents of the system, bigwigs...

To commence operations when the Testament has been read everywhere.

Collect and classify a mass of misdeeds and crimes, and show in what sense it is systematic.

Atrocious [ ] of the worker; degeneration of the races.—Corruption of women and girls.—Strike down all these great culprits.

The sensual, selfish, obscene life of the exploiting aristocracy.

Games, dances, concerts, spectacles, feasts [ ] to all tastes; rest, pleasure, the seven deadly sins and all their progeny; that is what they cultivate. The institutions have committed them to the guard and management of an immense capital, [ ]; ils ne domptent qu'à la [ ]. Like [ ], whom I cite in my notebook, they only exist for [ ] and [ ]. Their maxim is that of Sardanapalus: Drink, eat, play and f...

It is necessary to exterminate [ ]. They are fattened for the sacrifice, said [ ]. It is time;--whoever adheres in their heart to the principles contained in this Testament, is part of the Society of Avengers; they are [ ].

Also, do not forget the reprisals.

Every culprit struck should be a notorious enemy of the Revolution, and bear on their corpse a sign that indicates that they have been sacrificed by an avenger.

Every prosecution directed against an individual as a suspect of having, for this reason, struck a great criminal, will give rise, if it ends in a conviction, in reprisals.

If the killer has been seized in flagrante delicto, and if it is proven that the individual is an avenger, he should be released under penalty of reprisals practiced as much against the judges, imperial prosecutors, public prosecutors, examining magistrates, as on the jurors.

-- Some will rail against the society.—Let them rail.—The grievances are there; let them refute them.—The principles are there;--let them recognized them.—The reforms are there; and [manuscript breaks here.]

Overview of the innovations and reforms

Main points, easy to remember, on which the Revolution must first of all undertake and finish in less than three months.

1. Public debt.—bankruptcy of ½; reimbursement of the ruined, interest reduced to ½ %.

2. Expropriation of Grandes Compagnies.—Liquidation, on the same principle.—[ ] of the great [ ].

3. Bank.—Reduction of interest to ½ — 1%.—Confiscation du capital.

4. Dette hypothécaire.—Reduction of 50%.—[ ] like the debt.

5. Rente foncière.—reduction of land tax: 1/3 of the rente of property; 1/3 to [ ] ; 1/3 to the State. Domain congéable.

6. Loyers.—reduction de 50 p.%.—Organization of its maconnieres.

[7 more points ; to be transcribed]

By what sign shall we recognize that an individual who has been struck has been struck by the society of avengers: if notorious depraved, or corrupt, or criminal, or villain; if an enemy of the people; if of a political importance that corresponds to their criminality; if a sign is left on the corps; if they are not stripped or robbed; if no author of the murder can be assumed from self-interest, rivalry, etc.

All these signs may exist together, or only exist in part.

-- Classification of persons to be harmed.

In the government, the administration, the police, the magistracy, the clergy, finance, industry, commerce, property, the army, la [ ].

Ten or twelve classes in all.

-- How, in each class, to choose the subjects to strike.

There are men of good faith everywhere.

We must not forget that a provisional order is necessary to society; we can suppose that every public functionary who only fulfills their duty according to the [ ] is inoffensive, and consequently innocent.

The same in property, etc.—Inequality is universal; all have wished it; lui [ ] the [ ] liberals, good people.

But add them, the [ ], the impious, the enemies of morals and liberty, devoted as [to] infernal gods.

The vengeance will stop when political liberties are established, and the Right [ ] unique [ ] (in seven or eight articles.)

Order and distribution

Legitimate complaints of the proletariat, starting from the birth of the socialist schools; bloody reaction, of the bourgeoisie; massacres, despotism, tyranny, transportation, crimes; under the Empire as well as under the Presidency and Cavaignac.

General economic principles, in the name of which we make our demands.

(Critique of the principle of property;

Law of collective force;

Theory of interest, discount, credit, taxation, and international exchange.

Church, army.

Principle of Human right, immanent.

Series of reforms, to be accomplished immediately.

Means of constraint.

Around one hundred pages, at most. Autographic reproduction, with 25 or 50 copies (25 to my friends as gifts; 25 to reliable people, who will reproduce it.)

Results of that economic revolution: Everything is renewed from top to bottom. Customs changed; poverty abolished; true liberty, internal and external, established; equality created; labor organized.

Justice

The just man has a right of life and death over the criminal, the father over the rebellious child, the husband over the adulterous wife and her accomplice, the brother over the immodest sister and her seducer, the citizen over the traitor and usurper.

Every citizen is a censor of customs, a guardian of peace and order.

—à fonder : Federations;

Universal suffrage;

The mnémosyne ;

The judiciary.

(The mnémosyne pour le cas dû pas d'autorisation.

Thus, we will make a monthly column for politics and political economy.

It will be weekly for everything else.

Do not forget the courts.

1846

Proudhon To Marx

Lyon, 17 May 1846

My dear Monsieur Marx,

I gladly agree to become one of the recipients of your correspondence, whose aims and organization seem to me most useful. Yet I cannot promise to write often or at great length: my varied occupations, combined with a natural idleness, do not favour such epistolary efforts. I must also take the liberty of making certain qualifications which are suggested by various passages of your letter.

First, although my ideas in the matter of organization and realization are at this moment more or less settled, at least as regards principles, I believe it is my duty, as it is the duty of all socialists, to maintain for some time yet the critical or dubitive form; in short, I make profession in public of an almost absolute economic anti-dogmatism.

Let us seek together, if you wish, the laws of society, the manner in which these laws are realized, the process by which we shall succeed in discovering them; but, for God's sake, after having demolished all the *a priori* dogmatisms, do not let us in our turn dream of indoctrinating the people; do not let us fall into the contradiction of your compatriot Martin Luther, who, having overthrown Catholic theology, at once set about, with excommunication and anathema, the foundation of a Protestant theology. For the last three centuries Germany has been mainly occupied in undoing Luther's shoddy work; do not let us leave humanity with a similar mess to clear up as a result of our efforts. I applaud with all my heart your thought of bringing all opinions to light; let us carry on a good and loyal polemic; let us give the world an example of learned and far-sighted tolerance, but let us not, merely because we are at the head of a movement, make ourselves the leaders of a new intolerance, let us not pose as the apostles of a new religion, even if it be the religion of logic, the religion of reason. Let us gather together and encourage all protests, let us brand all exclusiveness, all mysticism; let us never regard a question as exhausted, and when we have used our last argument, let us begin again, if need be, with eloquence and irony. On that condition, I will gladly enter your association. Otherwise — no!

I have also some observations to make on this phrase of your letter: *at the moment of action.* Perhaps you still retain the opinion that no reform is at present possible without a *coup de main*, without what was formerly called a revolution and is really nothing but a shock. That opinion, which I understand, which I excuse, and would willingly discuss, having myself shared it for a long time, my most recent studies have made me abandon completely. I believe we have no need of it in order to succeed; and that consequently we should not put forward *revolutionary action* as a means of social reform, because that pretended means would simply be an appeal to force, to arbitrariness, in brief, a contradiction. I myself put the problem in this way: *to bring about the return to society, by an economic combination, of the wealth which was withdrawn from society by another economic combination.* In other words, through

Political Economy to turn the theory of Property against Property in such a way as to engender what you German socialists call *community* and what I will limit myself for the moment to calling *liberty* or *equality*. But I believe that I know the means of solving this problem with only a short delay; I would therefore prefer to burn Property by a slow fire, rather than give it new strength by making a St Bartholomew's night of the proprietors...

Your very devoted
Pierre-Joseph Proudhon

1847

On the Jews

Translated by Mitchell Abidor[13]

December 26, 1847: Jews. Write an article against this race that poisons everything by sticking its nose into everything without ever mixing with any other people. Demand its expulsion from France with the exception of those individuals married to French women. Abolish synagogues and not admit them to any employment. Demand its expulsion Finally, pursue the abolition of this religion. It's not without cause that the Christians called them deicides. The Jew is the enemy of humankind. They must be sent back to Asia or be exterminated. H. Heine, A. Weill, and others are nothing but secret spies ; Rothschild, Crémieux, Marx, Fould, wicked, bilious, envious, bitter, etc. etc. beings who hate us. The Jew must disappear by steel or by fusion or by expulsion. Tolerate the elderly who no longer have children. Work to be done – What the peoples of the Middle Ages hated instinctively I hate upon reflection and irrevocably. The hatred of the Jew like the

---

[13] Translator's note: Though some twentieth century writers have maintained that Proudhon was not an anti-Semite, we find in his notebooks proof of the contrary. In this selection from his notebooks Proudhon's anti-Semitism goes far beyond that of Marx at approximately the same time, calling not for the end of what Jews represent, i.e., capitalism, but of the Jews as a people. Proudhon's privately expressed thoughts were elaborated on in the same year as this entry by his follower Alphonse Toussenel in his "Les Juifs, Rois de l'Epoque," The Jews, Kings of the Era. After reading the passage translated here it can come as no surprise that the founder of the royalist group Action Française, the Jew-hater Charles Maurras, drew inspiration from Proudhon.

hatred of the English should be our first article of political faith. Moreover, the abolition of Judaism will come with the abolition of other religions. Begin by not allocating funds to the clergy and leaving this to religious offerings. – And then, a short while later, abolish the religion.

1848

Letter to Jeanne Deroin

Madame.

You have understood me perfectly: what I pursue under the name of the abolition of usury and of property, is the restoration of the family, it is the advent of the man-king, and of the woman-queen.

Until this great reform is accomplished, men and women will not love one another: cupidity will infect their union, and behind cupidity comes brutality of the senses. Libertinism replaces love, and murder, finally, takes its place at the domestic hearth, and chases off devotion, sanctity and decency. I say nothing to you of my religious opinions: that is too grueling and difficult a text. But what does that matter to you, if I want everything that is, according to you, desired by the Divinity?

But it is not enough, Madame, to discuss these things: it is necessary to put them into practice, and do what will not be done by the men on whom the destinies of France, at this moment, depend.

Poverty increases, winter approaches and if we do not bring about a quick and efficacious remedy for the growing pauperism, the industrial and financial disorder, we run the risk, in a few months, of finding ourselves like the castaways of the Medusa, obliged to commandeer everything, put ourselves on rations and live in community until we decide to live in liberty, equality and fraternity, under the law of labor and devotion.

Thus it is appropriate that the citizens, both male and female, who take to heart the interests of the People and the Revolution, seek to put themselves in a position to oppose these calamitous times, to which I still do not see an end several months from now and which will inevitable worsen

We must, in a word, organize, if not labor, at least aid and charity.

Let women sustain one another, let them create relief funds; in addition, let them continue to labor, even at a reduced price, for it will be better to gain five cents than to do nothing; let them solicit the return of work by this decline; finally, let them engage in a sort of mutual and fraternelle association until we escape from poverty.

Let us not remain spectators to the fire that consumes us: let us work at the pumps, and try to extinguish the flames. Let us resign ourselves for awhile to a sort of division of goods; but at the same time let us strive to use our time, and, since one part of our brethren must be fed by the other, let us occupy the first with something, make it labor, even if that labor must be given for nothing.

It is with this thought, Madame, that I would pray you to welcome the visit that I have enlisted a poor widow, Mme Gueyffier, to make you: being absolutely unable to occupy myself with private distresses, in this moment when I have to uphold the question of the general poverty, and to defend myself against the enemies of the Republic and their cowardly auxiliaries.

I am, Madame, your very humble servant.

P.-J. PROUDHON.

P. S. – Madame, I would receive with pleasures any communications that you would make to me in the name of the meeting where you preside regarding the organization of mutual aid that I have proposed to you. It is by organization, by labor, that we will vanquish the enemy. To date, we have spoken too much, but we have done nothing.

Mme Jeanne Dervin,

Rue Miromesnil, 4.

The Malthusians, the Representatives of the People

Dr. Malthus, an economist, an Englishman, once wrote the following words:

> "A man who is born into a world already possessed, if he cannot get subsistence from his parents on whom he has a just demand, and if the society do not want his labor, has no claim of *right* to the smallest portion of food, and, in fact, has no business to be where he is. At nature's mighty feast there is no vacant cover for him. She tells him to be gone, and will quickly execute her own orders..."[14]

As a consequence of this great principle, Malthus recommends, with the most terrible threats, every man who has neither labor nor income upon which to live to take himself away, or at any rate to have no more children. A family, — that is, love, — like bread, is forbidden such a man by Malthus.

Dr. Malthus was, while living, a minister of the Holy Gospel, a mild-mannered philanthropist, a good husband, a good father, a good citizen, believing in God us firmly as any man in France. He died (heaven grant him peace) in

---

[14] Tucker supplies a slightly different version of this passage, having translated Proudhon's quotation of Joseph Garnier's French translation of Malthus back into English. This passage, which Malthus struck from subsequent editions of his *Essay on the Principle of Population*, appears in the 1803 edition. From Andy Carloff.

1834. It may be said that he was the first, without doubt, to reduce to absurdity all political economy, and state the great revolutionary question, the question between labor and capital. With us, whose faith in Providence still lives, in spite of the century's indifference, it is proverbial — and herein consists the difference between the English and ourselves — that "everybody must live." And our people, in saying this, think themselves as truly Christian, as conservative of good morals and the family, as the late Malthus.

Now, what the people say in France, the economists deny; the lawyers and the litterateurs deny; the Church, which pretends to be Christian, and also Gallican, denies; the press denies; the large proprietors deny; the government which endeavors to represent them, denies.

The press, the government, the Church, literature, economy, wealth, — everything in France has become English; everything is Malthusian. It is in the name of God and his holy providence, in the name of morality, in the name of the sacred interests of the family, that they maintain that there is not room in the country for all the children of the country, and that they warn our women to be less prolific. In France, in spite of the desire of the people, in spite of the national belief, eating and drinking are regarded as privileges, labor a privilege, family a privilege, country a privilege.

M. Antony Thouret said recently that property, without which there is neither country, nor family, nor labor, nor morality, would be irreproachable as soon as it should cease to be a privilege; a clear statement of the fact that, to abolish all the privileges which, so to speak, exclude a portion of the people from the law, from humanity, we must abolish, first of all, the fundamental privilege, and change the constitution of property.

M. A. Thouret, in saying that, agreed with us and with the people. The State, the press, political economy, do not view the matter in that light; they agree in the hope that property, without which, as M. Thouret says, there is no labor, no family, no Republic, may remain what it always has been, — a privilege.

All that has been done, said, and printed today and for the last twenty years, has been done, said, and printed in consequence of the theory of Malthus.

The theory of Malthus is the theory of political murder; of murder from motives of philanthropy and for love of God. There are too many people in the world; that is the first article of faith of all those who, at present, in the name of the people, reign and govern. It is for this reason that they use their best efforts to diminish the population. Those who best acquit themselves of this duty, who practice with piety, courage, and fraternity the maxims of Malthus, are good citizens, religious men, those who protest against such conduct are anarchists, socialists, atheists.

That the Revolution of February was the result of this protest constitutes its inexpiable crime. Consequently, it shall be taught its business, this Revolution which promised that all should live. The original, indelible stain on this Republic is that the people have pronounced it anti-Malthusian. That is why the Republic is so especially obnoxious to those who were, and would become again, the toadies and accomplices of kings — *grand eaters of men*, as Cato called them. They would make monarchy of your Republic; they would devour its children.

There lies the whole secret of the sufferings, the agitations, and the contradictions of our country.

The economists are the first among us, by an inconceivable blasphemy, to establish as a providential dogma the theory of Malthus. I do not reproach them; neither do I abuse them. On this point the economists act in good faith and from the best intentions in the world. They would like nothing better than to make the human race happy; but they cannot conceive how, without some sort of an organization of homicide, a balance between population and production can exist.

Ask the Academy of Moral Sciences. One of its most honorable members, whose name I will not call, — though he is proud of his opinions, as every honest man should be, — being the prefect of I know not which department, saw fit one day, in a proclamation, to advise those within his province to have thenceforth fewer children by their wives. Great was the scandal among the priests and gossips, who looked upon this academic morality as the morality of swine! The *savant* of whom I speak was none the less, like all his fellows, a zealous defender of the family and of morality; but, he observed with Malthus, at the banquet of Nature there is not room for all.

M. Thiers, also a member of the Academy of Moral Sciences, lately told the committee on finance that, if he were minister, he would confine himself to *courageously and stoically passing through the crisis,* devoting himself to the expenses of his budget, enforcing a respect for order, and carefully guarding against every financial innovation, every socialistic idea, — especially such as the right to labor, — as well as every revolutionary expedient. And the whole committee applauded him.

In giving this declaration of the celebrated historian and statesman, I have no desire to accuse his intentions. In the present state of the public mind, I should succeed only in serving the ambition of M. Thiers, if he has any left. What I wish to call attention to is that M. Thiers, in expressing himself in this wise, testified, perhaps unconsciously, to his faith in Malthus.

Mark this well, I pray you. There are two millions, four millions of men who will die of misery and hunger, if some means be not found of giving them work. This is a great misfortune, surely, and we are the first to lament it, the Malthusians tell you; but what is to be done? It is better that four millions of men should die than that privilege should be compromised; it is not the fault of capital, if labor is idle; at the banquet of credit there is not room for all.

They are courageous, they are stoical, these statesmen of the school of Malthus, when it is a matter of sacrificing workers by the millions. Thou hast killed the poor man, said the prophet Elias to the king of Israel, and then thou hast taken away his inheritance. *Occidisti et possedisti.*[15] To-day we must reverse the phrase, and say to

---

[15] 1 Kings 21:19. From Andy Carloff.

those who possess and govern: You have the privilege of labor, the privilege of credit, the privilege of property, as M. Thouret says; and it is because you do not wish to be deprived of these privileges, that you shed the blood of the poor like water: *Possedisti et occidisti!*

And the people, under the pressure of bayonets, are being eaten slowly; they die without a sigh or a murmur; the sacrifice is effected in silence. Courage, workers! sustain each other: Providence will finally conquer fate. Courage! the condition of your fathers, the soldiers of the republic, at the sieges of Genes and Mayence, was even worse than yours.

M. Leon Faucher, in contending that journals should be forced to furnish securities and in favoring the maintenance of taxes on the press, reasoned also after the manner of Malthus. The serious journal, said he, the journal that deserves consideration and esteem, is that which is established on a capital of from four to five hundred thousand francs. The journalist who has only his pen is like the worker who has only his arms. If he can find no market for his services or get no credit with which to carry on his enterprise, it is a sign that public opinion is against him; he has not the least right to address the country: at the banquet of public life there is not room for all.

Listen to Lacordaire, that light of the Church, that chosen vessel of Catholicism.[16] He will tell you that socialism is

---

[16] Abbé Henri Lacordaire (1802-1861), who, together with Lamennais, was one of the leading lights of nineteenth-century

antichrist. And why is socialism antichrist? Because socialism is the enemy of Malthus, whereas Catholicism, by a final transformation, has become Malthusian.

The gospel tells us, cries the priest, that there will always be poor people, *Pauperes semper habebitis vobsicum*,[17] and that property, consequently in so far as it is a privilege and makes poor people, is sacred. Poverty is necessary to the exercise of evangelical charity; at the banquet of this world here below there cannot be room for all.

He feigns ignorance, the infidel, of the fact that *poverty*, in Biblical language, signified every sort of affliction and pain, not hard times and the condition of the proletarian. And how could he who went up and down Judea crying, *Woe to the rich!* be understood differently? In the thought of Jesus Christ, woe to the rich means woe to the Malthusians.

If Christ were living today, he would say to Lacordaire and his companions: "You are of the race of those who, in all ages, have shed the blood of the just, from Abel unto Zacharias. Your law is not my law; your God is not my God!..." And the Lacordaires would crucify Christ as a seditious person and an atheist

Almost the whole of journalism is infected with the same ideas. Let *Le National*, for example, tell us whether it has

---

Catholic liberalism. From Andy Carloff.

[17] Loose quotation of the Latin version of the famous phrase repeated, with variations, in Matthew 26:11, Mark 14:7, John 12:8. From Andy Carloff.

not always believed, whether it does not still believe, that pauperism is a permanent element of civilization; that the enslavement of one portion of humanity is necessary to the glory of another; that those who maintain the contrary are dangerous dreamers who deserve to be shot; that such is the basis of the State. For, if this be not the secret thought of *Le National,* if *Le National* sincerely and resolutely desires the emancipation of workers, why these anathemas against, why this anger with, the genuine socialists — those who, for ten and twenty years, have demanded this emancipation?

Further, let the Bohemian of literature, today the myrmidons of Journalism, paid slanderers, courtiers of the privileged classes, eulogists of all the vises, parasites living upon other parasites, who prate so much of God only to dissemble their materialism, of the family only to conceal their adulteries, and whom we shall see, out of disgust for marriage, caressing monkeys when Malthusian women fail, — let these, I say, publish their economic creed, in order that the people may know them.

Faites des filles, nous les aimons, — beget girls, we love them, — sing these wretches, parodying the poet. But abstain from begetting boys; at the banquet of sensualism there is not room for all.

The government was inspired by Malthus when, having a hundred thousand workers at its disposal, to whom it gave gratuitous support, it refused to employ them at useful labor, and when, after the civil war, it asked that a law be passed for their transportation. With the expenses of the pretended national workshops, with the costs of war, lawsuits, imprisonment, and transportation, it might have given the insurgents six months income, and thus changed our whole economic system. But labor is a monopoly; the government does not wish revolutionary industry to compete with privileged industry; at the workbench of the nation there is not room for all.

Large industrial establishments ruin small ones; that is the law of capital, that is Malthus.

Wholesale trade gradually swallows the retail; again Malthus.

Large estates encroach upon and consolidate the smallest possessions: still Malthus.

Soon one half of the people will say to the other:

The earth and its products are my property.

Industry and its products are my property.

Commerce and transportation are my property.

The State is my property.

You who possess nether reserve nor property, who hold no public offices and whose labor is useless to us, TAKE YOURSELVES AWAY! You have really no business on the earth; beneath the sunshine of the Republic there is not room for all.

Who will tell me that the right to labor and to live is not the whole of the Revolution?

Who will tell me that the principle of Malthus is not the whole of the Counter-Revolution?

And it is for having published such things as these, — for having exposed the evil boldly and sought the remedy in good faith, that speech has been forbidden me by the government, the government that represents the Revolution!

That is why I have been deluged with the slanders, treacheries, cowardice, hypocrisy, outrages, desertions, and failings of all those who hate or love the people! That is why I have been given over; for a whole month, to the mercy of the jackals of the press and the screech-owls of the platform! Never was a man, either in the past or in the present, the object of so much execration as I have become, for the simple reason that I wage war upon cannibals.

To slander one who could not reply was to shoot a prisoner. Malthusian carnivora, I discover you there! Go on, then; we have more than one account to settle yet. And, if calumny is not sufficient for you, use iron and lead. You may kill me; no one can avoid his fate, and I am at your discretion. But you shall not conquer me; you shall never persuade the people, while I live and hold a pen, that, with the exception of yourselves, there is one too many on the earth. I swear it before the people and in the name of the Republic!

Toast to the Revolution

October 17, 1848

Citizens,

When our friends of the democratic republic, apprehensive of our ideas and our inclinations, cry out against the qualification of *socialist* which we add to that of *democrat*, of what do they reproach us? — They reproach us for not being revolutionaries.

Let us see then if they or we are in the tradition; whether they or we have the true revolutionary practice.

And when our adversaries of the middle class, concerned for their privileges, pour upon us calumny and insult, what is the pretext of their charges? It is that we want to totally destroy property, the family, and civilization.

Let us see then again whether we or our adversaries better deserve the title of conservatives.

Revolutions are the successive manifestation of justice in human history. — It is for this reason that all revolutions have their origins in a previous revolution.

Whoever talks about revolution necessarily talks about progress, but just as necessarily about *conservation*. From this it follows that revolution is always in history and that, strictly speaking, there are not several revolutions, but only one permanent revolution.

The revolution, eighteen centuries ago, called itself the gospel, the Good News. Its fundamental dogma was the *Unity of God*; its motto, *the equality of all men before God*. Ancient slavery rested on the antagonism and inequality of gods, which represented the relative inferiority of races, in the state of war. Christianity created the rights of peoples, the brotherhood of nations; it abolished simultaneously idolatry and slavery.

Certainly no one denies today that the Christians, revolutionaries who fought by testimony and by martyrdom, were men of progress. They were also conservatives.

The polytheist initiation, after civilizing the first humans, after converting these men of the woods, *sylvestres homine*, as the poet says, into men of the towns, became itself, through sensualism and privilege, a principle of corruption and enslavement. Humanity was lost, when it was saved by the Christ, who received for that glorious mission the double title of *Savior* and *Redeemer*, or as we put it in our political language, conservative and revolutionary.

That was the character of the first and greatest of revolutions. It renewed the world, and in renewing it conserved it.

But, supernatural and spiritual as it was, that revolution nevertheless only expressed the more material side of justice, the enfranchisement of bodies and the abolition of slavery. Established on faith, it left thought enslaved; it was not sufficient for the emancipation of man, who is body and spirit, matter and intelligence. It called for another revolution. A thousand years after the coming of Christ, a new upheaval began, within the religion the first revolution founded, a prelude to new progress. Scholasticism carried within it, along with the authority of the Church and the scripture, the authority of reason! In about the 16th century, the revolution burst out.

The revolution, in that epoch, without abandoning its first given, took another name, which was already celebrated. It called itself philosophy. Its dogma was *the liberty of reason*, and its motto, which follows from that, was *the equality of all before reason*.

Here then is man declared inviolable and free in his double essence, as soul and as body. Was this progress? Who but a tyrant could deny it? Was it an act of conservation? The question does not even merit a response.

The destiny of man, a wise man once said, is to contemplate the works of God. Having known God in his heart, by faith, the time had come for man to know him with his reason. The Gospel had been for man like a primary education; now grown to adulthood, he needed a higher teaching, lest he stagnate in idiocy and the servitude that follows it.

In this way, the likes of Galileo, Arnaud de Bresce, Giordano Bruno, Descartes, Luther — all that elite of thinkers, wise men and artists, who shone in the 15th, 16th and 17th centuries as great revolutionaries — were at the same time the conservatives of society, the heralds of civilization. They continued, in opposition to the representatives of Christ, the movement started by Christ, and for it suffered no lack of persecution and martyrdom!

Here was the second great revolution, the second great manifestation of justice. It too renewed the world — and saved it.

But philosophy, adding its conquests to those of the Gospel, did not fulfill the program of that eternal justice. Liberty, called forth from the heart of God by Christ, was still only individual: it had to be established in the tribunal. Conscience was needed to make it pass into law.

About the middle of the last century then a new development commenced and, as the first revolution had been religious and the second philosophical, the third revolution was political. It called itself the social contract.

It took for its dogma *the sovereignty of the people*: it was the counterpart of the Christian dogma of *the unity of god*.

Its motto was *equality before the law*, the corollary of those which it had previously inscribed on its flag: equality before God and equality before reason.

Thus, with each revolution, liberty appeared to us always as the instrument of justice, with equality as its criterion. The third term — the aim of justice, the goal it always pursues, the end it approaches — is brotherhood.

Never let us lose sight of this order of revolutionary development. History testifies that brotherhood, supreme end of revolutions, does not impose itself. It has as conditions first liberty, then equality. It is as if just said to us all: Men, be free; citizens, become equal; brothers, embrace one another.

Who dares deny that the revolution undertaken sixty years ago by our fathers, and which the heroic memory makes our hearts beat with such force that we almost forget our own sense of duty — who denies, I ask, that that revolution was a progress? Nobody. Very well, then. But was it not both progressive and conservative? Could society have survived with its time-worn despotism, its degraded nobility, its corrupt clergy, with its egotistical and undisciplined parliament, so given to intrigue, with a people in rags, a race which can be exploited at will?

Is it necessary to blot out the sun, in order to make the case? The revolution of '89 was the salvation of humanity; it is for that reason that it deserves the title of revolution.

But, citizens, if our fathers have done much for liberty and fraternity, and have even more profoundly opened up the road of brotherhood, they have left it to us to do even more.

Justice did not speak its last word in '89, and who knows when it will speak it?

Are we not witnesses, our generation of 1848, to a corruption worse than that of the worst days of history, to a misery comparable to that of feudal times, an oppression of spirit and of conscience, and a degradation of all human faculties, which exceeds all that was seen in the epochs of most dreadful cruelty? Of what use are the conquests of the past, of religion and philosophy, and the constitutions and codes, when in virtue of the same rights that are guaranteed to us by those constitutions and codes, we find ourselves dispossessed of nature, excommunicated from the human species? What is politics, when we lack bread, when even the work which might give bread is taken from us? What to us is the freedom to go or to become, the liberty to think or not to think, the guarantees of the law, and the spectacles of the marvels of civilization? What is the meager education which is give to us, when by the withdrawal of all those objects on which we might practice human activity, we are ourselves plunged into an absolute void; when to the appeal of our senses, our hearts, and our reason, the universe and civilization reply: *Néant!* Nothing!

Citizens, I swear it by Christ and by our fathers! Justice has sounded its fourth hour, and misfortune to those who have not heard the call!

— Revolution of 1848, what do you call yourself?

— I am the *right to work!*

— What is your flag?

— *Association!*

— And your motto?

1848: Toast to the Revolution

— *Equality before fortune!*

— Where are you taking us?

— *To Brotherhood!*

— *Salut* to you, Revolution! I will serve you as I have served God, as I have served Philosophy and Liberty, with all my heart, with all my soul, with all my intelligence and my courage, and will have no other sovereign and ruler than you!

Thus the revolution, having been by turns religious, philosophical and political, has become economic. And like all its predecessors it brings us nothing less than a contradiction of the past, a sort of reversal of the established order! Without this complete reversal of principles and beliefs, there is no revolution; there is only mystification. Let us continue to interrogate history, citizens.

Within the empire of polytheism, slavery had established and perpetuated itself in the name of what principle? In the name of religion. — Christ appeared, and slavery was abolished, precisely in the name of religion.

Christianity, in its turn, made reason subject to faith; philosophy reversed that order, and subordinated faith to reason.

Feudalism, in the name of politics, controlled everything, subjecting the laborer to the bourgeois, the bourgeois to the noble, the noble to the king, the king to the priest, and the priest to a dead letter. — In the name of politics again, '89 subjected everyone to the law, and recognized among men only citizens.

Today labor is at the discretion of capital. Well, then! The revolution tells you to change that order. It is time for capital to recognize the predominance of labor, for the tool to put itself at the disposition of the worker.

Such is this revolution, which has suffered sarcasm, calumny and persecution, just like any other. But, like the others, the Revolution of 1848 becomes more fertile by the blood of its martyrs. *Sanguis martyrun, semen christianorum!* exclaimed one of the greatest revolutionaries of times past, the indomitable Tertullien. Blood of republicans, seed of republicans.

Who does not dare to acknowledge this faith, sealed with the blood of our brothers, is not a revolutionary. The failure is an infidelity. He who dissembles regarding it is a renegade. To separate the Republic from socialism is to willfully confuse the freedom of mind and spirit with the slavery of the senses, the exercise of political rights with the deprivation of civil rights. It is contradictory, absurd.

Here, citizens, is the genealogy of social ideas: are we, or are we not, in the revolutionary tradition? It is a question of knowing if at present we are also engaged in revolutionary practice, if, like our fathers, we will be at once men of conservation and of progress, because it is only by this double title that we will be men of revolution.

We have the revolutionary principle, the revolutionary dogma, the revolutionary motto. What is it that we lack in order to accomplish the work entrusted to our hands by Providence? One thing only: revolutionary practice!

But what is that practice which distinguishes the epochs of revolution from ordinary times?

What constitutes revolutionary practice is that it no longer proceeds by technicality and diversity, or by imperscriptible transitions, but by simplifications and enjambments. It passes over, in broad equations, those middle terms which suggest the spirit of routine, whose application should normally have been made during the former time, but that the selfishness of the privilege or the inertia of the governments pushed back.

These great equitations of principles, these enormous shifts in mores, they also have their laws, not at all arbitrary, no more left to chance than the practice of revolutions.

But what, in the end, is that practice?

Suppose that the statesmen we have seen in power since February 24, that these short-sighted politicians of small means, of narrow and meticulous routines, had been in the place of the apostles. I ask you citizens, what would they have done?

They would have fallen into agreement with the innovators of the individual conferences, in secret consultations, that the plurality of gods was an absurdity.

They would have said, like Cicero, that it is inconceivable that two augurs could look at one another without laughter; they would have condemned slavery very philosophically, and in a deep voice.

But they would have cried out against the bold propaganda which, denying the gods and all that society has sanctified, raised against it superstition and all the interests; they would have trusted in good policy, rather than tackling the old beliefs, and interpreting them; they would have knelt before Mercury the thief, before impudent Venus and incestuous Jupiter. They would have talked with respect and esteem of the Floralia and the Bacchanalia. They would have made a philosophy of polytheism, retold the history of the gods, renewed the personnel of the temples, published the payments for sacrifices and public ceremonies, according, as far as it was in them, reason and morality to the impure traditions of their fathers, by dint of attention, kindness and human respect; instead of saving the world, they would have caused it to perish.

There was, in the first centuries of the Christian era, a sect, a party powerful in genius and eloquence, which, in the face of the Christian revolution, undertook to continue the idolatry in the form of a moderate and progressive republic; they were the Neo-Platonists, to whom Apollonius of Tyana and the Emperor Julian attached themselves. It is in this fashion that we have seen with our own eyes certain preachers attempt the renovation of Catholicism, by interpreting its symbols from the point of view of modern ideas.

A vain attempt! Christian preaching, which is to say revolutionary practice, swept away all the gods and their hypocritical admirers; and Julian, the greatest politician and most beautiful spirit of his time, bears in the histories the name of *apostate*, for having been madly opposed to evangelical justice.

Let us cite one more example.

Let us suppose that in '89, the prudent counselors of despotism, the well-advised spirits of the nobility, the tolerant clergy, the wise men of the middle class, the most patient of the people — let us suppose, I say, that this elite of citizens, with the most upright vision and the most philanthropic views, but convinced of the dangers of abrupt innovations, had agreed to manage, following the rules of high policy, the transition from despotism to liberty. What would they have done?

They would have passed, after long discussion and mature deliberation, letting at least ten years elapse between each article, the promised charter; they would have negotiated with the pope, and with all manner of submissiveness, the civil constitution of the clergy; they would have negotiated with the convents, by amicable agreement, the repurchase of their goods; they would have opened an investigation into the value of feudal rights, and on the compensation to be accorded to the lords; they would have sought compensation to the privileged for the rights accorded to the people. They would have made the work of a thousand years what revolutionary practice might accomplish overnight.

All of this is not just empty talk: there was no lack of men in '89 willing to connect themselves to this false wisdom of revolution. The first of all was Louis XVI, who was as revolutionary at heart and in theory as anyone, but who did not understand that the revolution must also be practiced. Louis XVI set himself to haggle and quibble over everything, so much and so well, that they revolution, growing impatient, swept him away!

Here then is what I mean, today, by revolutionary practice.

The revolution of February proclaimed *the right to work*, the predominance of labor over capital.

On the basis of that principle, I say that before overriding all reforms, we have to occupy ourselves with a generalizing institution, which expresses, on all the points of social economy, the subordination of capital to labor; which, in lieu of making, as it has been, the capitalist the sponsor of the laborer, makes the laborer the arbiter and commander of the capitalist, an institution which changes the relation between the two great economic powers, labor and property, and from which follows, consequently, all other reforms.

Will it then be revolutionary to propose an agricultural bank serving, as always, the monopolizers of money; there to create a certified loan office, monument to stagnation and unemployment; elsewhere, to found an asylum, a pawn-shop, a hospital, a nursery, a penitentiary, or a prison, to increase pauperism by multiplying its sources?

Will it be a work of Revolution to finance a few millions, sometimes a company of tailors, sometimes of masons; to reduce the tax on drink and increase it on properties; to convert obligations into losses; to vote seeds and pick-axes for twelve thousand colonists leaving for Algeria, or to subsidize a trial phalanstery?

Will it be the speech or act of a revolutionary to argue for four months whether the people will work or will not, if capital hides or if it flees the country, if it awaits confidence or if it is confidence that awaits it, if the powers will be divided or only the functions, if the president will be the superior, the subordinate or the equal of the national assembly, if the first who will fill this role will be the nephew of the emperor or the son of the king, or if it would not be better, for that good use, to have a soldier or a poet; if the new sovereign will be named by the people or by the representatives, if the ministry of reaction which goes out merits more confidence than the ministry of *conciliation* which comes, if the Republic will be blue, white, red, or tricolor?

Will it be revolutionary, when it is a question of returning to labor the fictive production of capital, to declare the net revenue inviolable, rather than to seize it by a progressive tax; when it is necessary to organize equality in the acquisition of goods, to lay the blame on the mode of transmission; when 25,000 tradesmen implore a legal settlement, to answer them by bankruptcy; when property no longer receives rent or farm rent, to refuse it further credit; when the country demands the centralization of the banks, to deliver that credit to a financial oligarchy which only knows how to make a void in circulation and to maintain the crisis, while waiting for the discouragement of the people to bring back confidence?

Citizens, I accuse no one.

I know that to all except for us social democrats, who have envisioned and prepared for it, the Revolution of February has been a surprise; and if it is difficult for the old constitutionals to pass in so short a time from the monarchical faith to republican conviction, it is still more so for the politicians of the other century to comprehend anything of the practice of the new Revolution. Other times have other ideas. The great maneuvers of '93, good for the time, do not suit us now any more than the parliamentary tactics of the last thirty years; and if we want to abort the revolution, you have no surer means than to take up again these errors.

Citizens, you are still only a minority in this country. But already the revolutionary flood grows with the speed of the idea, with the majesty of the ocean. Again, some of that patience that made your success, and the triumph of the Revolution is assured. You have proven, since June, by you discipline, that you are politicians. From now on you will prove, by your acts, that you are organizers. The government will be enough, I hope, with the National Assembly, to maintain the republican form: such at least is my conviction. But the revolutionary power, the power of conservation and of progress, is no longer today in the hands of the government; it is not in the National Assembly: it is in you. The people alone, acting upon themselves without intermediary, can achieve the economic Revolution begun in February. The people alone can save civilization and advance humanity!

1849

God is Evil, Man is Free

Translated by Shawn P. Wilbur

Introduction by Shawn P. Wilbur

Proudhon was fond of scandal and provocation — and it got him, and his friends, into hot water. In his *System of Economic Contradictions*, he wrapped his already provocative thesis about the evolution of institutions around a scandalous narrative about "the hypothesis of God." Proudhon was fascinated with Christianity, and wrote about it from a variety of perspectives and in a variety of tones, but he is probably best remembered for writings like his "Hymn to Satan" and the final chapter of the first volumes of the *Economic Contradictions*, where he worked himself up to a sort of declaration of war against the very idea of God:

> "If God did not exist" — it is Voltaire, the enemy of religions, who says so, — "it would be necessary to invent him." Why? "Because," adds the same Voltaire, "if I were dealing with an atheist prince whose interest it might be to have me pounded in a mortar, I am very sure that I should be pounded." Strange aberration of a great mind! And if you were dealing with a pious prince, whose confessor, speaking in the name of God, should command that you be burned alive, would you not be very sure of being burned also? Do you forget, then, anti-Christ, the Inquisition, and the Saint Bartholomew, and the stakes of Vanini

and Bruno, and the tortures of Galileo, and the martyrdom of so many free thinkers? Do not try to distinguish here between use and abuse: for I should reply to you that from a mystical and supernatural principle, from a principle which embraces everything, which explains everything, which justifies everything, such as the idea of God, all consequences are legitimate, and that the zeal of the believer is the sole judge of their propriety.

"I once believed," says Rousseau, "that it was possible to be an honest man and dispense with God; but I have recovered from that error." Fundamentally the same argument as that. of Voltaire, the same justification of intolerance: Man does good and abstains from evil only through consideration of a Providence which watches over him; a curse on those who deny its existence! And, to cap the climax of absurdity, the man who thus seeks for our virtue the sanction of a Divinity who rewards and punishes is the same man who teaches the native goodness of man as a religious dogma.

And for my part I say: The first duty of man, on becoming intelligent and free, is to continually hunt the idea of God out of his mind and conscience. For God, if he exists, is essentially hostile to our nature, and we do not depend at all upon his authority. We arrive at knowledge in spite of him, at comfort in spite of him, at society in spite of him; every step we take in advance is a victory in which we crush Divinity.

Let it no longer be said that the ways of God are impenetrable. We have penetrated these ways, and there we have read in letters of blood the proofs of God's impotence, if not of his malevolence. My reason, long humiliated, is gradually rising to a level with the infinite; with time it will discover all that its inexperience hides from it; with time I shall be less and less a worker of misfortune, and by the light that I shall have acquired, by the perfection of my liberty, I shall purify myself, idealize my being, and become the chief of creation, the equal of God. A single moment of disorder which the Omnipotent might have prevented and did not prevent accuses his Providence and shows him lacking in wisdom; the slightest progress which man, ignorant, abandoned, and betrayed, makes towards good honors him immeasurably. By what right should God still say to me: Be holy, for I am holy? Lying spirit, I will answer him, imbecile God, your reign is over; look to the beasts for other victims. I know that I am not holy and never can become so; and how could you be holy, if I resemble you? Eternal father, Jupiter or Jehovah, we have learned to know you; you are, you were, you ever will be, the jealous rival of Adam, the tyrant of Prometheus.

So I do not fall into the sophism refuted by St. Paul, when he forbids the vase to say to the potter: Why hast thou made me thus? I do not blame the author of things for having made me an inharmonious creature, an incoherent assemblage; I could exist only in such a condition. I content myself with crying out to him: Why do you deceive me? Why, by your silence, have you unchained egoism within me? Why have you submitted me to the torture of universal doubt by the bitter illusion of the antagonistic ideas which you have put in my mind? Doubt of truth, doubt of justice, doubt of my conscience and my liberty, doubt of yourself, O God! and, as a result of this doubt, necessity of war with myself and with my neighbor! That, supreme Father, is what you have done for our happiness and your glory; such, from the beginning, have been your will and your government; such the bread, kneaded in blood and tears, upon which you have fed us. The sins which we ask you to forgive, you caused us to commit; the traps from which we implore you to deliver us, you set for us; and the Satan who besets us is yourself.

You triumphed, and no one dared to contradict you, when, after having tormented in his body and in his soul the righteous Job, a type of our humanity, you insulted his candid piety, his prudent and respectful ignorance. We were as naught before your invisible majesty, to whom we gave the sky for a canopy and the earth for a footstool. And now here you are dethroned and broken. Your name, so long the last word of the savant, the sanction of the judge, the force of the prince, the hope of the poor, the refuge of the repentant sinner, — this incommunicable name, I say, henceforth an object of contempt and curses, shall be a hissing among men. For God is stupidity and cowardice; God is hypocrisy and falsehood; God is tyranny and misery; God is evil. As long as humanity shall bend before an altar, humanity, the slave of kings and priests, will be condemned; as long as one man, in the name of God, shall receive the oath of another man, society will be founded on perjury; peace and love will be banished from among mortals. God, take yourself away! for, from this day forth, cured of your fear and become wise, I swear, with hand extended to heaven, that you are only the tormentor of my reason, the specter of my conscience.

Naturally, this riled folks up. And Proudhon wasn't the only to feel the heat. The perception was that his friends, and socialism in general, were getting a black eye from his provocative writing. So he was under some pressure to clear things up. But Proudhon wasn't always real good at giving the people what they wanted, so his reply (*le Peuple*, May 6, 1849) may not have exactly smoothed things over. But it's a lot of fun...

God is Evil

My friends beg me, in the interest of our common ideas, and to remove any pretext for slander, to make my opinion known on the divinity and Providence, and at the same time to explain certain passages from the *System of [Economic] Contradictions*, that the reactionary tartuffes have for a year constantly exploited against socialism with simple and credulous souls.

I surrender to their solicitations. I will even say that if I have for so long let the *Constitutionnel* and its consorts make of me a Vanini even more ferocious that the original, attacking at once God and the Devil, — the family and property, — I had my reasons for that. First I wanted to lead certain schools, up to then considered enemies, to confess themselves their perfect resemblance; I wanted, in a word, it to be demonstrated to the eyes of all that doctrinaire and Jesuit, it is all one. Also, as a metaphysician by profession, I was not unhappy to take advantage of the circumstances in order to judge, by a decisive test, where our century really is with regard to religion. It is not given to everyone to engage in such experiments in social psychology, and to examine, as I have for six months, public reason. Few men are in a position for that; and besides, it is too costly. Thus I was curious to know if, among a people such as our own, who, for two centuries, have banished religious disputes from among them; who have posited in principle the absolute liberty of conscience, that is to say the most determined skepticism; who, through the mouthpiece of the present head of the ministry, M. Odilon-Barrot, have put God and religion beyond the law; who salary all the faiths existing in their territory, while waiting for them to fade away; among a people where one no longer swears but by *honor* and *conscience*; where education, justice, power, literature and art, everything, finally, is religious indifference, if not atheism, the minds of the citizens were on a level with the institutions.

There is, I said to myself, a man who exactly fulfills his civic duties; who, above all things, respects the family of his fellow man; who keeps himself pure for the good of others; who makes a rule of never disguising his thoughts, even at the risk of his respect; who has sworn himself to the improvement of his fellows; well! What could it matter to the people to know if this man is or is not an atheist? How could that modify their opinion? Especially if one considers that the word *atheist* is as poorly defined, as obscure, as the word *God*, of which it is the negation.

For a mind enamored with philosophical and social trifles, the question deserves to be examined deeply.

Now, I have seen that, thank God! — if you'll excuse the expression — the bulk of the people in France have been stirred very little by the transcendent interests of the supreme being, and that there remains hardly anyone but the *Constitutionnel* and the Jesuits, M. Thiers and M. de Montalembert, to take up the cause of the divinity. Here, in order to conceal nothing, is all that I gathered from my researches.

> 1. Four petitions have arrived at the National Assembly, holding thirty to forty signatures, and demanding my expulsion from the Assembly for cause of atheism. As if I did not have the right to be atheist!... If the National Assembly ever occupies itself with these petitions, my honorable colleagues will laugh about it like the gods.

> 2. I have received two anonymous letters in which I have been warned, with plenty of biblical citations in support, that if I continue, as I have, to blaspheme, the heavens will strike me. — OK! I say, If the heavens intervene, I am a goner!

> 3. Finally, here is the Constitutionnel, number of May 3, which tells me to beware, that *if I push Providence too far, she will chastise me,* delivering me up to the delirium of my pride. — Indeed, merely to be

occupied with her, that is good reason to become mad.

That is all that I have been able to gather of the indignation of the devout; the rest, the immense majority of the French people, jeer at the Providence of Constitutionnel and of the good God of the Jesuits, like an ass with a fistful of nettles.

However, it is time that the comedy finishes; and, since my friends wish it and our colleagues in socialism desire it, I will address to them my profession of faith. God and the people pardon me! What I am going to say is a serious thing; but such is the sacrilegious hypocrisy of my adversaries, that I am almost ashamed of my action, as if I had just taken the holy water.

Man is Free

There is my first proposition. Liberty is thought; I only translate the *Cogito, ergo sum,* of Descartes. I am free, therefore I am. All the propositions that will follow, follow from that one, with the rigor of a geometric demonstration.

By virtue of his liberty, man adheres to or resists the *divine order*, which is nothing but the order of *nature* delivered to itself.

By his adhesion to the divine order, as by the modifications that it imposes on him, man enters into a share of government of the universe. He becomes himself, like God, of whom he is the eternal reflection, *creator* and *revealer*; he is a form of the divinity.

All that which does not come to modify the free action of man falls exclusively under the law of God.

Reciprocally, all that which surpasses the force of nature is the proper work of the will of man.

God is *eternal* reason; man is *progressive* reason.

These two reasons are necessary to one another; they complete one another.

Their *agreement* constitutes what I call the government of Providence.

Providence is not, then, like God and man, whose convergence it represents, a simple idea; it is a complex idea. — It is the harmony between the order of nature and the order of liberty, a thing that the popular proverb expresses by saying: *Help yourself, heaven will aid you!*

All that man does on encountering the divine law is *arbitrary*; all that happens without man's knowledge, or despite it, is a matter of *fatality*.

Depending on whether Humanity is more or less *autonomous*, that is to say mistress and legislator of itself; whether its share of initiative is more or less great and reasoned, and the course of events more or less freed from the unconscious laws of nature, the amount of *good* increased or diminished in the world. So that order, in its highest expression, or, as the ancient philosophers said, the Sovereign Good, results from the perfect accord between the two sovereign powers, God and man, and the extreme *wretchedness* of their complete scission.

The *progress* in Humanity can then be defined, the incessant struggle of man with nature, eternal opposition, producing and eternal conciliation.

Everywhere where man misunderstood the law of nature where it is lacking, it is inevitable that nature and society fall into dissolution. The perfection of the physical world is linked to the perfection of the social world, and *vise versa*. A God, a world, without humanity, is impossible; a Humanity-God is a contradiction. Confusion, exclusion, there is (the) evil.

God, eternal and infinite, is *everywhere*, Humanity, immortal and progressive, is *somewhere*.

Neither can the divine order be fully absorbed in human law, nor can free will resolve itself entirely in fatalism. These two orders should develop in parallel, sustain one another, harmonize, not blend: the *antinomy* between man and God is unsolvable.

The *absolute* is a conception necessary for the reason, not without reality. In other terms, God, considered as the synthesis of the faculties of the finite and infinite, does not exist. From yet another point of view, man is not the *weakened* image, but the *reversed* image of God.

The *equality* of relations between God and man; the distinction and the *antagonism* of their natures; the obligatory *convergence* of their wills; the progress of their agreement, are the fundamental dogmas of the *democratic and social philosophy*.

Christianity has been the *prophecy*, and socialism is the *realization*.

Atheism is the negation of Providence, as it results from the agreement between the inflexible laws of nature and the incessant aspirations of liberty, and as I have attempted to define it.

Atheism is, in general, the doctrine that, in an infinite variety of forms, materialism and spiritualism, Catholicism and paganism, deism, pantheism, idealism, skepticism and mysticism, etc., denies by turns equality, la contemporaneity, the necessity of the two powers, God and man, their distinction, their solidarity, tends continually either to subordinate one to the other, or to isolate them, or to resolve them.

God, eternal and inevitable reason, not being conceivable without man; and man, progressive and free reason, not being conceivable without God; and that duality being inconvertible and insoluble, every theory that detracts from it is atheism.

Thus, atheism is the opposite of *anti-theism*, which is nothing other than socialism itself, which is to say the theory Providence, or, as St. Augustine would have said, the organization of the City of God.

After that, the vulgar who relate everything to a superior will, to a Supreme Being, of which man will only be the creature and plaything, profoundly religious as to consciousness, is atheist in beliefs. The supremacy of God is a mutilation of Humanity: it is atheism.

It is as true today to say that the world does not know God, as it was at the birth of Jesus Christ.

Bossuet, in his *Discours sur l'histoire universelle*, where he glorifies the creator to the detriment of humanity, attributing everything to God, and making man the passive instrument of his designs, Bossuet, without wanting or knowing it, is an atheist.

Jean-Jacques Rousseau is an atheist, when, after having misanthropically denied civilization, that is, the participation of humanity in the government of the universe, he prostrates himself before nature and returns civilized society to the savage state. The philosopher of Geneva has not seen that the knowledge of God is progressive like society, that it is really because of the progress of that society.

And as in every state of civilization the political form has for point of departure the theological or metaphysical idea, — as in society *government* is produced according to the example of religion, — we constantly see the varieties of atheism become so many varieties of *despotism*.

Thus Bossuet, after having made the theory of divine absolutism in his *Discours sur l'histoire universelle*, has been carried by the force of his principle to make the theory of monarchical absolutism in his *Politique tirée de l'Écriture sainte*. Thus Jean-Jacques Rousseau, the theoretician of deism, a kind of compromise between reason and faith, can be considered as the father of *constitutionalism*, an arbitrary transaction between monarchy and democracy. Rousseau is the predecessor of M. Guizot: besides, the *Social Contract* is only a contradiction on the part of the philosopher of Geneva. And as deism is the worst of hypocrisies, constitutionalism is the worst of governments.

The present society, finally, a society without energy, without philosophy, without an idea of God or of itself, living from day to day on some extinct traditions, rejecting every intervention of free will in its industrial economy, awaiting its salvation only from the fatality of nature, as it awaits the sun and rain, is profoundly atheist.

And the most detestable of atheists, although they do not cease to claim to follow God and Church, are those who envy the people liberty and knowledge; who make them march at the points of their bayonets, who preach resignation and renunciation to them, the respect of parasitism and submission to the foreigner. — It is those who say to them: Make love but do not make children, because you cannot feed them; labor, but save, because you are not certain that you can always work.

It is time that we knew them, these detractors of divine and human Providence, who pose as defenders of religion, and who always deny one of the faces of the infinite; who award themselves the title of *party of order*, but who have never organized anything but conspiracies...

The readers of the *Peuple* understand at present why, in a recent article, where I brought out the deep and incurable powerlessness of these men, I called their tyrannical domination the *reign of God!* Aren't they fatalists, indeed? Don't they oppose every effort of liberty! Don't they want us to relate it exclusively to the force of things? Don't they have, as maxims, these simple phrases:

Laissez faire, laissez passer!

Chacun chez soi, chacun pour soi! [Every one for his home, every one for himself]

Qui vivra verra! [Time will tell!]

and a thousand others, which are so many acts of despair, so many professions of atheism?

Similarly, the readers of the *Peuple* will understand how, in a work where I will proceeded to the determination of the socialist dogma by the analysis of the contradictions, I have successively been able to make the critique of God and Humanity, and to show that, either by one, or by the other, the order in society, or what I today call *Providence*, was impossible: the convergence of both is required. I showed on that occasion that the God of the deists and of the Catholics, the God of the *Constitutionnel* and the *Univers*, is as impossible, as contradictory and immoral as the man of Rousseau or Lamettrie; that such a God would be the negation of God himself, and would deserve to be called *Satan* or *Evil*. In what sense have I failed my principles? How have I offended the intimate belief of Humanity?

One has so often cited, in horror of socialism, that passage of the *Economic Contradictions*, that the readers of the *Peuple* will be grateful to have me explain it. The true ideas could not be spread about too much or too early: it is the remedy against atheism, against superstition, oppression and exploitation in all its forms.

The author of the *Economic Contradictions* begins by positioning himself in the catholic hypothesis, namely that God's reason is like that of man, although infinitely superior, and he addresses this question to his adversaries:

> Would God be guilty if, after having created the world according to the laws of geometry, he had put it into our minds, or even allowed us to believe without fault of our own, that a circle may be square or a square circular, though, in consequence of this false opinion, we should have to suffer an incalculable series of evils? Again, undoubtedly.

> Well! that is exactly what God, the God of Providence, has done in the government of humanity; it is of that that I accuse him. He knew from all eternity — inasmuch as we mortals have discovered it after six thousand years of painful experience — that order in society — that is, liberty, wealth, science — is realized by the reconciliation of opposite ideas which, were each to be taken as absolute in itself, would

> precipitate us into an abyss of misery: why did he not warn us? Why did he not correct our judgment at the start? Why did he abandon us to our imperfect logic, especially when our egoism must find a pretext in his acts of injustice and perfidy? He knew, this jealous God, that, if he exposed us to the hazards of experience, we should not find until very late that security of life which constitutes our entire happiness: why did he not abridge this long apprenticeship by a revelation of our own laws? Why, instead of fascinating us with contradictory opinions, did he not reverse experience by causing us to reach the antinomies by the path of analysis of synthetic ideas, instead of leaving us to painfully clamber up the steeps of antinomy to synthesis?

The reasoning is this: If God is such as the theists claim, sovereignly good, fair and provident, how has he not prevented evil? That is the standard argument of the materialists. Now what with the conclusion of the author be? It is here that he completely separates himself from his precursors.

> If, as was formerly thought, the evil from which humanity suffers arose solely from the imperfection inevitable in every creature, or better, if this evil were caused only by the antagonism of the potentialities and inclinations which constitute our being, and which reason should teach us to master and guide, we should have no right to complain. Our condition being all that it could be, God would be justified.

But, in view of this willful delusion of our minds, a delusion which it was so easy to dissipate and the effects of which must be so terrible, where is the excuse of Providence? Is it not true that grace failed man here? God, whom faith represents as a tender father and a prudent master, abandons us to the fatality of our incomplete conceptions; he digs the ditch under our feet; he causes us to move blindly: and then, at every fall, he punishes us as rascals. What do I say? It seems as if it were in spite of him that at last, covered with bruises from our journey, we recognize our road; as if we offended his glory in becoming more intelligent and free through the trials which he imposes upon us. What need, then, have we to continually invoke Divinity, and what have we to do with those satellites of a Providence which for sixty centuries, by the aid of a thousand religions, has deceived and misled us?

What does that argumentation mean? Nothing but this: Reason, in God, is constructed otherwise than it *becomes* each day in man; apart from that, God would be inexcusable. — Note that the author guards himself well from concluding after the manner of the atheist materialists: Providence is unjustifiable; thus there is no God. He says on the contrary: If God and Providence are not justified, it is because we do not understand them; it is because God and Providence are different than the priests and philosophers say that they are.

The discussion continues on this terrain, and soon we see that not only does reason, in God, not *resemble* that of man, but that it is precisely the *inverse* of man's intelligence.

When the theists, in order to establish their dogma of Providence, cite the order of nature as a proof, although this argument is only a begging of the question, at least it cannot be said that it involves a contradiction, and that the fact cited bears witness against the hypothesis. In the system of the world, for instance, nothing betrays the smallest anomaly, the slightest lack of foresight, from which any prejudice whatever can be drawn against the idea of a supreme, intelligent, personal motor. In short, though the order of nature does not prove the reality of a Providence, it does not contradict it.

It is a very different thing with the government of humanity. Here order does not appear at the same time as matter; it was not created, as in the system of the world, once and for eternity. It is gradually developed according to an inevitable series of principles and consequences which the human being himself, the being to be ordered, must disengage spontaneously, by his own energy and at the solicitation of experience. No revelation regarding this is given him. Man is submitted at his origin to a pre-established necessity, to an absolute and irresistible order. That this order may be realized, man must discover it; that it may exist, he must have divined it. This labor of invention might be abridged; no one, either in heaven or on earth, will come to man's aid; no one will instruct him. Humanity, for hundreds of centuries, will devour its generations; it will exhaust itself in blood and mire, without the God whom it worships coming once to illuminate its reason and abridge its time of trial. Where is divine action here? Where is Providence?

What, then, is the progression of this discussion?

It is: 1° that before an error, invincible and that it was so easy to dissipate, the inaction of Providence (as the catholic atheists understand it) is not justified; 2° that from this it is necessary to conclude, not that God does not exist, but that we do not understand God; 3° that in fact, the reason that has presided over the order of nature is obviously otherwise, the reason that presides over the development of human destinies is otherwise. Soon we will see, and that will be the conclusion of the chapter, that reason in God is different from that in man, not in its *extent*, but it is *quality*; from which this consequence, that God and man, necessary to one another, contemporary with one another, at once inseparable and irreducible, are in a state of perpetual antagonism, so that the supreme perfection in the one is adequate to the supreme infirmity in the other, and that the destiny of man is, by unceasingly studying Divinity, to resemble it as little as possible.

Here is the passage where that consequence is found developed, and which has so scandalized the devout:

> And for my part I say: The first duty of man, on becoming intelligent and free, is to continually hunt the idea of God out of his mind and conscience. For God, if he exists, is essentially hostile to our nature, and we do not depend at all upon his authority. We arrive at knowledge in spite of him, at comfort in

spite of him, at society in spite of him; every step we take in advance is a victory in which we crush Divinity.

Let it no longer be said that the ways of God are impenetrable. We have penetrated these ways, and there we have read in letters of blood the proofs of God's impotence, if not of his malevolence. My reason, long humiliated, is gradually rising to a level with the infinite; with time it will discover all that its inexperience hides from it; with time I shall be less and less a worker of misfortune, and by the light that I shall have acquired, by the perfection of my liberty, I shall purify myself, idealize my being, and become the chief of creation, the equal of God.

It is impossible to better bring to light, on the one hand, the progressivity of human reason, and, on the other, the *immobility* of divine reason. How have some serious men been able to see, in all that, only an atheistic declamation, in the style of those by Diderot or the Baron d'Holbach?

A single moment of disorder which the Omnipotent might have prevented and did not prevent accuses his Providence and shows him lacking in wisdom; the slightest progress which man, ignorant, abandoned, and betrayed, makes towards good honors him immeasurably. By what right should God still say to me: *Be holy, for I am holy?* Lying spirit, I will answer him, imbecile God, your reign is over; look to the beasts for other victims. I know that I am not holy and never can become so; and how could you be holy, if I resemble you? Eternal father, Jupiter or Jehovah, we have learned to know you; you are, you were, you ever will be, the jealous rival of Adam, the tyrant of Prometheus.

So I do not fall into the sophism refuted by St. Paul, when he forbids the vase to say to the potter: Why hast thou made me thus? I do not blame the author of things for having made me an inharmonious creature, an incoherent assemblage; I could exist only in such a condition. I content myself with crying out to him: Why do you deceive me? Why, by your silence, have you unchained egoism within me? Why have you submitted me to the torture of universal doubt by the bitter illusion of the antagonistic ideas which you have put in my mind? Doubt of truth, doubt of justice, doubt of my conscience and my liberty, doubt of yourself, O God! and, as a result of this doubt, necessity of war with myself and with my neighbor!

Is there need at present to warn the reader that this does not really fall on God and Providence? — How, if the author was atheist, would he reproach God for having made him *doubt him,* and then to have made him fall into sin! That would not make sense. Under the names of God and Providence, it is Catholicism and deism, principles of Malthusian economy and of the constitutional theory, that the writer attacks. The catholic papers are not mistaken. The lines that follow, and which are the paraphrase of the Sunday oration, could not in that regard leave them in doubt.

That, supreme Father, is what you have done for our happiness and your glory (*Ad majorent Dei gloriam!*); such, from the beginning, have been your will and your government; such the bread, kneaded in blood and tears, upon which you have fed us. The sins which we ask you to forgive, you caused us to commit; the traps from which we implore you to deliver us, you set for us; and the Satan who besets us is yourself.

On the one hand, capital, authority, wealth, science; on the other, poverty, obedience, ignorance: that is the fatal antagonism that it is a question of bringing to an end; that is Malthusian fatalism, that is Catholicism! That is all that socialism has sworn to lay waste. Listen to his oath:

You triumphed, and no one dared to contradict you, when, after having tormented in his body and in his soul the righteous Job, a type of our humanity, you insulted his candid piety, his prudent and respectful ignorance. We were as naught before your invisible majesty, to whom we gave the sky for a canopy and the earth for a footstool. And now here you are dethroned and broken. Your name, so long the last word of the savant, the sanction of the judge, the force of the prince, the hope of the poor, the refuge of the repentant sinner, — this incommunicable name, I say, henceforth an object of contempt and curses, shall be a hissing among men. For God is stupidity and cowardice; God is hypocrisy and falsehood; God is tyranny and misery; God is evil.

As long as humanity shall bend before an altar, humanity, the slave of kings and priests, will be condemned; as long as one man, in the name of God, shall receive the oath of another man, society will be founded on perjury; peace and love will be banished from among mortals. God, take yourself away! for, from this day forth, cured of your fear and become wise, I swear, with hand extended to heaven, that you are only the tormentor of my reason, the specter of my conscience.

It is useless to prolong this citation, the sense of which can no longer be in doubt.

A few weeks ago, at the news of the liquidation of the Bank of the People, the *Constitutionnel* let out a cry of joy and nearly presented me as a huckster. — I responded by producing my resources and my accounts: the Constitutionnel was silent.

Some time after, I published in the *Peuple* a plan for a *Code de la résistance*; and *Constitutionnel* cried out that this was the organization of social disorganization. I then demonstrated that the organization of the resistance, the right of insurrection and conspiracy was the pure spirit of the constitutional system: the *Constitutionnel* was silent.

The other day, I proved, by a review of the year 1848, that all the evil that has been produced from February 22 until May 1, 1849, was due to the providential theory, current in the world of the Catholics and doctrinaires. The *Constitutionnel* accused me on that occasion of atheism, and found nothing better, to justify its dire, than to cite a passage were I had intended precisely to establish that the true atheism is Catholicism, the religion of the *Univers* and the Constitutionnel.

Will the *Constitutionnel* deign just once, instead of always slandering, to seriously discuss the Bank of the People, doctrinaire theory, and the Catholic faith?

In Connection with Louis Blanc: The Present Use and Future Possibility of the State

There is something odd about the fate of the writer of these lines. No matter how little he may be tempted to take pride in an all but unprecedented situation, he would be compelled to believe that, just at the moment, everybody, excepting only himself, has taken leave of their senses; or that he himself, through some inexplicable freak, has gone mad, albeit a madness of the most erudite, considered, thought out, conscientious, philosophical sort and (in terms of its principle, its purpose, its deductions) the sort that conforms most closely to pure science and common sense.

But God forbid that we should mentally entertain this presumptuous alternative: and would do better to investigate whether the contradiction currently existing between public belief and the views we hold might not be the effect of some sort of misunderstanding. Every idea delivered into this world for the very first time, even though it may be derived from the universal consciousness, is a deduction from previous tradition and, at the moment it first appears, is nonetheless regarded, by the one who articulates it, as his own personal creation and for that reason he assumes sole responsibility for it. At which point the notion appears to sit outside of the general belief and is dubbed a *paradox*. But in next to no time that paradox is acknowledged; little by little common sense overtakes it. The idea is absorbed into the public mind which then grants it credibility and leave to circulate. There is not one of us who has not witnessed such a shift in public consciousness at least once in our lives. So might we not, today, be witnessing just such a shift?

What have we been saying since February? What has *La Voix du Peuple*, founded to carry on the work of its older siblings, *Le Peuple* and *Le Représentant du Peuple*, been saying for the last three months?[18]

That the Revolution in the nineteenth century has a dual purpose:

1. In economic terms, it seeks the utter subordination of capital to labor, the assimilation of worker and capitalist, through democratization of credit, the abolition of interest, and the reduction of all dealings relating to the instruments of labor and products to equal and honest exchange. In this sense, we were the first to point out and remark that henceforth there are but two parties in France: the party of labor and the party of capital.

2. In political terms, the object of the Revolution is to absorb the State into society, which is to say, to put paid to all authority and do away with the entire machinery of government through the abolition of taxes, simplification of administration, and the separate centralization of each and every class of function, or, to put this another way, the organization of universal suffrage. In which regard we

---

[18] All three of these papers were suppressed by the state, as was its next incarnation *Le Peuple de 1850* (Editor)

say that now there are but two parties in France: the party of freedom and the party of government.

There, summed up in two articles, you have our declaration of social and political faith.

Yes, the future requires that the worker aspect and the capitalist or proprietor aspect of every producer be made equal and clear. Just as in a bygone age the serf was bound to the land, so today, by an inversion of relationships, capital should be bound to the worker. There you have the most positive pledge and most authentic tendency of the Revolution. Socialism and democracy are of like mind with us on this count.

Yes, freedom and authority must be equal in every citizen: otherwise, there would be no equality and equality would be compromised; and the sovereignty of the people, vested in a small number of representatives, would be a fiction. Here again we have the pledge as well as the irrepressible and irresistible tendency of the Revolution, even though opinion has yet to wake up entirely to the way in which this parity between freedom and authority is to be established. In this respect, let the bourgeoisie look to tradition: let it cast its mind back to its own long exertions against despotism, its deep-seated hatred of government; let those who were the first on February 22nd to bellow *Long live Reform!* and who, even before Ledru-Rollin himself, laid the first foundation stone of universal suffrage, let them answer for us: let them say whether we have truth on our side!

Now, this double pledge, this trend, detected and acknowledged, is what we are still affirming! What is the loftier and definitive conclusion we afford the Revolution?

That between labor and liberty, like capital and government, there is a kinship and identification: so that instead of four parties such as we had in the land but recently, placing us in turn in the economic point of view and in the political point of view, there are really only two: the party of labor or liberty and the party of capital or government. And these two propositions — *abolition of man's exploitation of his fellow-man and abolition of the man's government of his fellow-man* — amount to one and the same proposition; that finally the revolutionary IDEA, despite the dualism in its formula, is one and indivisible, as is the Republic itself: universal suffrage implying negation of capital's preponderance and equality of wealth, just as equality of wealth and the abolition of interest are implicit in negation of government.

We need not spell out the identity of these ideas for any logical mind to acknowledge and embrace it; it represents the point of transition between the capitalist, governmental age which is nearing its end and the era of freedom and equality which is just beginning. And, so to speak, history's apogee and the humanitarian equator.

Our entire opposition, our polemic, our revolutionary science flows from this fact: just as, further along, all philosophical advancement, every manifestation of religion — should society still need to manifest itself in this manner — will flow from it. With all of our might we are striving for, on the one hand, the abolition of interest and for lending to be free and, on the other, the obliteration of government. *La Voix du Peuple* has no other reason for its existence.

Now, this is what has befallen us.

As a result of one of those contradictions so frequent during times of great intellectual endeavor, it turns out that at present the laboring class, that which resists capital, and for whose benefit the Revolution is primarily made, is unwittingly sliding, due to a communism in its thinking and thanks above all to the ineptitude of its leaders, into the preservation of authority: the old monarchist instinct is still around, in the form of Dictatorship, Convention or whatever, to delude the people; whereas the middle class, or bourgeoisie, eternally hostile to authority, having baptized itself the liberal party, is tilting, as a consequence of its economic routine and the servility of its interests, towards perpetuation of capitalist and proprietary exploitation.

So that we who, in the name of the Revolution and of the principle invoked by every single one of the parties who stand for it, are also and simultaneously striving for the abolition of capital and of the State, at a time when we should be rallying every opinion, find ourselves at odds with each of them and upbraided and opposed by all of the very people whose cause we serve! Politics! If you want to get surely to power then refrain from being in the right against everybody.

And so the Revolution that the middle class and the proletariat, by virtue of their shared ideas and needs, seemed to be competing to accomplish, has been stopped in its tracks by the short-sighted, illogical parting of the ways between their views and their interests. Since 26th February, when it looked as if everyone was agreed upon giving it a formidable forward thrust, the Revolution has been faced with the entire nation split into two antagonistic camps — those who, with Messieurs Dunoyer, Frédéric Bastiat, etc., following in the footsteps of J.-B. Say, were ready to surrender the State, were championing capital; and the rest, who, together with the provisional government, Louis Blanc, Pierre Leroux and the entire democratic and utopian tradition, were bent on turning the State into the creator of freedom and order.

For, and we can say this without fear of misquotation and calumny, it was in all seriousness that Pierre Leroux who rejects man's governance of his fellow man, or so he assures us, nevertheless craves, in the name of the Triad and the consent of each one, to establish over *all* the sovereignty of THE FEW. The draft for a Triadic Constitution published by Pierre Leroux, which we will some day make time to examine, reeks of its author's governmental tendencies. And it was also with the utmost seriousness that Louis Blanc, for all his celebrated dictum about going "from the *master-State* to the *servant-State*", wants an authority formed, as all authorities are, through delegation by the citizenry; a State that is the organ and representative of society: in short, a government that may be to the people as the head is to the body, which is to say, master and sovereign.

This is the contradiction which we are striving with all the vigor of our consciousness and all the might of our reason to banish. Whilst the political thinking by which the middle class is prompted and the economic rationale pursued by the people should, through mutual complementation, resolve into one and the same notion that would thus encapsulate the Revolution's past and its future and reconcile those two classes, these two ideas are at war with each other and by virtue of their clash, stopping movement and jeopardizing public safety.

And this also lies at the root of the recriminations that our polemic has sparked every time that, contrary to one of the half-baked ideas competing for influence, it falls to us to expand upon one of the great principles of February. On our right we find the old liberalism, inimical to the authorities, but protective of interest and exclusive property; on our left, the governmentalist democrats, inimical, like us, to man's exploitation of his fellow man, but full to the brim with faith in dictatorship and the omnipotence of the State; and in the center ground stands absolutism, its banners emblazoned with the two faces of the counter-revolution; and, bringing up the rear, the moderates whose phony wisdom is always ready to compromise with all shades of opinion.

Each party ascribing its own contradictions to us, we are simultaneously accused by the democratic socialists of treason; by the liberal economists, of frivolity; by the moderates, of exaggeration. The first take us to task for preaching individualism after having opposed property. They tell us: you see only one term in the republican equation of *Liberty, Equality, Fraternity*; this AN-ARCHY of yours is Monsieur Dupin's *every man for himself, each to his own*; what you attack under the name of government is the core idea of the age, association.

The economists, in turn, ask us how it is that, rejecting State initiative, we could nonetheless look to the initiative of the people; they contend that putting society in the place of government through the organization of the free interplay of wills and interests, still amounts to going around in the same circles and to opposing freedom.

The moderates acknowledge the correctness of our reasoning: they give their blessing to our principles; but they refuse to follow us all the way to our conclusions. Following a principle through to its every consequence is, they say, tantamount to sacrificing truth on the altar of logic and venturing beyond the target one wishes to reach and going astray through exaggeration.

As for the absolutists, they are, of all our adversaries, the ones who best understand us. They level no charges against us and do not slander us; they take the line that we are playing into their hands by making our *reductio ad absurdum* of all of the notions shared by pubic opinion, democracy, constitutional monarchy, economism, socialism and philosophism; and, bedazzled by their illusions, they gravely wait for us to be converted and repent our errors. However, the situation must become clear and this already too long-lived error must come to its end.

Who, then, is contradicting himself, us, or the governmental socialists whose noxious tendencies we have been denouncing these past twenty months and whose every defeat we have foretold? Us, or the liberal economists whose errors we have been refuting these past ten years? Us, or the pig-headed doctrinaires whom we are forever telling that their alleged moderation is nothing but impotence and arbitrariness? Who is it that needs to win his adversary over — we who have kept to the broad thoroughfares of progress all the way, or the supporters of absolutism, as rigid as milestones, at the furthest extremity of the horizon?

All doubts will be dispelled and the public spared many a discussion if, just the same way as we agree in acknowledging, on the one hand, the bourgeoisie's liberal inclinations and, on the other, the proletariat's egalitarian tendencies, we might yet agree that they are one and the same.

Is it true that socialism, an expression of the proletariat, is at war for all eternity against capital, indeed, against property? — Yes.

Is it a fact that liberalism, an expression of the middle class, has, since time immemorial, been resisting the factiousness of government, the ventures of the authorities, the prerogatives of the State? — Again, yes.

Those two points made, what say we?

That what, in politics, goes under the name of *Authority* is analogous to and synonymous with what is termed, in political economy, *Property*; that these two notions overlap one with the other and are identical.

That an attack upon one is an attack upon the other.

That the one is incomprehensible without the other, and *vise versa*.

That if you do away with the former, you still have to do away with the latter, and vise versa.

That where capital is stripped of all interest, government is rendered useless and impossible; and, on the other hand, capital, in the absence of a government to support it, cloak it with its prerogatives and guarantee it the exercise of its privileges must, of necessity, remain unproductive and all usury unfeasible.

Finally, that Socialism and Liberalism are the two halves of the wholesale opposition that Liberty has, ever since the world began, mounted against the principle of AUTHORITY as articulated through property and through the State.

Are we wrong now, are we being frivolous, disloyal to our cause and treacherous to our principles when we champion this grand, magnificent conclusion? Is it our fault if the proletariat and the middle class, divided right now by the selfishness of their respective tendencies, are, in essence, of one mind on principles as well as on aims and on means?

And just because self-styled revolutionaries, capitalizing upon hatred, service this factious antagonism for the benefit of their own despicable ambitions are we supposed to stay silent about our ideas, the same ideas as

February? Should we cravenly shy away from the risk of calumny and unpopularity?

But, they tell us, you are forever mistaking civilization's *trends* for its *laws* and this is where you go astray: that is the origins of the contradictions, inconsistencies and exaggerations of which the entire people accuses you.

Thus one socialist says, it is correct, and we were delighted to welcome this truth, that capital and products should circulate free of charge and that use of the instruments of labor should be guaranteed for all at no cost other than what covers the costs of depreciation. This, indeed, is one of the laws of society: and you yourself have demonstrated it mathematically. But, by the same token, it is not true that society can and should dispense with government. In the absence of government, in the absence of the State, who would then extend loans to the worker, organize commerce and ensure that everyone gets education and work?

But, responds an economist from the liberal school, that is the very opposite of what is true. The abolition of governments is what societies dream about; and the elicitation of order by means of the boundless spread of freedom is their law. As for reducing interest, the phenomenon of social economics should be seen as a mere tendency rather than as a principle of amelioration. Rent on capital dwindles as capital proliferates; this is a fact. But it is nonsensical to claim that interest ever falls to zero; in that case who would be willing to make loans? Who would save? Who would work? Discard your political and egalitarian mirages, therefore, socialist, and follow freedom's banner: the banner of 1789 and 1830!

THE SOCIALIST: You do not want a social Revolution! You support usury! You actually advocate man's exploitation of his fellow man! There is enough intelligence, initiative and patriotism within the people for it to be able to complete the Revolution on its own. It will be able to do without a suspect alliance: it will never tag along behind the bourgeoisie.

THE ECONOMIST: Liberty is indebted to the bourgeois for all its gains; it is to it that the laboring class is beholden for the welfare and the rights that it enjoys, Thus far, it is this valiant and disciplined bourgeoisie that has, all unaided, shouldered the burden of Revolution: it will never allow itself to be overtaken, nor dragged along. It will never be carried along in the wake of the proletariat.

Now, now, citizens. If you cannot see eye to eye with one another, then at least try to see eye to eye with common sense. How can you fail to see that every *tendency* points to a law? That tendency is law itself, not in the form of a latency, but in the form of action? Aristotle used to teach that the first cause of motion is the intelligible heavens, by which he meant pure Idea, Reason, Law. Thus what we describe in bodies as *attraction*, or in man as *love* or *passion*, is in society, *tendency* or *progress*; in organized creatures, *life*; in the universe, *destiny*. All of which is nothing more than a manifestation of the Idea, the Law, the Intelligible Heavens, commanding the creature, nurturing it, shaping it and magnetically commanding obedience...

1849: In Connection with Louis Blanc: The Present Use and Future Possibility of the State

But let us put psychology, ontology and metaphysics to one side. Let us turn to facts and evidence. For as long as the proletariat and the bourgeoisie, in their mutual suspicion, hold each other in check, the Revolution, instead of growing peaceably, will do so in fits and starts; and at every step society will be in danger of a general dislocation. Let us show them both, therefore, that their principle is one and the same, their tendency one and the same and their pride one and the same: that whatever the one might do in the pursuit of its own interests would amount to a realization of the wishes of the other, just as the victory of the one over the other would spell the suicide of them both.

Odd, is it not, that, in order to break through universal ostracism, we should now need to effect a universal reconciliation?

Interest and Principal: A Loan is a Service

On the one hand, it is very true, as you have unquestionably established, that a loan is a *service*. And as every service has a *value*, and, in consequence, is entitled by its nature to a reward, it follows that a loan ought to have its *price*, or, to use the technical phrase, ought to *bear interest*.

But it is also true, and this truth is consistent with the preceding one, that he who tends, under the ordinary conditions of the professional lender, does not *deprive* himself, as you phrase it, of the capital which be lends. He lends it, on the contrary, precisely because the loan is not a deprivation to him; he lends it because he has no use for it himself, being sufficiently provided with capital without it; be lends it, finally, because he neither intends nor is able to make it valuable to him personally,--because, if he should keep it in his own hands, this capital, sterile by nature, would remain sterile, whereas, by its loan and the resulting interest, it yields a profit which enables the capitalist to live without working. Now, to live without working is, in political as well as moral economy, a contradictory proposition, an impossible thing.

The proprietor who possesses two estates, one at Tours, and the other at Orleans, and who is obliged to fix his residence on the one which he uses, and consequently to abandon his residence on the other, can this proprietor claim that he deprives himself of anything, because he is not, like God, ubiquitous in action and presence? As well say that we who live in Paris are deprived of a residence in New York! Confess, then, that the privation of the capitalist is akin to that of the master who has lost his slave, to that of the prince expelled by his subjects, to that of the robber who, wishing to break into a house, finds the dogs on the watch and the inmates at the windows.

Now, in the presence of this affirmation and this negation diametrically opposed to each other, both supported by arguments of equal validity, but which, though not harmonizing, cannot destroy each other, what course shall we take?

You persist in your affirmation, and say: "You do not wish to pay me interest? Very well! I do not wish to lend you my capital. Try working without capital." On the other hand, we persist in our negation, and say: "We will not pay you interest, because interest, in social economy, is a premium on idleness, the primary cause of misery and the inequality of wealth." Neither of us is willing to yield, we come to a stand-still.

This, then, is the point at which Socialism takes up the question. On the one hand, the commutative justice of interest; on the other, the organic impossibility, the immorality of interest; and, to tell you the truth at once, Socialism aims to convert neither party--the Church, which denies interest, nor the political economy, which supports it--especially as it is convinced that both are right. Let us see, now; how it analyzes the problem, and what it proposes, in its turn, that is superior to the arguments of the old moneylenders, too vitally *interested* to be worthy of belief, and to the ineffectual denunciations uttered by the Fathers of the Church.

Since the theory of usury has finally prevailed in Christian as well as in Pagan countries; since the hypothesis, or fiction, of the productivity of capital has become a practical fact among nations--let us accept this economic fiction as we have accepted for thirty-three years the constitutional fiction, and let us see what it results in when carried to its ultimate. Intead of simply rejecting the idea, as the Church has done --a futile policy--let us make from it a historical and philosophical deduction; and, since the word is more in fashion than ever, let us trace the evolution.

Moreover, this idea must correspond to some reality; it must indicate some necessity of the mercantile spirit; else nations never would have sacrificed to it their dearest and most sacred beliefs.

See, then, how Socialism, entirely convinced of the inadequacy of the economic theory as well as of the ecclesiastical doctrine, treats in its turn the question of usury.

First, it observes that the principle of the productivity of capital is no respecter of persons, grants no privileges; it applies to every capitalist, regardless of rank or dignity. That which is legitimate for Peter is legitimate for Paul; both have the same right to usury as well as to labor. When, then,--l go, back to the example which you have used,--when you lend me, at interest, the plane which you have made for smoothing your planks, if, in my turn, I lend you the saw which I have made for cutting up my lumber, I also shall be entitled to interest.

The right of capital is alike for all; all, in the proportion that they lend and borrow, ought to receive and pay interest. Such is the first consequence of your theory, which would not be a theory, were not the right which it establishes universal and reciprocal; this is self-evident.

Let us suppose, then, that of all the capital that I use, whether in the form of machinery or of raw material, half is lent to me by you; suppose also that of all the capital used by you half is lent to you by me; it is clear that the interests which we must pay will offset each other; and, if equal amounts of capital are advanced, the interests canceling each other, the balance will be zero.

In society, it is true things do not go on precisely in this way. The loans that the producers reciprocally make to each other are not always equal in amount, therefore the interests that they have to pay are also unequal; hence the inequality of conditions and fortunes.

But the question is to ascertain whether this equilibrium in the loaning of capital, labor, and skill, and, consequently, equality of income for all citizens, perfectly admissible in theory, is capable of realization in practice; whether this realization is in accordance with the tendencies of society; whether, finally and unquestionably, it is not the inevitable result of the theory of usury itself.

Now, this is what Socialism affirms, now that it has arrived at an understanding of itself, the Socialism which no longer distinguishes itself from economic science, studied at once in the light of its accumulated experience and in the power of its deductions. In fact, what does the history of civilization, the history of political economy, tell us concerning this great question of interest?

It tells us that the mutual loaning of capital, material, or immaterial, tends more and more towards equilibrium, owing to the various causes enumerated below, which the most conservative economists cannot dispute:--

First--The division of labor, or the separation of industries, which, infinitely multiplying both tools and raw material, multiplies in the same proportion the loans of capital.

Second--The accumulation of capital, an accumulation which results from diversity of industries, producing between capitalists a competition similar to that between merchants, and, consequently, effecting gradually a lowering of the rent of capital, a reduction of the rate of interest.

Third--The continually increasing power of circulation which capital acquires through the use of specie and bills of exchange.

Fourth--Finally, public security.

Such are the general causes which, for centuries have developed among producers a reciprocity of loans tending more and more to equilibrium and consequently to a more and more even balance of interests, to a continual diminution of the price of capital.

These facts cannot be denied; you yourself admit them; only you mistake their principle and purport, by giving capital the credit for the progress made in the domain of industry and wealth, whereas this progress is caused not by capital, but by the circulation of capital.

The facts being thus analyzed and classified Socialism asks whether, in order to bring about this equilibrium of credit and income, it is not possible to act directly, not on capital, remember, but on circulation; whether it is not possible so to organize this circulation as to inaugurate, at one blow, between capitalists and producers (two classes now hostile, but theoretically identical) equivalence of loans, or, in other words, equality of fortunes.

To this question Socialism again replies: Yes, it is possible, and in several ways.

Suppose, in the first place, to confine ourselves to the present conditions of credit, the operations of which are carried on mainly through the intervention of specie--suppose that all the producers in the republic, numbering more than ten millions, tax themselves, each one, to the amount of only one percent of their capital. This tax of one percent upon the total amount of the capital of the country, both real and personal, would amount to more than a thousand million of francs.

Suppose that by means of this tax a bank be founded, in competition with the Bank (miscalled) of France, discounting and giving credit on mortgages at the rate of one-half of one percent.

1849: Interest and Principal: A Loan is a Service

It is evident, in the first place, that the rate of discount on commercial paper, the rate of loans on mortgages, the dividend of invested capital, etc., being one-half of one percent, the cash capital in the hand of all usurers and moneylenders would be immediately struck with absolute sterility; interest would be zero, and credit gratuitous.

If commercial credit and that based on mortgages--in other words, if money capital, the capital whose exclusive function is to circulate--was gratuitous, house capital would soon become so; in reality, houses no longer would be capital; they would be merchandise, quoted in the market like brandy and cheese, and rented or sold--terms which would then be synonymous--at cost.

If houses, like money, were gratuitous--that is to say, if use was paid for as an exchange, and not as a loan--land would not be slow in becoming gratuitous also; that is, farmrent, instead of being rent paid to a non-cultivating proprietor, would be the compensation for the difference between the products of superior and inferior soils; or, better, there no longer would exist, in reality, either tenants or proprietors; there would be only husbandmen and wine-growers, just as there are joiners and machinists.

Do you wish another proof of the possibility of making all capital gratuitous by the development of economic institutions?

Suppose that instead of our system of taxes, so complex, so burdensome, so annoying, which we have inherited from the feudal nobility, a single tax should be established, not on production, circulation, consumption, habitation, etc., but in accordance with the demands of justice and the dictates of economic science, on the net capital falling to each individual. The capitalist, losing by taxation as much as or more than he gains by rent and interest, would be obliged either to use his property himself or to sell it; economic equilibrium again would be established by this simple and moreover inevitable intervention of the treasury department.

Such is, substantially, Socialism's theory of capital and interest.

Not only do we affirm, in accordance with this theory (which, by the way, we hold in common with the economists) and on the strength of our belief in industrial development, that such is the tendency and the import of lending at interest; we even prove, by the destructive results of economy as it is, and by a demonstration of the causes of poverty, that this tendency is necessary, and the annihilation of usury inevitable.

In fact, rent, reward of capital, interest on money, in one word, usury, constituting, as has been said, an integral part of the price of products, and this usury not being the same for all, it follows that the price of products, composed as it is of wages and interest, cannot be paid by those who have only their wages, and no interest to pay it with; so that, by the existence of usury, labor is condemned to idleness and capital to bankruptcy.

This argument, one of that class which mathematicians call the *reductio ad absurdum*, showing the organic impossibility of lending at interest, has been repeated a hundred times by Socialism.

Why do not the economists notice it? Do you really wish to refute the ideas of Socialism on the question of interest? Listen, then, to the questions which you must answer:--

1. Is it true that, though the loaning of capital, when viewed objectively, is a *service* which has its value, and which consequently should be paid for, this loaning, when viewed subjectively, does not involve an actual sacrifice on the part of the capitalist; and consequently that it does not establish the right to set a price on it?

2. Is it true that usury, to be unobjectionable, must be equal; that the tendency of society is towards this equalization; so that usury will be entirely legitimate only when it has become equal for all,--that is, nonexistent?

3. Is it true that a national bank, giving credit and discount *gratis,* is a possible institution?

4. Is it true that the effects of the gratuity of credit and discount, as well as that of taxation when simplified and restored to its true form, would be the abolition of rent of real estate, as well as of interest on money?

5. Is it true that the old system is a contradiction and a mathematical impossibility?

6. Is it true that political economy, after having, for several thousand years, opposed the view of usury held by

theology, philosophy, and legislation, comes, by the application of its own principles, to the same conclusion?

7. Is it true, finally, that usury has been, as a providential institution, simply an instrument of equality and progress, just as, in the political sphere, absolute monarchy was an instrument of liberty and progress, and as, in the judicial sphere, the boiling-water test, the duel, and the rack were, in their turn, instruments of conviction and progress?

These are the points that our opponents are bound to examine before charging us with scientific and intellectual weakness; these, Monsieur Bastiat, are the points on which your future arguments must turn, if you wish them to produce a definite result. The question is stated clearly and categorically: permit us to believe that, after having examined it, you will perceive that there is something in the Socialism of the nineteenth century that is beyond the reach of your antiquated political economy.

Interest and Principal: Arguments Drawn from the Operations of the Bank of France

It is not true--and the facts just cited prove beyond a doubt that it is not--that the decrease of interest is proportional to the increase of capital. Between the *price* of merchandise and *interest* of capital there is not the least analogy; the laws governing their fluctuations are not the same; and all your dinning of the last six weeks in relation to capital and interest has been utterly devoid of sense. The universal custom of banks and the common sense of the people give you the lie on all these points in a most humiliating manner.

Now, would you believe, sir,--for indeed you do not seem to be well-informed about anything,--that the Bank of France, an association composed of honest people, philanthropists, God-fearing men, utterly incapable of compromising, with their consciences, continues to charge four percent on all its discounts without allowing the public to derive the slightest bonus therefrom? Would you believe that it regulates the dividends of its stockholders, and quotes its stock in the money-market, on this basis of four percent on a capital of four hundred and thirty-one millions not its own? Say, is that robbery, yes or no?

But we have not reached the end. I have not begun to tell you of the crimes of this society of stock-jobbers, founded by Napoleon for the express purpose of supporting parasitic officials and proprietors and sucking the nation's life-blood. A few millions, more or less, are not sufficient to affect dangerously a population of thirty-six millions of men. That portion of the robberies committed by the Bank of France which I have exposed is but a trifle: only the results are worthy of consideration.

The fortune and destiny of the country is today in the hands of the Bank of France. If it would relieve industry and commerce by a decrease of its rate of discount proportional to the increase of its reserves; in other words, if it would reduce the price of its credit to three-fourths of one percent, which it must do in order to quit stealing,--this reduction would instantly produce, throughout the republic and all Europe, incalculable results. They could not be enumerated in a volume: I will confine myself to the indications of a few.

If, then, the credit of the Bank of France, when that bank has become a National Bank, should be loaned at three-fourths of one percent instead of at four percent, ordinary bankers, notaries, capitalists, and even the stockholders of the bank itself, would be immediately compelled by competition to reduce their interest, discount, and dividends to at least one percent, including incidental expenses and brokerage. What harm, think you, would this reduction do to borrowers on personal credit, or to commerce and industry, who are forced to pay, by reason of this fact alone, an annual tax of at least two thousand millions?

If financial circulation could be effected at a rate of discount representing only the cost of administration, drafting, registration, etc., the interest charged on purchases and sales on credit would fall in its turn from six percent to zero,--that is to say, business would then be transacted on a cash basis: there would be no more debts. Again, to how great a degree, think you, would that diminish the shameful number of suspensions, failures, and bankruptcies?

But as in society *net* product is undistinguishable from *raw* product, so in the light of the sum total of economic facts capital is undistinguishable from product. These two terms do not, in reality, stand for two distinct things; they designate relations only. Product is capital; capital is product; there is a difference between them only in private economy; none whatever in public economy.

If, then, interest, after having fallen, in the case of money, to three-fourths of one percent,--that is, to zero, inasmuch as three-fourths of one percent represents only the service of the bank,--should fall to zero in the case of merchandise also, by analogy of principles and facts it would soon fall to zero in the case of real estate: rent would disappear in becoming one with liquidation. Do you think, sir, that that would prevent people from living in houses and cultivating land?

If, thanks to this radical reform in the machinery of circulation, labor was compelled to pay to capital only as much interest as would be a just reward for the service rendered by the capitalist, specie and real estate being deprived of their reproductive properties and valued only as products,--as things that can be consumed and replaced,--the favor with which specie and capital are now looked upon would be wholly transferred to products; each individual, instead of restricting his consumption, would strive only to increase it. Whereas, at present, thanks to the restriction laid upon consumable products by interest, the means of consumption are always very much limited, then, on the contrary, production would be insufficient: Labor would then be secure in fact as well as in right.

The laboring class, gaining at one stroke the five thousand millions, or thereabouts, now taken in the form of interest from the ten thousand which it produces, plus five thousand millions which this same interest deprives it of by destroying the demand for labor, plus five thousand millions which the parasites, cut off from a living, would then be compelled to produce, the national production would be doubled and the welfare of the laborer increased four-fold. And you, sir, whom the worship of interest does not prevent from lifting your thoughts to another world,--what say you to this improvement of affairs here below?

Do you see now that it is not the multiplication of capital which decreases interest, but on the contrary, that the decrease of interest multiplies capital?

But all this is displeasing to the capitalists and distasteful to the bank. The bank holds in its hand the horn of plenty which the people have entrusted to it: that horn is the three hundred and forty-one millions of specie accumulated in its vaults, which testify so loudly to the power of the public credit. To revive labor and diffuse wealth everywhere, the bank needs to do but one thing; namely, reduce its rate of discount to such a figure that the sum total of the interest it receives shall be equal to four percent of ninety millions. It will not do it. For the sake of a few millions more to distribute among its stockholders, and which it steals, it prefers to cause an annual loss to the country of ten thousand millions. In order to reward parasitism, remunerate crime, satisfy the intemperate cravings of two millions of officials, stock-jobbers, usurers, prostitutes, and spies, and preserve this leper of a Government, it will cause, if necessary, thirty-four millions of men to rot in poverty. Once more, I ask, is that robbery? Is that rapine, plunder, premeditated and willful murder?

Have I told all?--No; that would require ten volumes, but I must stop. I will close by considering a stroke which seems to me a masterpiece of its kind, and to which I ask your undivided attention. A defender of capital, you are not acquainted with its tricks.

The amount of specie, I will not say existing, but circulating in France, including the bank's reserve, does not exceed, by common estimation, one thousand millions.

At four percent interest--I am reasoning on the supposition of paid credit--the laboring people should pay forty millions annually for the use of this capital.

Can you, sir, tell me why, instead of forty millions, we are paying sixteen hundred millions--I say *sixteen hundred millions*--as the reward of this capital?

"Sixteen hundred millions! One hundred and sixty percent! Impossible!" you exclaim. Did I not tell you, sir, that you knew nothing about political economy? This is the fact, though to you, I am sure, it is still an enigma.

The amount of mortgages, according to the most reliable authorities, is twelve thousand millions; some put it at fourteen thousand millions;

> We will say: 12,000 millions.
>
> Amount of notes of hand, at least: 6,000 millions.
>
> Amount invested in sleeping partnership, about: 2,000 millions.
>
> To which should be added the public debt: 8,000 millions.
>
> Total: 28,000 millions.

which agriculture, manufactures, and commerce, in a word, labor, which produces everything, and the State, which produces nothing and is supported by labor, owe to capital.

All these debts--note this point--arise from money loaned, or said to have been loaned, at four, five, six, eight, twelve, and even fifteen percent.

Taking six percent as the average rate of interest on the first three items, which amount to twenty thousand millions, they would yield twelve hundred millions. Add the interest on the public debt, which is about four hundred millions, and we have altogether sixteen hundred millions of interest *per annum* on a capital of one thousand millions. Now, then, tell me, is it in this case also the scarcity of specie that causes the enormous amount of interest? No, for all these amounts were loaned, as we have seen, at an average rate of six percent. How, then, has an interest, stipulated at six percent, become an interest of one hundred and sixty percent? I will tell you.

You, sir, who regard all capital as naturally and necessarily productive, know that this productivity is not possessed by all kinds of property in the same degree; that it belongs mainly to two kinds, the kind known as real estate (land and houses), if we have a chance to lease them (which is not always easy or always safe), and the kind known as money. Money, money especially! that is the capital *par excellence,* the capital which is lent, which is hired, which is paid for, which produces all those wonderful financiers whom we see maneuvering at the bank, at the stock exchange, and at all the interest and usury shops.

But money is not, like land, capable of cultivation, nor, like houses or clothes, can it be consumed by use. It is only a *token of exchange,* receivable by all merchants and producers, and with which a shoemaker, for example, can buy him a hat. In vain, through the agency of the bank, does paper, little by little and with universal consent, get substituted for specie: the prejudice sticks fast, and if bank paper is received in lieu of specie, it is only because the opinion prevails that it can be exchanged at will for specie. Specie alone is in demand.

When I lend money, then, it is really the power to exchange my unsold product of today or of the future which I lend: money, in itself, is useless. I take it only to expend it; I neither consume nor cultivate it. The exchange once consummated, the money again becomes transferable, and capable, consequently, of being loaned anew. Thus it goes on, and as, by the accumulation of interest, money-capital, in the course of exchange, always returns to its source, it follows that the new loan, always made by the same hand, always benefits the same persons.

Do you say that, inasmuch as money serves to facilitate the exchange of capital and products, the interest paid on it is a compensation not so much for the money itself as for the capital exchanged; and that, thus viewed, the sixteen hundred millions of interest paid an one thousand millions of specie represent really the reward of from twenty-five to thirty thousand millions of capital? That has been said or written somewhere by an economist of your school.

Such an allegation cannot be sustained for one moment. How happens it, I ask you, that houses are rented, that lands are leased, that merchandise sold on credit bears interest? Just because of the use of specie; specie, which intervenes, as a fiscal agent, in all transactions; specie, which prevents houses and lands from being exchanged instead of loaned, and merchandise from being sold for cash. Specie, then, intervening everywhere as a supplementary capital, as an agent of circulation, as a means of security,--this it is precisely that we pay for, and the remuneration of the service rendered by it is exactly the point now in question.

And since in another place we have seen from an explanation of the workings of the Bank of France and the consequences of the accumulation of its metallic reserve, that a capital of ninety millions of specie, having to produce an annual interest of four percent, admits of a rate of discount of three, two, one, or even three-fourths of one percent, according to the amount of business transacted by the bank, it is very evident, further, that the sixteen hundred millions of interest which the nation pays to its usurers, bankers, bondholders, notaries, and sleeping-partners are simply the rent of one thousand millions of gold and silver, unless you prefer to acknowledge with me that these sixteen hundred millions are obtained by robbery.

Interest and Principal: The Origin of Ground Rent

I said before that in ancient times the landed proprietor, when neither he nor his family farmed his land, as was the case among the Romans in the early days of the Republic, cultivated it through his slaves: such was the general practice of patrician families. Then slavery and the soil were chained together; the farmer was called *adscrpitus gleboe*, joined to the land; property in men and things was undivided. The price of a farm depended (1) upon its area and quality of its soil, (2) upon the quantity of stock, and (3) upon the number of slaves.

When the emancipation of the slave was proclaimed, the proprietor lost the man and kept the land; just as today, in freeing the blacks, we leave the master his property in land and stock. Nevertheless, from the standpoint of ancient law as well as of natural and Christian right, man, born to labor, cannot dispense with the implements of labor; the principles of emancipation involved an agrarian law which guarantees them to him and protects him in their use: otherwise, this pretended emancipation was only an act of hateful cruelty, an infamous deception, and if, as Moses said, interest, or the yearly income from capital, reimburses capital, might it not be said that servitude reimburses property? The theologians and the law-givers of the time did not understand this, and by an irreconcilable contradiction, which still exists, they continued to rail at usury, but gave absolution to rent.

1849: Interest and Principal: The Origin of Ground Rent

The result was that the emancipated slave, and, a few centuries later, the enfranchised serf, without means of existence, was obliged to become a tenant and pay tribute. The master grew still richer. I will furnish you, he says, with land; you shall furnish the labor; and we will divide the products. It was a reproduction on the farm of the ways and customs of business. I will lend you ten talents, said the moneyed man to the workingman; you shall use them; and then either we will divide the profits, or else, as long as you keep my money, you shall pay me a twentieth; or, if you prefer, at the expiration of the loan, you shall return double the amount originally received. From this sprang ground-rent, unknown to the Russians and the Arabs. The exploitation of man by man, thanks to this transformation, passed into the form of law: Usury, condemned in the form of lending at interest, tolerated in the *contrat a la grosse,* was extolled in the form of farm-rent. From that moment commercial and industrial progress served to make it only more and more customary. This was necessary in order to exhibit all the varieties of slavery and robbery, and to establish the true law of human liberty.

Once engaged in this practice of *interesse,* so strangely understood, so improperly applied, society began to revolve in the circle of its miseries. Then it was that inequality of conditions seemed a law of civilization, and evil a necessity of our nature.

Two ways, however, seemed open to laborers to free themselves from exploitation by the capitalist: one was, as we said above, the gradual balancing of values and consequently a decrease in the price of capital; the other was the reciprocity of interest.

But it is evident that the income from capital, represented mainly by money, cannot be totally destroyed by decreasing it; for, as you well say, sir, if my capital brought me nothing, instead of lending it I should keep it, and the laborer, in consequence of having refused to pay the tithe, would be out of work. As for the reciprocity of usury, it is certainly possible between contractor and contractor, capitalist and capitalist, proprietor and proprietor; but between proprietor, capitalist, or contractor, and the common laborer, it is utterly impossible. It is impossible, I say, as long as in commerce interest on capital is added to the workingman's wages as a part of the price of merchandise, for the workingman to repurchase what he has himself produced. To *live by working* is a principle which, as long as interest exists, involves a contradiction.

Society once driven into this corner, the absurdity of the capitalistic theory is shown by the absurdity of its consequences; the inherent iniquity of interest results from its homicidal effects, and while property begins and ends in rent and usury, its affinity with robbery will be established. Can it exist under other conditions? For my own part, I say no: but this is an inquiry entirely foreign to the question now under discussion, and I will not enter upon it.

Look now at the situation of both capitalist and laborer, resulting from the invention of money, the power of specie, and the established similarity between the lending of money and the renting of land and houses.

The first,--for it is necessary to justify him, even in your eyes,--controlled by the prejudice in favor of money, cannot gratuitously dispossess himself of his capital in favor of the laborer. Not that such dispossession is a sacrifice, for, in his hands, capital is unproductive; not that he incurs any risk of loss, for, by taking a mortgage as security, he is sure of repayment; not that this loaning costs him the slightest trouble, unless you consider as such counting the money and verifying the security; but because, by dispossessing himself for ever so short a time of his money,--of this money which, by its prerogative, is, as has been so justly said, *power*,--the capitalist lessens his strength and his safety.

This would be otherwise, if, gold and silver were only ordinary merchandise; if the possession of coin was regarded as no more desirable than the possession of wheat, wine, oil, or leather; if the simple ability to labor gave a man the same security as the possession of money. While this monopoly of circulation and exchange exists, usury is necessary to the capitalist. His motives, in the light of justice, are not reprehensible: when his money leaves his own vault, his safety goes with it.

Now, this necessity, which is laid upon the capitalist by an involuntary and widespread prejudice, is, as respects the laborer, the most shameful of robberies, as well as the most hateful of tyrannies, the tyranny of force.

1849: Interest and Principal: The Origin of Ground Rent

What are, indeed, the theoretical and practical consequences to the working-class, to this vital, productive, and moral portion of society, of lending at interest and its counterpart, farm-rent? I today confine myself to the enumeration of some of them, to which I call your attention, and which hereafter, if agreeable to you, shall be the subject of our discussion.

And first, it is the principle of interest, or of *net* product, that enables an individual really and legitimately to live without working: that is the conclusion of your last letter but one, and such, in fact, is the condition to which every one today aspires.

Again: If the principle of *net* product is true of the individual, it must be true also of the nation; for example, the capital of France, both real and personal, being valued at one hundred and thirty-two billions, which yields, at five percent, an annual income of sixty-six hundred millions, at least half of the French nation might, if it pleased, live without working; in England, where the amount of accumulated capital is much larger than in France, and the population much smaller, the entire nation, from Queen Victoria down to the lowest hanger-on of the son of Liverpool, might live on the product of its capital, promenading with cane in hand, or groaning in public meetings. Which leads to this conclusion, evidently an absurd one, that, thanks to its capital, such a nation has more income than its labor can produce.

Again: The total amount of wages paid annually in France being in the neighborhood of six thousand millions, and the total amount of revenue yielded by capital being also six thousand millions, making the market value of the annual product of the nation twelve thousand millions, the producers, who are also consumers, can and must pay, with the six thousand millions of wages allowed them, the twelve thousand millions which commerce demands of them as the price of its merchandise, and without which the capitalists would find themselves minus an income.

Again: Interest being perpetual in its nature, and never being regarded, as Moses wished, as a repayment of the original capital, and further, it being possible to place each year's income at interest in its turn, thus forming a new loan, and consequently giving rise to a new income, the smallest amount of capital may, in time, yield sums so enormous as to exceed in value a mass of gold as large as the globe on which we live. Price demonstrated this in his theory of liquidation.

Again: The productivity of capital being the immediate and sole cause of the inequality of wealth, and the continual accumulation of capital in a few hands, it must be admitted, in spite of the progress of knowledge, in spite of Christian revelation and the extension of public liberty, that society is naturally and necessarily divided into two classes--a class of exploiting capitalists and a class of exploited laborers.

Interest and Principle: The Circulation of Capital, Not Capital Itself, Gives Birth to Progress

Thus it is with interest on capital, legitimate when a loan was a service rendered by citizen to citizen, but which ceases to be so when society has acquired the power to organize credit gratuitously for everybody. This interest, I say, is contradictory in its nature, in that, on the one hand, the service rendered by the lender is entitled to remuneration, and that, on the other, all wages suppose either a production or a sacrifice, which is not the case with a loan. The revolution which is effected in the legitimacy of lending originates there. That is how Socialism states the question; that, therefore, is the ground on which the defenders of the old regime must take their stand.

To confine one's self to tradition, to limit one's self to saying a loan is a service rendered which ought, therefore, to be compensated, without entering into the considerations which tend to annihilate interest, is not to reply. Socialism, with redoubled energy, protests, and says: I have nothing to do with your service,--service for you, but robbery for me,--as long as it is possible for society to furnish me with the same advantages which you offer me, and that without reward. To impose on me such a service in spite of myself, by refusing to organize the circulation of capital, is to make me submit to an unjust discount, is to rob me.

Thus your whole argument in favor of interest consists in confounding epochs,--I mean to say, in confounding that which is legitimate in lending with that which is not,--whereas I, on the contrary, carefully distinguish between them. I will proceed to make this intelligible to you by an analysis of your letter.

I take up your arguments one by one. In my first reply I made the observation that he who lends does not *deprive* himself of his capital. You reply: What matters it, if he has created his capital for the express purpose of lending it?

In saying that you betray your own cause. You acquiesce, by those words, in my *antithesis,* which consists in saying: The hidden reason why lending at interest, legitimate yesterday, is no longer so today, is because lending, in itself, does not involve privation. I note this confession.

But you cling to the intention: What matters it, you says if the lender has created his capital for the express purpose of lending it?

To which I reply: And what do I care, indeed, for your intention, if I have really no need of your service, if the pretended service which you wish to do me becomes necessary only through the ill-will and incapacity of society? Your credit resembles that which the pirate gives to his captive, when he gives him his liberty in return for a ransom. I protest against your credit at five per cent, because society is able and ought to give it to me at zero per cent; and, if it refuses to do so, I accuse it, as well as you, of robbery; I say that it is an accomplice, an abettor, an organizer of robbery.

Comparing a loan to a *sale,* you say: Your argument is as valid against the latter as against the former, for the hatter who sells hats does not *deprive* himself.

No, for he receives for his hats--at least he is reputed to receive for them--their exact value immediately, neither *more* nor *less.* But the capitalist lender not only is not deprived, since he recovers his capital intact, but he receives more than his capital, more than he contributes to the exchange; he receives in addition to his capital an interest which represents no positive product on his part. Now, a service which costs no labor to him who renders it is a service which may become gratuitous: this you have already told us yourself.

After having recognized the *non-privation* attendant upon a loan, you admit further "that *it is not theoretically impossible that interest,* which today constitutes an integral part of the price of commodities, *may become the same for all,* and thereby be *abolished."* "But," you add, "for this other things are needed than a new bank. Let Socialism endow all men with equal activity, skill, honesty, economy, foresight, needs, desires, virtues, vises, and chances even, and then it will have succeeded."

So that you enter upon the question only to immediately avoid it. Socialism, at the point which it has now reached, justly claims that it is by means of a reform in banking and taxation that we can arrive at this balance of interests. Instead of passing over, as you do, this claim of Socialism, stop here and refute it: you will thereby demolish all the utopias of the world. For Socialism affirms--and without this affirmation Socialism could not exist, it would be a nonentity--that it is not by endowing all men with equal "activity, skill, honesty, economy, foresight, needs, desires, virtues, vises, and chances even" that we shall succeed in balancing interest and equalizing incomes; it maintains that we must, on the contrary, begin by centralizing credit and abolishing interest, in order to equalize faculties, needs, and chances. Let there be no more robbers among us, and we shall be all virtuous, all happy! That is Socialism's creed. I feel the keenest regret in telling you of it, but really your acquaintance with Socialism is so slight that you run against it without seeing it.

You persist in attributing to capital all social progress in the domain of wealth, while I, for my part, attribute it to circulation; and you say that here I mistake the cause for the effect.

But, in maintaining such a proposition, you unwittingly refute your own argument. J. B. Say has shown--and of this fact you are not ignorant--that the *transportation* of a value, be that value called money or merchandise, is a value in itself; that it is as real a product as wheat and wine; that consequently the service of the merchant and banker deserves to be remunerated equally with that of the husband-man and wine-grower. It is on this ground that you stand when you claim wages for the capitalist who, by lending his capital, the return of which is guaranteed him, performs the office of transportation, of circulation. In lending, you said in your first letter, I render a service, I create a value. Such were your words, which we have admitted: in this respect we both agreed with the master.

I am justified, then, in saying that it is not capital itself, but the circulation of capital,--that kind of service, product, merchandise, value, or reality, which political economy calls *movement* or *circulation,* and which, indeed, constitutes the whole subject-matter of economic science,--that causes wealth. We remunerate all who render this service; but we affirm that, as far as capital, properly speaking, or money is concerned, it is society's duty to render it to us gratuitously; that if it does not do so, there is fraud and robbery. Do you now understand the real point on which the social question turns?

After having expressed your regret at the division of capitalists and laborers into two hostile classes,--which surely is not the fault of Socialism,--you take the very useless trouble of showing me by illustrations that every laborer is in some degree a capitalist, and does a work of capitalization,--that is, usury. And who, pray, ever dreamed of denying it? Who has told you that what we recognize as legitimate once in the capitalist, we condemn at the same time in the laborer?

Yes, we know that the price of all merchandise and service may be analyzed at the present day as follows:--

1. Raw material;

2. Compensation of tools, and incidental expenses;

3. Wages of labor.

4. Interest of capital.

Thus it is in all kinds of business,--agriculture, industry, commerce, and transportation. These are the *fourches caudines* of every one who is not a parasite, be he capitalist or laborer. You need not enter into long details upon this subject, very interesting though they are and clearly delightful to your imagination.

I repeat: The problem of Socialism is to make this fourth element which enters into the price of commodities--interest on capital--equal for all producers, and consequent nugatory. We maintain that this is possible; that, if this is possible, it is society's duty to procure gratuitous credit for all; that, failing to do this, it will not be a society, but a conspiracy of capitalists against laborers, a compact for purposes of robbery and murder.

Understand then, once for all, that it is not necessary to show us how capital is formed, how it accumulates through interest, how interest enters into the price of products, how all laborers are themselves guilty of the sin of usury: we have long known all these things, just as we are convinced of the personal honesty of annuitants and proprietors.

We say: The economic system based on the fiction of the productivity of capital, justifiable once, is henceforth illegitimate. Its inefficacy and malfeasance have been exposed; it is the cause of all existing misery, the present mainstay of that old fiction of representative government which is the last form of tyranny among men.

1849: Interest and Principle: The Circulation of Capital, Not Capital Itself, Gives Birth to Progress

I will not detain myself with the purely religious considerations with which your letter closes. Religion, allow me to say, has nothing to do with political economy. A real science is sufficient unto itself; otherwise, it cannot exist. If political economy needs the sanction of religion to make up for the inadequacy of its theories, and if, in its turn, religion, as an excuse for the barrenness of its dogmas, pleads the exigencies of political economy, the result will be that political economy and religion, instead of mutually sustaining each other, will accuse each other, and both will perish.

Begin, then, by doing justice, and liberty, fraternity, and wealth will increase; even the happiness of another life will be only the surer. Is the inequality of capitalistic income, yes or no, the primary cause of the physical, moral, and intellectual poverty which today afflicts society? Is it necessary to equalize the income of all men, to make the circulation of capital gratuitous by assimilating it to the exchange of products, and to destroy interest? That is what Socialism asks, and it must have an answer.

Socialism, in its most positive conclusions, furnishes the solution in the democratic centralization and gratuity of credit, combined with a single tax, to replace all other taxes, and to be levied on capital.

Let this solution be verified; let its application be tried. That is the only way to refute Socialism; except that is done, we shall shout louder than ever our war-cry: *Property is robbery!*

Letter to Pierre Leroux

My dear Pierre Leroux,

I really must forgive you your incessant accusations, for you do not know me and do not engage in debate.

For a start, you haven't read me, so you have a cheek attacking me; next, I think you need telling and everything that you have written over the past month is there to prove it: you have absolutely no method. As a result of rehashing your empty formulas, wallowing in your sterile imaginings and focusing your thoughts upon some world beyond the senses, you have rendered yourself incapable of grasping other people's thinking; the upshot being that, all unbeknownst to yourself, your criticisms amount, I am sorry to say, to unrelenting demonization.

On the basis of a few snatches of text quarried from my books and utterly misconstrued, you have cast me as an adversary of your own devising — anti-democratic, anti-socialist, counter-revolutionary, Malthusian and atheistic. This is the imaginary creature to which you address your arguments, without in the least bothering if the man you depict thus to proletarians fits the description. Sometimes you credit me with saying things that I never said, or you credit me with conclusions diametrically opposed to my actual ones; at other times, you take the trouble to lecture me on what no one living in this century could honestly be ignorant of; all in order to banish me benignly from the democratic and social community.

Meanwhile, the well-intentioned readers who follow you, and the malicious ones — and of the latter sort there is no shortage — pick up on your accusations, passing comment on them, inflating them and exploiting them. So much so that, ultimately and thanks to you, today I find myself the Satan of socialism, just as, as year ago, I was the Satan of property. Socialism's main business at this point in time is to demolish Proudhon, or so one of your disciples, Madame Pauline Roland,[19] is telling all who are prepared to listen. How much more clear-sighted socialism will be, won't it?, once this renegade Proudhon has been cast down; whereupon Pierre Leroux's tittle-tattle merchants, eaten up by hypochondria, will take their seats among the denizens of the Assembly of representatives of the People!

So, my dear Pierre Leroux, would you care to see this controversy brought to an end? The crucial thing is that the debate be kept on track, that, in each particular, we deal first with one issue and then with the next, rather than rant about them all, and then some, as you do in every one of your articles; without this, our exchanges will inevitably become a laughing-stock for the Malthusians and scandalize the proletarians. As for myself, I will freely

---

[19] Pauline Roland (1805-1852), a Saint-Simonian socialist, feminist, and associate of Leroux, also wrote a column for Proudhon's *Le Représentant du peuple*, but was later to write a critique of Proudhon's antifeminism, *La femme a-t-elle le droit à la liberté?* (*Does Woman Have the Right to Liberty?*, 1851). From Andy Carloff.

confess to you that I find it impossible to keep up such a polemic, squandering my time and my paper on relentlessly clarifying facts, reconstructing texts, clearing up your misunderstandings, rebutting your whimsy and translating your high-falutin' style into common parlance.

Thus you take me to task for having made a distinction between the labor question and the question of the State, two questions which are, at bottom, identical and susceptible to one and the same solution.

If you were as eager to acknowledge the common ground between your thoughts and mine as you are to highlight where they differ, you wouldn't have had any difficulty persuading yourself that, when it comes to the questions of labor and the State, as well as on a host of other matters, our two outlooks have no reason to feel jealous of each other. When I state, say, that the capitalist principle and the monarchist or governmental principle are one and the same principle; that the abolition of the exploitation of man by man and the abolition of the government of man by man are one and the same formula; when, taking up arms against communism and absolutism alike, those two kindred faces of the authority principle, I point out that, if the family was the building block of feudal society, the workshop is the building block of the new society; it must be as plain as day that I, like you, look upon the political question and the economic question as one and the same. What you upbraid me for not knowing on this score is your own sheer ignorance of my own thinking and, what is worse, it is a waste of time.

But does it follow from the fact that the labor question and the State question resolve each other and are, fundamentally, one and the same issue, that no distinction should be made between them and that each does not deserve its own resolution? Does it follow from these two questions being, in principle, identical, that we must arrive at a particular mode of organizing the State rather than the State being subsumed by labor? Neither of those conclusions holds water. Social questions are like problems of geometry; they may be resolved in different ways, depending on how they are approached. It is even useful and vital that these differing solutions be devised so that, in adding further dimensions to theory, they may add to the sum of science.

And as to the State, since, despite this multi-faceted character, the ultimate conclusion is that the question of its organization is bound up with that of the organization of labor, we may, we must, further conclude that a time will come when, labor having organized itself, in accordance with its own law, and having no further need of law-maker or sovereign, the workshop will banish government. As I argue and into which we shall look into, my dear philosopher, whenever, paying rather more heed to the other fellow's ideas and being a little less sensitive about your own, you may deign to enter into a serious debate about one or other of these two things, about which you are forever prattling without actually saying anything: Association and the State.

The government question and the labor question being identical, you rightly remark that such identity is articulated in the following terms: *The Question of the organization of Society.*

Now, read through chapter one of *Contradictions Économiques* and you will find it formally spelled out that it is incorrect to say that labor is organized or that it is not; that it is *forever* self-organizing; that society is an ongoing striving for organization; that such organization is at one and the same time the principle, the life and the purpose of society. So, my dear Pierre Leroux, be so kind as to think me somewhat less of an ignoramus and above all less of a sophist than I may seem to your frightened imagination: it will lay to rest three quarters of our quarrel.

There can be nothing easier than justifying the orthodoxy of this proposition as penned by me and upon which you seize so contemptuously and irrationally: "The February Revolution has posed two crucial questions: one economic, namely, the question of labor and property; and the other political, to wit, the question of government and the State." I merely needed to issue a reminder of the message implicit in all my words, that politics and political economy are one and the same science, the former being the more personal, arbitrary or subjective; the latter more substantial and positive. However, that interpretation of the February Revolution strikes you as *dry* and *narrow*: it lacks that certain something beyond the government and economics of societies, without which any idea looks satanic to you and every proposition fit for the pyre. That certain something is the sense of the divine, the theological and religious sense. Topped off with a quotation from some homily by Monsieur de Lamartine, and one of your usual commentaries on God, religion, the head of Christ, the Convention and the Republic.

At a time of your choosing, my dear Pierre Leroux, I shall give you such a sermon on God, his Spirit and his Word, as will draw tears from socialism's blue-stockings and their concierges; I can play that instrument every bit as deftly as you and Monsieur de Lamartine. But permit me not to throw theology into the pot with Political Economy, or, as the proverb has it, serve up *God with plums*. Such abuse of religiosity is one of the mystifications of our age and one that it behooves socialism to purge from its literature and press. Talking religion to men when the task in hand is to lay the foundations of social, mathematical and objective science amounts to a muddying of minds; and to perpetrating against the People the very same crime as the notorious Mazarin[20] was accused of having committed against the person of the young Louis XIV.

What is your God?

What is your religion, your ritual, your dogma?

What is the meaning of this constant invocation of Christ and Church?

---

[20] Jules Mazarin (1602-61) was an Italian cardinal who served as the chief minister of France from 1642 until his death first under King Louis XIII and then Louis XIV. As the later was only five years old when he became King, Mazarin functioned essentially as the co-ruler of France alongside the queen. From Andy Carloff.

You do not know the first thing about these things; you cannot see a single drop of them in your own thinking and all this other-worldly lyricism is nothing but a cover for the wretchedness of your alleged faith and the nullity of your means. You only prattle so much about God, of whom you, the anti-Christian, know nothing, to spare yourself the need to talk about matters here below, *non ut aliquid dicatur sed ne taciturn*.²¹

Yes, I tell you, the February Revolution (and I am sticking to my formula precisely on account of its concrete simplicity and its very materiality), the February Revolution has posed two questions; one political and the other economic. The first is the question of government and freedom; the second that of labor and capital. I defy you to express bigger issues in fewer words. So leave the Supreme Being to heaven and religion to conscience, to the household, a matter for the mother of the family and her offspring.

Let me add — and there is nothing in me to validate your entertaining doubts, the way you do, about my feelings on this score — that once those two major issues have been resolved, the republican catch-cry, *Liberty, Equality, Fraternity*, is a reality. If this is what you refer to as *God's kingdom on earth*, let me say to you, indeed, that I have no quarrel with that. It is a real comfort to me to find out at last that the kingdom of God is the kingdom of liberty,

---

²¹ A slight misquotation of St. Augustine's *De Trinitate*: "Dictum est tamen tres personae, non ut aliquid diceretur, sed ne taceretur" ("We shall speak of [God as having] three persons, not in order to say anything, but in order not to be silent"). From Andy Carloff.

equality and fraternity. But could you not express yourself in everyday language?

You have me saying, and I really do not know where you could have found this, that *ownership of the instruments of labor must forever stay vested in the individual and remain unorganized*. These words are set in italics, as if you had lifted them from somewhere in my books. And then, on the back of this alleged quotation, you set about answering me that society, or the State that stands for it, has the right to buy back all property assets, that it has a duty to pursue such *buy backs* and that it will do so.[22]

But it does not follow at all from my speaking on the basis of socialism in order to reject the buy back of such assets as nonsensical, illegitimate and poisonous that I want to see individual ownership and non-organization of the instruments of labor endure for all eternity. I have never penned nor uttered any such thing: and have argued the opposite a hundred times over. I make no distinction, as you do, between real ownership and phony ownership: from the lofty heights of righteousness and human destiny, I deny all kinds of proprietary domain. I deny it, precisely because I believe in an order wherein the instruments of labor will cease to be appropriated and instead become shared; where the whole earth will be depersonalized; where, all functions having become interdependent

---

[22] The French word translated here as *buy back* and *buyback*, "rachat," can also have a theological dimension, as in the English words *redeem* and *redemption*: the phrase "redeemed by the blood of Jesus Christ," in French, is "rachat par le sang de Jésus-Christ." From Andy Carloff.

[*solidaires*], the unity and personhood of society will be articulated alongside the personality of the individual. True, were I not familiar with the candor of your soul, I should think, dear Pierre Leroux, that such misrepresentation of my meaning and my words were done on purpose.

But how is such solidarity of possession and labor to be achieved? How are we to make a reality of such personhood of society, which must result from the disappropriation, or de-personalizing of things?

That plainly is the issue, the big question of the revolution.

Together with Louis Blanc, you make noises about *association* and *buy back*: but association, such as it must emerge from fresh reforms, is as much a mystery as religion, and all the attempts at association made by the workers before our very eyes and more or less modeling themselves on the forms of companies defined by our civil and commercial codes, can only be deemed transitory. In short, we know nothing about association. But, besides its requiring the acquiescence of all property-owners, by all the citizenry — which is an impossibility — buying back assets is a notion of mathematical nonsensicality. What is the State supposed to use to pay for assets? Why, assets. An across-the-board buyback amounts to universal expropriation without public utility and WITHOUT COMPENSATION. Yet your sense of caution, Pierre Leroux, has no misgivings about being compromised by fostering such claptrap!

There is a more straightforward, more effective and infinitely less onerous and less risky way of transferring ownership, of achieving Liberty, Equality and Fraternity: that way is, as I have indicated many times, to put an end to capital's role in production by the democratic organization of credit and a simplification of taxation.[23]

Capital having been divested of its power of usury, economic solidarity is gradually created, and with it, an equality of wealth.

Next comes the spontaneous, popular formation of groups, workshops or workers' associations;

Finally, the last to be conjured and formed is the over-arching group, comprising the nation in its entirety, what you term the State because you invest it in a representative body outside of society, but which, to me, is no longer the State.

That, dear philosopher, is how I see the Revolution going; this is how we should shift from Liberty to Equality and thence to Fraternity. Which is why I so forcefully insist upon the importance of economic reform, a reform that I have given this makeshift designation: *Free credit*.

---

[23] The term Proudhon uses, "la productivité du capital," is literally "the productivity of capital" but such a literal translation unfortunately implies that he simply wishes to end returns to capital. Rather, he wants to achieve production without the mediation of capital and the chosen translation reflects this. From Andy Carloff.

And that too we might have scrutinized methodically, and have thrashed out item by item, had you but once managed to stand back from your amorous ecstasies and turn your attention to the sordid practice of loans and discounts. But you deemed it more purposeful, more urgent to have it out and repeat everywhere that I am a foe of Socialism, a foe of Democracy, a foe of Revolution, a hidden disciple of Malthus, determined to preserve *bourgeoisism* and *proprietarism*.

Hang on, Pierre Leroux: do I need to tell you what I think of your role and mine in this mammoth drama of the nineteenth century? I am the thresher of the February Revolution: the proletarians who are listening to us will be the millers and the bakers and you, with your triad,[24] and the rest with their tub-thumping claptrap, all of you are merely pastry cooks.

Yours, etc.,

P-J PROUDHON

---

[24] In Leroux's philosophy the fundamental principle was that of what he called the "triad" – a triplicity which he finds to pervade all things, which in God is "power, intelligence and love," in man "sensation, sentiment and knowledge." In society, he pointed to the division of the human race into three great classes, philosophers, artists and industrial chiefs, to be paid according to their capacity, labor, and capital. From Andy Carloff.

Parliamentary Isolation

I entered the National Assembly with the timidity of a child, with the ardor of a neophyte. Assiduous, from nine o'clock in the morning, at the meetings of bureaux and committees, I did not quit the Assembly until the evening, and then I was exhausted with fatigue and disgust. As soon as I set foot in the parliamentary Sinai, I ceased to be in touch with the masses; because I was absorbed by my legislative work, I entirely lost sight of the current of events. I knew nothing, either of . the situation of the national workshops, or the policy of the government, or of the intrigues that were grow-ing up in the heart of the Assembly. One must have lived in that isolator which is called a National Assembly to realize how the men who are most completely ignorant of the state of the country are almost always those who represent it... Most of my colleagues of the left and the extreme left were in the same perplexity of mind, the same ignorance of daily facts. One spoke of the national workshops only with a kind of terror, for fear of the people is the sickness of all those who belong to authority; the people, for those in power, are the enemy.

The Coming Era of Mutualism

If I am not deceived, my readers must be convinced at least of one thing, that Social Truth is not to be looked for either in Utopia or in the Old Routine; that Political Economy is not the Science of Society, and yet that it contains the elements of such a science, even as chaos before creation contained the elements of the universe; and finally, that in order to arrive at the definitive organization which would appear to be the destiny of our race upon this globe, it is only necessary to make a general equation of all our contradictions.

But what shall be the formula of this equation?

Already we have been enabled to perceive, that it must be a Law of Exchange, a theory of Mutualism, a system of Guarantees, which dissolves the old forms of society civil and commercial, and satisfies all the conditions of efficiency, progress and justice, which criticism has pointed out; a Society no longer merely conventional, but real, which substitutes for the present piecemeal divisions of property a scientific distribution; which abolishes the servitude [of] machinery, and prevents the crises engendered by new inventions; which converts competition into a benefit and makes of monopoly a pledge of universal security; which by the power of its principle, instead of demanding credit for capital and protection for the state, subjects both capital and the state to the uses of labor; which by the truthful honesty of the exchanges produces a real solidarity among nations;

which without interdicting individual enterprise and without prohibiting domestic expenditure, incessantly restores to society the wealth that private appropriation diverts from it; which by the rapid turning over, the outflux and influx of capital, insures the political and industrial equality of citizens, and by a grand system of public education produces,—while constantly elevating the general level,—an equality of functions and an I equivalence of skill; which regenerating human conscience by justice, well being and virtue, ensures harmony and the equilibrium of generations; a society, in a word, which being at once organized and transitional, avoids what is merely provisional, guarantees all, yet leaves the way open for improvement.

This theory of Mutualism, that is to say of exchange in kind, of which the simplest form is the loan of articles of consumption is, when the collective being of society is regarded, a synthesis of the two ideas of appropriation and of communism; a synthesis as ancient as the elements of which it is composed, inasmuch a as it is only a return of society to its primitive practices, across a labyrinth of inventions and systems, the result of six thousand years of meditation upon this fundamental proposition, A equals A.

All is prepared to day for this solemn restoration; every thing announces that the reign of delusions is ended, and that society is about to return to its natural sincerity. Monopoly has swelled to a world-wide size; and monopoly embracing the world can not remain exclusive; it must either popularize itself or explode and disappear. Hypocrisy, venality, prostitution, robbery, form the very foundations of the public conscience, and unless humanity learns to live upon that which is its bane, we must believe that the era of justice and expiation draws nigh.

Already Socialism, feeling the unsatisfactoriness of Utopian dreams, applies itself to realities and facts; laughs at its own follies in Paris; plunges into discussions in Berlin, Cologne, Leipzig, Breslau; rages in England; thunders from across the Atlantic; stands ready for martyrdom in Poland; makes governmental experiments at Berne and Lausanne. Socialism, penetrating the masses, has become transformed; the people care little for the honor of particular schools; they demand work, knowledge, well-being, equality. Little reck they of systems, if only the end they seek is gained. When the people have set their will upon a certain good, and the only question is how to obtain it, we have not long to wait before it comes; prepare to see the grand masquerade break up and vanish. —Translated for *The Spirit of the Age.*

The Nature and Destination of Government

There must, says holy Scripture, be factions [*partis*] [1]: For there must be heresies [*Oportet enim hoereses esse*]. – Terrible. *There must!* writes Bossuet [2] in profound adoration, without daring to search for the reason behind this *There must!*

A little reflection has revealed to us the principle and the significance of factions: the point is to know their goal and their end.

All men are equal and free: society, by nature and destination, is thus autonomous, one might say, ungovernable. If the sphere of activity of each citizen is determined by the natural division of labor and the choice one makes of a profession, social functions are combined so as to produce an effect of harmony, and the order results from the free action of all; there is no government. Whosoever lays a hand on me in order to govern me is a usurper and a tyrant; I declare him my enemy.

But social physiology does not at first contain this egalitarian organization: the idea of Providence, among the first to appear in society, is repugnant to it. Equality happens to us by a succession of tyrannies and governments, in which Freedom is continually in a struggle with absolutism, like Israel with Jehovah. Equality is thus born, for us, continually out of inequality. Freedom's father is Government.

1849: The Nature and Destination of Government

Once the first men assembled on the edges of the forests to found the first societies, they did not say to one another, as shareholders of a company [*commandite*]: "Let us organize our rights and our duties in such a way as to provide each of us with the greatest amount of well-being, and to bring along our equality and our independence as well." So much reason was beyond the grasp of the first men, and in contradiction with the theory of those preaching revelation. The language we used was quite different: "Let us constitute among ourselves an authority that will watch over and govern us, *Constituamus super nos regem*! It is in this way that our peasants heard it, on December 10, 1848, when they gave their votes to Louis Bonaparte. The voice of the people is the voice of power, while waiting for it to become the voice of liberty. Also, all authority is by divine right, *Omnis potestas à Deo*, says Saint Paul.

> Authority, then, behold that which was the first social idea of human kind. And the second was to work immediately for the abolition of authority, each person wanting to make it an instrument to his or her own freedom against the freedom of others: such is the work and the destiny of Factions.

Authority was not long inaugurated in the world, when it became the object of universal competition. Authority, Government, Power, State, – these words all designate the same thing; – each sees in them the means to oppress and exploit his fellows. Absolutists, doctrinaires, demagogues and socialists, all incessantly turn their regard to authority, as if towards their shared magnetic pole.

From this comes the aphorism of the radical faction, which the doctrinaires and absolutists assuredly would not disavow: *The social revolution is the goal; the political revolution* (that is to say, the change of authority) *is the means*. This means: "Give us the right of life and death over your persons and your belongings, and we will make you free!."..For more than six thousand years the kings and priests have been repeating that line!

Thus the Government and the factions, are, reciprocally one to the other, Cause, End and Means. They exist for each other; they have a common destiny: it is to call the populace to emancipation each day; it is to energetically solicit their initiative at the expense of their faculties; it is to mold [*façonner*] their minds and push them continually towards progress by prejudice, by restrictions, and with a calculated resistance to all their ideas, to all their needs. You will not do this; you will abstain from that: the Government, no matter which faction reigns, has never known how to say anything else. *Interdiction* has been, since Eden, the educational system of humanity. But, once man reaches the age of majority, the Government and the Factions must disappear. This conclusion arrives with the same logical force, the same necessary tendency as we saw socialism come out of absolutism, philosophy be born of religion, and equality find purchase [*se poser*] on inequality itself.

When, by philosophical analysis, one wants to take account of authority, of its principle, its forms, its effects, one recognizes quickly enough that the constitution of authority, spiritually and temporally, is nothing other than a preliminary organism [*organisme préparatoire*], in essence parasitic and corruptible, incapable of producing anything by itself but tyranny and misery, whatever form it takes, whatever ideas it represents. Philosophy affirms in consequence that, contrary to faith, the constitution of authority over the people is but a transitional establishment, that power not being a conclusion of science, but a product of spontaneity, disintegrates as soon as it is discussed, that, far from strengthening and growing with time, as suppose the rival factions that besiege it, it must be reduced indefinitely and be absorbed into the organization of industry. In consequence, it must not be placed on, but under society; and, turning the aphorism of the radicals on its head, it concludes: *The political revolution, the abolition of authority among men, is the goal, the social revolution is the means.*

It is for this reason, adds the philosopher, that all factions, without exception, as much as they affect power, are variations of absolutism, and that there will not be freedom for citizens, order for societies, unity among workers, until the renunciation of authority has replaced the political catechism of faith in authority.

No more factions;

No more authority;

Absolute freedom for man and citizen.

In three phrases, I have made my political and social profession of faith.

It is in this spirit of governmental negation that one day I spoke thus to a man who, though he was of rare intelligence, had the weakness of wanting to be a minister:

> "Conspire with us for the demolition of the government. Make yourself a revolutionary for the transformation of Europe and the world, and remain a journalist. (*Représentant du Peuple*, June 5, 1848)

He replied:

> "There are two ways of being a revolutionary: *from above*, which is to say the revolution by initiative, by intelligence, by progress, by ideas; – *from below*, which is to say the revolution by insurrection, by force, by desperation, by throwing cobble stones.
>
> "I was, I still am a revolutionary *from above*, I have never been, I never will be a revolutionary *from below*.
>
> "Do not count on me to ever conspire for the demolition of any government, my spirit [*esprit*] would refuse. It is open to but one thought: improve the government." (*Presse*, June 6, 1848).

There is in this distinction, *from above, from below,* much rattling and very little truth. Mr. de Girardin, in expressing himself thus, thought he was saying something as new as it was profound. He has only reproduced the eternal illusion of demagogues who, thinking that they were advancing revolutions, with the help of those in power, have only ever managed to push them back. Let us examine Mr. de Girardin's thought more closely.

It pleases this ingenious publicist to call a revolution by initiative, intelligence, progress and ideas, *a revolution from above*; it pleases him to call a revolution by insurrection and despair, *a revolution from below*. It is precisely the opposite which is true.

From above, in the thought of the author that I cite, is evidently the power; *from below* means the people. On one side, the action of the government, on the other, the initiative of the masses. What is at issue, then, is which of these two initiatives, that of the government and that of the people, is more intelligent, more progressive, more peaceful.

But, the revolution from above is inevitably – I will say the reason why later – a revolution by the capricious pleasure [*bon plaisir*] of the prince, by the arbitrariness of a minister, by the tentative groping [*tâtonnements*] of an assembly, by the violence of a club; it is revolution by dictatorship and despotism.

Louis XIV, Napoleon, Charles X practiced it thus; so Mr. Guizot, Louis Blanc, Leon Faucher want it. The whites, the blues, the reds, they are all in agreement on this point.

The revolution by the initiative of the masses is a revolution by concerted citizens, by the experience of workers, by the diffusion of enlightenment – a revolution by freedom. Condorcet, Turgot, Robespierre sought the revolution from below, real democracy. One of the men who revolutionized the most, and who governed the least was Saint Louis. France, at the time of Saint Louis, made herself what she is; like a grapevine grows its buds, she produced her lords and her vassals: When the king published his famous rules, he was nothing but the recorder of the public wills.

Socialism has given in completely to the illusion of radicalism. The divine Plato, over two thousand years ago, is a sobering [*triste*] example. Saint-Simon, Fourier, Owen, Cabet, Louis Blanc, all partizans of the organization of work by the State, by capital, by any authority, call for, like my Mr. de Girardin, the revolution from above. Instead of teaching the people how to organize themselves, to appeal to their experience and their reason, they demand power from them. In what way do they differ from the despots? They are also utopian, like all despots: the latter cannot last, the former cannot take root.

The implication is that the Government can never be revolutionary, and for the very simple reason that it is government. Only society, the mass of the people penetrated by intelligence, can revolutionize itself, because only it can rationally deploy its spontaneity, analyze its situation, explain the mystery of its destiny and its origin, change its faith and its philosophy; because it alone, ultimately, is capable of struggling against its author, to produce its fruit. Governments are the scourges of God, established to discipline the world; and you want them to destroy themselves, to create freedom, to make revolutions!

It cannot be that way. All revolutions from the coronation of the first king to the Declaration of the Rights of Man, were accomplished by the spontaneity of the people. Governments have always impeded [*empêché*], always suppressed [*comprimé*], always struck with force [*frappé*], never have they revolutionized anything. Their role is not to bring about movement, but to hold it back. Even if they were to have the revolutionary science, social science, to which they are averse, they could not apply it, they would not have the right. It would first be necessary to disseminate their science among the people, so that they could obtain the consent of the citizens; to expect this is to misunderstand the nature of authority and power.

The facts come to confirm the theory here. The nations which are most free are those where the power has the least initiative, where its role is the most restrained: let us cite only the United States of America, Switzerland, England, Holland. On the contrary, the most subjugated nations are those where the power is the best organized and the strongest, we can witness. And yet we complain ceaselessly about not being governed, we demand always a stronger power, always stronger!

Long ago the church said, speaking like a tender mother: Everything for the people, but everything by the priests.

The monarchy came after the church: Everything for the people, but everything by the prince.

The doctrinaires : Everything for the people, but everything by the bourgeoisie.

The radicals have not changed the principles for having changed the formula: Everything for the people, but everything by the state.

It's always the same governmentalism, the same communism.

Who would dare say finally: All for the people, even the government? – All for the people: Agriculture, commerce, industry, philosophy, religion, police, etc. All by the people: the government, religion, just as much as agriculture and commerce.

Democracy is the abolition of all powers, spiritual and temporal, legislative, executive, judiciary, proprietary. Doubtless it is not the Bible that reveals it, but the logic of societies, the chain reaction of revolutionary acts; it is all modern philosophy.

Following Mr. de Lamartine, agreeing on this with Mr. de Genoude, it is for the government to say *I want*. The country has but to respond *I consent*.

And centuries of experience answers them, saying that the best governments are those which are most successful at rendering themselves useless. Do we need parasites to work and priests to speak to God? We have no more need of the elected officials who govern us.

The exploitation of man by man, someone said, is theft. Well, then! The government of man by man is servitude. And all positive religion, finding its end point in the dogma of papal infallibility, is nothing other than the worship of man by man – idolatry.

Absolutism, founding, all at once, the power of the altar, the throne, and the bank, has multiplied the network of chains on humanity. After the exploitation of man by man, after the government of man by man, after the worship of man by man, we have yet still:

The judgment of man by man,

The condemnation of man by man,

And to finish the series, the punishment of man by man.

These religious, political, and judiciary institutions, of which we are so proud, we must respect and obey until, by the progress of time, they wither and fall, like fruit falls during its season. They are the instruments of our apprenticeship, visible signs of the governance of Instinct over humanity, the weakened, but not disfigured remnants of the bloody customs that signal our base age. Anthropophagy has long since disappeared, but not without the resistance of authority, with its atrocious rites: anthropophagy subsists everywhere in the spirit of our institutions, I attest it in the sacrament of the Eucharist and the penal code.

Philosophical reason repudiates this symbolism of savages. It proscribes these exaggerated forms of *human respect*. And yet it does not claim, with the radicals and the doctrinaires, that we can undertake this reform by legislative authority; it does not concede that anyone has the right to prosecute the good of the people, in spite of the people, or that it be lawful to liberate a nation that wants to be governed. Philosophy only puts its trust in reforms coming out of the free will of societies: the only revolutions that it admits are those which precede from the initiative of the masses: it denies, in the most absolute manner, the revolutionary competency of governments.

In summary:

If we consult only faith, the schism [*scission*] of society appears as the terrible effect of the original fall of man. That is what Greek mythology expressed by the fable of the warriors born of snake's teeth who all killed each other at birth. God, according to this myth, left the government of humanity in the hands of antagonistic factions, such that discord establish its reign on earth, and that man learn, under perpetual tyranny, how to turn his thought towards another plane of existence [*séjor*].

Before reason, governments and factions are naught but the staging of the fundamental concepts of society, a realization of abstractions, a metaphysical pantomime whose meaning is FREEDOM.

I have made my profession of faith. You know the characters who, in this account of my political life, must play the principal roles. You know what subject they represent. Be attentive to what I will now recount to you.

The State: Its Nature, Object, and Destiny

Translated by Benjamin R. Tucker

The Revolution of February raised two leading questions: one economic, the question of labor and property; the other political, the question of government or the State.

On the first of these questions the socialistic democracy is substantially in accord. They admit that it is not a question of the seizure and division of property, or even of its repurchase. Neither is it a question of dishonorably levying additional taxes on the wealthy and property-holding classes, which, while violating the principle of property recognized in the constitution, would serve only to overturn the general economy and aggravate the situation of the proletariat. The economic reform consists, on the one hand, in opening usurious credit to competition and thereby causing capital to lose its income,—in other words, in identifying, in every citizen to the same degree, the capacity of the laborer and that of the capitalist; on the other hand, in abolishing the whole system of existing taxes, which fall only on the laborer and the poor man, and replacing them all by a single tax on capital, as an insurance premium.

By these two great reforms social economy is reconstructed from top to bottom, commercial and industrial relations are inverted, and the profits, now assured to the capitalist, return to the laborer. Competition, now anarchical and subversive, becomes emulative and fruitful; markets no longer being wanting, the workingman and employer, intimately connected, have nothing more to fear from stagnation or suspension. A new order is established upon the old institutions abolished or regenerated.

On this point the revolutionary course is laid out; the meaning of the movement is known. Whatever modification may appear in practice, the reform will be effected according to these principles and on these bases; the Revolution has no other issue. The economic problem, then, may be considered solved.

It is far from being the same with the political problem,—that is, with the disposal to be made in the future, of government and the State. On this point the question is not even stated; it has not been recognized by the public conscience and the intelligence of the masses. The economic Revolution being accomplished, as we have just seen, can government, the State, continue to exist? Ought it to continue to exist? This no one, either in democracy or out of it, dares to call in question; and yet it is the problem which, if we would escape new catastrophes, must next be solved.

We affirm, then, and as yet we are alone in affirming, that with the economic Revolution, no longer in dispute, the State must entirely disappear; that this disappearance of the State is the necessary consequence of the organization of credit and the reform of taxation; that, as an effect of this double innovation government becomes first useless and then impossible; that in this respect it is in the same category with feudal property, lending at interest, absolute and constitutional monarchy, judicial institutions, etc., all of which have served in the education of liberty, but which fall and vanish when liberty has arrived at its fullness. Others, on the contrary, in the front ranks of whom we distinguish Louis Blanc and Pierre Leroux, maintain that, after the economic revolution, it is necessary to continue the State, but in an organized form, furnishing however, as yet no principle or plan for its organization. For them the political question, instead of being annihilated by identification with the economic question always subsists, they favor an extension of the prerogatives of the State, of power, of authority, of government. They change names only; for example, instead of master-State they say servant-State, as if a change of words sufficed to transform things! Above this system of government, about which nothing is known, hovers a system of religion whose dogma is equally unknown, whose ritual is unknown, whose object, on earth and in heaven, is unknown.

This, then is the question which at present divides the socialistic democracy, now in accord, or nearly so, on other matters: Must the State continue to exist after the question of labor and capital shall be practically solved? In other words, shall we always have, as we have had hitherto, a political constitution apart from the social constitution?

We reply in the negative. We maintain that, capital and labor once identified, society exists by itself, and has no further need of government. We are, therefore, as we have more than once announced, anarchists. Anarchy is the condition of existence of adult society, as hierarchy is the condition of primitive society. There is a continual progress in human society from hierarchy to anarchy.

Louis Blanc and Pierre Leroux affirm the contrary. In addition to their capacity of socialists they retain that of politicians; they are men of government and authority, statesmen.

To settle the difference, we have, then, to consider the State, no longer from the point of view of the old society, which naturally and necessarily produced it, and which approaches its end, but from the point of view of the new society, which is, or must be, the result of the two fundamental and correlative reforms of credit and taxation.

Now if we prove that, from this last point of view, the State, considered in its nature rests on a thoroughly false hypothesis; that, in the second place, considered in its object, the State finds no excuse for its existence save in a second hypothesis, equally false; that, finally, considered in the reasons for its continuance, the State again can appeal only to an hypothesis as false as the two others, — these three points cleared up, the question will be settled, the State will be regarded as a superfluous, and consequently harmful and impossible, thing; government will be a contradiction.

Let us proceed at once with the analysis: —

I. Of the nature of the State

"What is the State?" asks Louis Blanc.

And he replies:—

"The State, under monarchical rule, is the power of one man, the tyranny of a single individual.

"The State, under oligarchical rule, is the power of a small number of men, the tyranny of a few.

"The State, under aristocratic rule, is the power of a class, the tyranny of many.

"The State, under anarchical rule is the power of the first comer who happens to be the most intelligent and the strongest; it is the tyranny of chaos.

"The State, under democratic rule, is the power of all the people, served by their elect, it is the reign of liberty."

Of the twenty-five or thirty thousand readers of Louis Blanc, perhaps there are not ten to whom this definition of the State did not seem conclusive, and who do not repeat, after the master: The State is the power of one, of a few, of many, of all, or of the first comer, according as the word State is prefaced by one of these other adjectives,—monarchical, oligarchical, aristocratic, democratic, or anarchical. The delegates of the Luxembourg—who think themselves robbed, it seems, when any one allows himself to hold an opinion different from theirs on the meaning and tendencies of the Revolution of February—in a letter that has been made public, have done me the honor to inform me that they regard Louis Blanc's answer as quite triumphant, and that I can say nothing in reply. It would seem that none of the citizen-delegates ever have studied Greek. Otherwise, they would have seen that their master and friend, Louis Blanc, instead of defining the State, has only translated into French the Greek words monos, one; aligoï, a few; aristoï, the great; démos, the people; and the privative a, which means no. It is by the use of these qualifying terms that Aristotle has distinguished the various forms of the State, which is designated by the word archê, authority, government, State. We ask pardon of our readers, but it is not our fault if the political science of the Luxembourg does not go beyond etymology.

And mark the artifice! Louis Blanc, in his translation, only had to use the word tyranny four times, tyranny of one, tyranny of many, etc., and to avoid it once, power of the people, served by their elect, to win applause. Every state save the democratic, according to Louis Blanc, is tyranny. Anarchy especially receives a peculiar treatment; it is the power of the first comer who happens to be the most intelligent and the strongest; it is the tyranny of chaos. What a monster must be this first comer, who, first comer that he is, nevertheless happens to be the most intelligent and the strongest, and who exercises his tyranny in chaos! After that who could prefer anarchy to this charming government of all the people, served so well, as we know, by their elect? How overwhelming it is, to be sure! at the first blow we find ourselves flat on the ground. O rhetorician! thank God for having created for your express benefit, in the nineteenth century, such stupidity as that of your so-called delegates of the working classes; otherwise you would have perished under a storm of hisses the first time you touched a pen.

What is the State? This question must be answered. The list of the various forms of the State, which Louis Blanc, after Aristotle, has prepared, has taught us nothing. As for Pierre Leroux, it is not worth while to interrogate him; he would tell us that the question is inconsiderate; that the State has always existed; that it always will exist,—the final reason of conservatives and old women.

The State is the EXTERNAL constitution of the social power.

By this external constitution of its power and sovereignty, the people does not govern itself; now one individual, now several, by a title either elective or hereditary, are charged with governing it, with managing it affairs, with negotiating and compromising in its name; in a word, with performing all the acts of a father of a family, a guardian, a manager, or a proxy, furnished with a general, absolute, and irrevocable power of attorney.

This external constitution of the collective power, to which the Greeks gave the name archê, sovereignty, authority, government, rests then on this hypothesis: that a people, that the collective being which we call society, cannot govern itself, think, act, express itself, unaided, like beings endowed with individual personality; that, to do these things, it must be represented by one or more individuals, who, by any title whatever, are regarded as custodians of the will of the people, and its agents. According to this hypothesis, it is impossible for the collective power, which belongs essentially to the mass, to express itself and act directly, without the mediation of organs expressly established and, so to speak, posted ad hoc. It seems, we say,—and this is the explanation of the constitution of the State in all its varieties and forms,—that the collective being, society, existing only in the mind, cannot make itself felt save through monarchical incarnation, aristocratic usurpation, or democratic mandate; consequently, that all special and personal manifestation is forbidden it.

Now it is precisely this conception of the collective being, of it life, its action, its unity, its individuality, its personality,—for society is a person, understand! just as entire humanity is a person,—it is this conception of the collective human being that we deny today; and it is for that reason that we deny the State also, that we deny government, that we exclude from society, when economically revolutionized, every constitution of the popular power, either without or within the mass, by hereditary royalty, feudal institution, or democratic delegation.

We affirm, on the contrary, that the people, that society, that the mass, can and ought to govern itself by itself; to thing, act, rise, and halt, like a man; to manifest itself, in fine, in its physical, intellectual, and moral individuality, without the aid of all these spokesmen, who formerly were despots, who now are aristocrats, who from time to time have been pretended delegates, fawners on or servants of the crowd, and whom we call plainly and simply popular agitators, demagogues.

In short:

We deny government and the State, because we affirm that which the founders of States have never believed in, the personality and autonomy of the masses.

We affirm further that every constitution of the State has no other object than to lead society to this condition of autonomy; that the different forms of the State, from absolute monarchy to representative democracy, are all only middle terms, illogical and unstable positions, serving one after another as transitions or steps to liberty, and forming the rounds of the political ladder upon which societies mount to self-consciousness and self-possession.

We affirm, finally, that this anarchy, which expresses, as we now see, the highest degree of liberty and order at which humanity can arrive, is the true formula of the Republic, the goal towards with the Revolution or February urges us; so that between the Republic and the government, between universal suffrage and the State, there is a contradiction.

These systematic affirmations we establish in two ways: first, by the historical and negative method, demonstrating that no establishment of authority, no organization of the collective force from without, is henceforth possible for us. This demonstration we commenced in the "Confessions of a Revolutionist," in reciting the fall of all the governments which have succeeded one another in France for sixty years, discovering the cause of their abolition, and in the last place signalizing the exhaustion and death of authority in the corrupted reign of Louis Philippe, in the inert dictatorship of the provisional government, and in the insignificant presidency of General Cavignac and Louis Bonaparte.

We prove our thesis, in the second place, by explaining how, through the economic reform, through industrial solidarity and the organization of universal suffrage, the people passes from spontaneity to reflection and consciousness; act, no longer from impulse and enthusiasm, but with design; maintains itself without masters and servants, without delegates as without aristocrats, absolutely as would an individual. Thus, the conception of person, the idea of the me, becomes extended and generalized; as there is an individual person or me, so there is a collective person or me; in the one case as in the other will, actions, soul, spirit, life, unknown in their principle, inconceivable in their essence, result from the animating and vital fact of organization. The psychology of nations and of humanity, like the psychology of man, becomes a possible science. It was this demonstration that we referred to in our publications on circulation and credit as well as in the fourteenth chapter of the manifesto of "La Voix du Peuple" relative to the constitution.

So, when Louis Blanc and Pierre Leroux assume the position of defenders of the State,—that is, of the external constitution of the public power,—they only reproduce, in a varied form peculiar to themselves which they have not yet made known, that old fiction of representative government, whose integral formula, whose completest expression, is still the constitutional monarchy. Did we, then, accomplish the Revolution of February in order to attain this retrogressive contradiction?

It seems to us—what do you say, readers?—that the question begins to exhibit itself in a somewhat clearer light; that the weak-minded, after what we have just said, will be able to form an idea of the State; that they will understand how republicans can inquire if it is indispensable, after an economic revolution which changes all social relations, to maintain, to please the vanity of pretended statesmen, and at a cost of two thousand millions per annum, this parasitic organ called government. And the honorable delegates of the Luxembourg, who, being seated in the arm-chairs of the peerage, therefore think themselves politicians, and claim so courageously an exclusive understanding of the Revolution, doubtless will fear no longer that we, in our capacity of the most intelligent and the strongest, after having abolished government, as useless and too costly, may establish the tyranny of chaos. We deny the State and the government; we affirm in the same breath the autonomy of the people and its majority. How can we be upholders of tyranny, aspirants for the ministry, competitors of Louis Blanc and Pierre Leroux?

In truth, we do not understand the logic of our adversaries. They accept a principle without troubling themselves about its consequences; they approve, for example, the equality of taxation which the tax on capital realizes; they adopt popular, mutual, and gratuitous credit, for all these terms are synonymous; they cheer at the dethronement of capital and the emancipation of labor; then, when it remains to draw the anti-governmental conclusions from these premises, they protest, they continue to talk of politics and government, without inquiring whether government is compatible with industrial liberty and equality; whether there is a possibility of a political science, when there is a necessity for an economic science! Property they attack without scruple, in spite of its venerable antiquity; but they bow before power like church-wardens before the holy sacrament. Government is to them the necessary and immutable a priori, the principle of principles, the eternal archeus.

Certainly, we do not offer our affirmations as proofs; we know, as well as any one, on what conditions a proposition is demonstrated. We only say that, before proceeding to a new constitution of the State, we must inquire whether, in view of the economic reforms which the Revolution imposes upon us, the State itself should not be abolished; whether this end of political institutions does not result from the meaning and bearing of economic reform. We ask whether, in fact, after the explosion of February, after the establishment of universal suffrage, the declaration of the omnipotence of the masses, and the henceforth inevitable subordination of power to the popular will, any government whatever is still possible, whether a government would not be placed perpetually in the alternative either of submissively following the blind and contradictory injunctions of the multitude, or of intentionally deceiving it, as the provisional government has done, as demagogues in all ages have done. We ask, at least, which of the various attributes of the State should be retained and strengthened, which abolished. For, should we find, as may still be expected, that, of all the present attributes of the State, not one can survive the economic reform, it would be quite necessary to admit, on the strength of this negative demonstration that, in the new condition of society, the State is nothing., can be nothing; in short, that the only way to organize democratic government is to abolish government.

Instead of this positive, practical, realistic analysis of the revolutionary movement, what course do our pretended apostles take? They go to consult Lycurgus, Plato, Orpheus, and all the mythological oracles; they interrogate the ancient legends; they appeal to remotest antiquity for the solution of problems exclusively modern, and then give us for answer the whimsical illuminations of their brain.

Once more: is this the science of society and of the Revolution which must, at first sight, solve all problems; a science essentially practical and immediately applicable; a science eminently traditional doubtless, but above all thoroughly progressive, in which progress takes place through the systematic negation of tradition itself?

II. Of the end or object of the State

We have just seen that the idea of the State, considered in its nature, rests entirely on an hypothesis which is at least doubtful,—that of the impersonality and the physical, intellectual, and moral inertia of the masses. We shall now prove that this same idea of the State, considered in its object, rests on another hypothesis, still more improbable than the first,—that of the permanence of antagonism in humanity, an hypothesis which is itself a consequence of the primitive dogma of the fall or of original sin.

We continue to quote "Le Nouveau Monde:"

"What would happen," asks Louis Blanc, "if we should leave the most intelligent or the strongest to place obstacles in the way of the development of the faculties of one who is less strong or less intelligent? Liberty would be destroyed.

"How prevent this crime? By interposing between oppressor and oppressed the whole power of the people.

"If James oppresses Peter, shall the thirty-four millions of men of whom French society is composed run all at once to protect Peter, to maintain liberty? To pretend such a thing would be buffoonery.

"How then shall society intervene?

"Through those whom it has chosen to REPRESENT it for this purpose.

"But these REPRESENTATIVES of society, these servants of the people, who are they? The State.

"Then the State is only society itself, acting as society, to prevent—what?—oppression; to maintain—what?—liberty."

That is clear. The State is a REPRESENTATION of society, externally organized to protect the weak against the strong; in other words, to preserve peace between disputants and maintain order. Louis Blanc has not gone, far, as we see, to find the object of the State. It can be traced from Grotius, Justinian, Cicero, etc., in all the authors who ever have written on public right. It is the Orphic tradition related by Horace:—

> Sylvestres homines sacer interpresque deorum.
>
> Cædíbus et victu fœdo deterruit Orpheus,
>
> Dictus ob hoc lenire tigres rabidosque leones,
>
> Dictus et Amphion, Thebanæ conditor arcis,
>
> Saxa movere sono testudinis, et prece blanda
>
> Ducere quo vellet...

"The divine Orpheus, the interpreter of the gods, called men from the depths of the forests and filled them with a horror of murder and of human flesh. Consequently it was said of him that he tamed lions and tigers, as later it was said of Amphion, founder of Thebes, that he moved the stones by the sound of his lyre, and led them whither he wished by the charm of his prayer."

Socialism, we know, does not require with certain people great efforts of the imagination. They imitate, flatly enough, the old mythologies; they copy Catholicism, while declaiming against it; they ape power, which they lust after; then they shout with all their strength: Liberty, Equality, Fraternity; and the circle is complete. One passes for a revelator, a reformer, a democratic and social restorer, one is named as a candidate for the ministry of progress,—nay, even for the dictatorship of the Republic!

So, by the confession of Louis Blanc, power is born of barbarism; its organization bears witness to a state of ferocity and violence among primitive men,—an effect of the utter absence of commerce and industry. To this savagism the State had to put an end by opposing to the force of each individual a superior force capable, in the absence of any other argument, of restraining his will. The constitution of the State supposes, then, as we have just said, a profound social antagonism, homo homini lupus. Louis Blanc himself says this when, after having divided men into the strong and the weak, disputing with each other like wild beasts for their food, he interposes between them, as a mediator, the State.

Then the State would be useless; the State would lack an object as well as a motive; the State would have to take itself away,—if there should come a day when, from any cause whatever, society should contain neither strong nor weak,— that is, when the inequality of physical and intellectual powers could not be a cause of robbery and oppression, independently of the protection, more fictitious than real by the way, of the State.

Now, this is precisely the thesis that we maintain today.

The power that tempers morals, that gradually substitutes the rule of right for the rule of force, that establishes security, that creates step by step liberty and equality, is, in a much higher degree than religion and the State, labor;

first, the labor of commerce and industry; next, science, which spiritualizes it; in the last analysis, art, its immortal flower. Religion by its promises and its threats, the State by its tribunals and its armies, gave to the sentiment of justice, which was too weak among primitive men, the only sanction intelligible to savage minds. For us, whom industry, science, literature, art, have corrupted, as Jean Jacques said, this sanction lies elsewhere; we find it in the division of property, in the machinery of industry, in the growth of luxury, in the overruling desire for well-being,—a desire which imposes upon all a necessity of labor. After the barbarism of the early ages, after the price of caste and the feudal constitution of primitive society, a last element of slavery still remained,—capital. Capital having lost its way, the laborer—that is, the merchant, the mechanic, the farmer, the savant, the artist—no longer needs protection; his protection is his talent, his knowledge is his industry. After the dethronement of capital, the continuance of the State, far from protecting liberty, can only compromise liberty.

He has a sorry idea of the human race—of its essence, its perfectibility, its destiny—who conceive it as an agglomeration of individuals necessarily exposed, by the inequality of physical and intellectual forces, to the constant danger of reciprocal spoliation or the tyranny of a few. Such an idea is a proof of the most retrogressive philosophy; it belongs to those days of barbarism when the absence of the true elements of social order left to the genius of the legislator no method of action save that of force; when the supremacy of a pacifying and avenging power appeared to all as the just consequence of a previous degradation and an original stain. To give our whole thought, we regard political and judicial institutions as the exoteric and concrete formula of the myth of the fall, the mystery of redemption, and the sacrament of penitence. It is curious to see pretended socialists, enemies or rivals of Church and State, copying all that they blaspheme,—the representative system in politics, the dogma of the fall in religion.

Since they talk so much of doctrine, we frankly declare that such is not ours.

In our view, the moral condition of society is modified and ameliorated at the same rate as its economic condition. The morality of a wild, ignorant, and idle people is one thing; that of an industrious and artistic people another: consequently, the social guarantees that prevail among the former are quite different from those that prevail among the latter. In a society transformed, almost unconsciously, by its economic development, there is no longer either strong or weak; there are only laborers whose faculties and means incessantly tend, through industrial solidarity and the guarantee of circulation, to become equalized. In vain, to assure the right and the duty of each, does the imagination go back to that idea of authority and government which attests the profound despair of souls long terrified by the police and the priesthood: the simplest examination of the attributes of the State suffices to demonstrate that, if inequality of fortunes, oppression, robbery, and misery are not our eternal inheritance, the first leprosy to be eradicated, after capitalistic exploitation, the first plague to be wiped out, is the State.

See, in fact, budget in hand, what the State is.

The State is the army. Reformer, do you need an army to defend you? If so, your idea of public security is Cæsar's and Napoleon's. You are not a republican; you are a despot.

The State is the police; city police, rural police, police of the waters and forests. Reformer, do you need police? Then your idea of order is Fouché's, Gisquet's, Carussidière's, and M. Carlier's. You are not a democrat, you are a spy.

The State is the whole judicial system; justices of the peace, tribunals of first instance, courts of appeal, court of cassation, high court, tribunals of experts, commercial tribunals, council of prefects, State council, councils of war. Reformer, do you need all this judiciary? Then your idea of justice is M. Baroche's, M. Dupin's, and Perrin Dandin's. You are not a socialist; you are a red-tapist.

The State is the treasury, the budget. Reformer, you do not desire the abolition of taxation? Then your idea of public wealth is M. Thiers's who thinks that the largest budgets are the best. You are not an organizer of labor; you are an exciseman.

The State is the custom-house. Reformer, do you need, for the protection of national labor, differential duties and toll-houses? Then your idea of commerce and circulation is M. Fould's and M. Rothschild's. You are not an apostle of fraternity; you are a Jew.

The State is the public debt, the mint, the sinking fund, the savings-banks, etc. Reformer, are these the foundation of your science? Then your idea of social economy is that of MM. Humann, Lacave-Laplagne, Garnier-Pagès, Passy, Duclerc, and the "Man with Forty Crowns." You are a Turcaret.

The State—but we must stop. There is nothing, absolutely nothing, in the State , from the top of the hierarchy to its foot, which is not an abuse to be reformed, a parasite to be exterminated, an instrument of tyranny to be destroyed. And you talk to us of maintaining the State, of extending the functions or the State, of increasing the power of the State! Go to, you are not a revolutionist; for the true revolutionist is essentially a simplifier and a liberal. You are a mystifier, a juggler; you are a marplot.

III. Of an ulterior destiny of the State

There arises in favor of the State a last hypothesis. The fact that the State, say the pseudo-democrats, hitherto has performed only a rôle of parasitism and tyranny is no reason for denying it a nobler and more humane destiny. The State is destined to become the principal organ of production, consumption, and circulation; the initiator of liberty and equality.

For liberty and equality are the State.

Credit is the State.

Commerce, agriculture, and manufactures are the State.

Canals, railroads, mines, insurance companies, as well as tobacco-shops and post-offices, are the State.

Public education is the State.

The State, in fine, dropping its negative attributes to clothe itself with positive ones, must change from the oppressor, parasite, and conservative it ever has been into an organizer, producer, and servant. That would be feudalism regenerated, the hierarchy of industrial associations, organized and graded according to a potent formula the secret of which Pierre Leroux still hides from our sight.

Thus, the organizers of the State suppose—for in all this they only go from supposition to supposition—that the State can change its nature, turn itself around, so to speak; from Satan become an archangel; and, after having lived for centuries by blood and slaughter like a wild beast, feed upon plants with the deer, and give suck to the lambs. Such is the teaching of Louis Blanc and Pierre Leroux; such, as we said long ago, is the whole secret of socialism.

"We love the tutelary, generous, devoted government, taking as its motto those profound words of the gospel, 'Whosoever of you will be the chiefest, shall be the servant of all;' and we hate the deprived, corrupting, oppressive government, making the people its prey. We admire it representing the generous and living portion of humanity; we abhor it when it represents the cadaverous portion. We revolt against the insolence, usurpation, and robbery involved in the idea of the MASTER-STATE; and we applaud that which is touching, fruitful, and noble in the idea of the SERVANT-STATE. Or better: there is a belief which we hold a thousand times dearer than life,—our belief in the approaching and final TRANSFORMATION of power. That is the triumphant passage from the old world to the new. All the government. of Europe rest today on the idea of the MASTER-STATE; but they are dancing desperately the dance of the dead."—"Le Nouveau Monde," November 16, 1849.

Pierre Leroux is a thorough believer in these ideas. What he wishes, what he teaches, and what he calls for is a regeneration of the State,—he has not told us yet whereby and by whom this regeneration should be effected,—just as he wishes and calls for a regeneration of Christianity without, as yet, having stated his dogma and given his credo.

We believe, in opposition to Pierre Leroux and Louis Blanc, that the theory of the tutelary, generous, devoted, productive, initiative, organizing, liberal and progressive State is a utopia, a pure illusion of their intellectual vision. Pierre Leroux and Louis Blanc seem to us like a man who, standing above a mirror and seeing his image reversed, should pretend that this image must become a reality some day and replace (pardon us the expression) his natural person.

This is what separates us from these two men, whose talents and services, whatever they may say, we have never dreamed of denying, but whose stubborn hallucination we deplore. We do not believe in the SERVANT-STATE: to us it is a flat contradiction.

Servant and master, when applied to the State, are synonymous terms; just as more and less, when applied to equality, are identical terms. The proprietor, by interest on capital, demands more than equality; communism, by the formula, to each according to his needs, allows less than equality: always inequality; and that is why we are neither a communist nor a proprietor. Likewise, whoever says master-State says usurpation of the public power; whoever says servant-State says delegation of the public power: always an alienation of this power, always a power, always an external, arbitrary authority instead of the immanent, inalienable, untransferable authority of citizens; always more or less than liberty. It is for this reason that we are opposed to the State.

Further, to leave metaphysics and return to the field of experience, here is what we have to say to Louis Blanc and Pierre Leroux.

You pretend and affirm that the State, that the government, can, and ought to be, wholly changed in its principle, in its essence, in its action, in its relations with citizens, as well as in its results that thus the State, a bankrupt and a counterfeiter, should be the sole source of credit; that for so many centuries an enemy of knowledge, and at the present moment still hostile to primary instruction and the liberty of the press, it is its business to officially provide for the instruction of citizens; that, after having left commerce, industry, agriculture, and all the machinery of wealth to develop themselves without its aid, often even in spite of its resistance, it belongs to it to take the initiative in the whole field of labor as in the world of ideas, that, in fine, the eternal enemy of liberty, it yet ought, not to leave liberty to itself, but to create and direct liberty. It is this marvelous transformation of the State that constitutes, in your opinion, the present Revolution.

There lies upon you, then, the twofold obligation: first, of establishing the truth of your hypothesis by showing its traditional legitimacy, exhibiting its historical titles, and developing its philosophy; in the second place, of applying it in practice.

Now, it appears already that both theory and practice, in your hypothesis, formally contradict the idea itself, and the facts of the past, and the most authentic tendencies of humanity.

Your theory, we say, involves a contradiction in its terms, since it pretends to make liberty a creation of the State, while the State, on the contrary, is to be a creation of liberty. In fact, if the State imposes itself upon my will, the State is master; I am not free; the theory is undermined.

It contradicts the facts of the past, since it is certain, as you yourselves admit, that everything that has been produced within the sphere of human activity of a positive, good, and beautiful character, was the product of liberty exclusively, acting independently of the State, and almost always in opposition to the State; which leads directly to this proposition, which ruins your system, that liberty is sufficient unto itself and does not need the State.

Finally, your theory contradicts the manifest tendencies of civilization; since, instead of continually adding to individual liberty and dignity by making every human soul, according to Kant's precept, a pattern of entire humanity, one face of the collective soul, you subordinate the private person to the public person; you submit the individual to the group; you absorb the citizen in the State.

It is for you to remove all these contradictions by a principle superior to liberty and to the State. We, who simply deny the State; who, resolutely, following the line of liberty, remain faithful to the revolutionary practice,—it is not for us to demonstrate to you the falsity of your hypothesis; we await your proofs. The master-State is lost; you are with us in admitting it. As for the servant-State, we do not know what it may be; we distrust it as supreme hypocrisy. The servant-State seems to us quite the same thing as a servant-mistress; we do not wish it; with our present light, we prefer to espouse Liberty in legitimate marriage. Explain, then, if you can, why, after having demolished the State through love of this adored liberty, we must now, in consequence of the same love, return to the State. Until you have solved this problem, we shall continue to protest against all government, all authority, all power; we shall maintain, through all and against all, the prerogative of liberty. We shall say to you: Liberty is, for us, a thing gained; now, you know the rule of law: Melior est conditio possidentis. Produce your titles to the reorganization of government; otherwise, no government!

To sum up:

The State is the external constitution of the social power.

The constitution supposes, in principle, that society is a creature of the mind, destitute of spontaneity, providence, unity, needing for its action to be fictitiously represented by one or more elected or hereditary commissioners: an hypothesis the falsity of which the economic development of society and the organization of universal suffrage agree in demonstrating.

The constitution of the State supposes further, as to its object, that antagonism or a state of war is the essential and irrevocable condition of humanity, a condition which necessitates, between the weak and the strong, the intervention of a coercive power to put an end to their struggles by universal oppression We maintain that, in this respect, the mission of the State is ended; that, by the division of labor, industrial solidarity, the desire for well-being, and the equal distribution of capital and taxation, liberty and justice obtain surer guarantees than any that ever were afforded them by religion and the State.

As for utilitarian transformation of the State, we consider it as a utopia contradicted at once by governmental tradition, and the revolutionary tendency, and the spirit of the henceforth admitted economic reforms. In any case, we say that to liberty alone it would belong to reorganize power, which is equivalent at present to the complete exclusion of power.

As a result, either no social revolution, or no more government; such is our solution of the political problem.

What is Government? What is God?

What is Government? What is its principle, its object, its right? -- This is incontestably the first question that the political man poses to himself.

Now, this question, which appears so simple and the solution of which seems so easy, we find that faith alone can answer. Philosophy is as incapable of demonstrating Government as it is of proving God. Authority, like Divinity, is not a matter of knowing; it is, I repeat, a matter of faith.

That insight, so paradoxical at first glance, and yet so true, merits some development. We are going to try, without any significant scientific apparatus, to make ourselves understood.

The principal attribute, the signal trait of our species, after THOUGHT, is belief, and above all things, the belief in God. Among the philosophers, some saw in that faith in a superior Being a prerogative of humanity, while others discovered there only its weakness. Whatever there is of merit or demerit in the belief in the idea of God, it is certain that the beginning of all metaphysical speculation is an act of worship of the Creator: it is that which the human mind, among all the Peoples, records in an invariable manner.

But what is God? That is what the philosopher and the believer immediately, and with an irresistible movement,

1849: What is Government? What is God?

demand. And, as a corollary to that first interrogation, this one arises immediately: What, of all the religions, is the best? Indeed, if there exists a Being superior to Humanity, there must also exist a system of relations between that Being and Humanity: what then is that system? The search for the best religion is the second step that the human mind makes in Reason and Faith.

To this double question, no response is possible. The definition of Divinity escapes the intelligence. Humanity has been by turns fetishist, idolater, Christian and Buddhist, Jew and Mohammedan, deist and pantheist: it has worshiped in turn plants, animals, stars, the heavens, the soul of the world, and, finally, itself: it has wandered from superstition to superstition, without managing to determine its God. The problem of the attributes and essence of God and of the worship that is proper to him, like a trap set for his ignorance, torments Humanity from its origin. The Peoples are sacrificed for their idols, society is exhausted by the elaboration of its beliefs, without the solution being advanced a step.

The deist and the pantheist, like the Christian and the idolater, is reduced to pure faith. One could even say, and it is the only progress we have made in this study, that it is repugnant to reason to know and understand God: it is only given to us to believe. And this is why in all eras, and under all religions, we encounter a small number of men, bolder in appearance than the others, who, not understanding God, have taken the part of denying him: we have given them the name of free spirits or atheists.

1849: What is Government? What is God?

But it is clear that atheism is still less logical than faith. The basic, conclusive fact of the spontaneous belief in the supreme Being remaining always, and the problem implied by that fact inevitably posing itself, atheism could not be accepted as a solution. Far from testifying to the strength of the mind, it would only prove its desperation. It is with atheism as it is with suicide: it has only been embraced by the smallest number. The People have always had a horror of it!

Things were thus. Humanity seemed eternally placed between an insoluble question and an impossible negation, when, at the end of the last century, a philosopher, Kant, as remarkable for his profound piety, as for the incomparable power of his reflection, realized how to attack the theological problem in an entirely new manner.

He no longer asked himself, as everyone had before him: What is God? and what is the true religion? From a question of fact he made a question of form, and he said to himself: Why does it happen that I believe in God? How, by virtue of what is that idea produced in my mind? What is its point of departure and its development? What are its transformations, and, if need be, its decline? How, finally, is it that, in the religious soul, the things, the ideas, come to be?

Such was the course of studies proposed, on God and Religion, by the philosopher of Kœnigsberg. Renouncing further pursuit of the content, or the reality of the idea of God, he set himself to writing, if I dare put it in this way, the biography of that idea. Instead of taking, like an anchorite, the idea of God for the object of his meditations,

1849: What is Government? What is God?

he analyzed the faith in God, as a religious period of six thousand years presented it to him. In short, he considered in religion, not an external and supernatural revelation of the infinite Being, but a phenomenon of our understanding.

From this moment the spell was broken: the mystery of religion was revealed to philosophy. What we seek and what we see in God, as Malebranche said, is not at all that being, or to speak more fairly, that chimerical entity, that our imagination constantly enlarges, and that, by the very fact that it must be after all the notion that our mind makes of it, cannot in reality be anything: it is our own ideal, the pure essence of Humanity.

What the theologian pursues, without knowing it, in the dogma that he teaches, is not the mysteries of the infinite: it is the laws of our collective and individual spontaneity. The human soul does not perceive itself at first by reflective contemplation on itself, as the psychologist believe; it perceives itself outside itself, as if it was a different being placed in front of it: it is that mirror image that it calls God.

Thus, morals, justice, order, laws, are no longer things revealed from on high, imposed on our free will by a so-called creator, unknown, unintelligible; they are things that are as proper and essential as our faculties and organs, as our flesh and blood. In short: Religion and Society are synonymous terms; Man is sacred pour himself as if he was God. Catholicism and Socialism, identical at base, differ only in form: in this was we explain faith, and the primitive face of the belief in God, and the indisputable progress of the religions.

Now, what Kant did nearly sixty years ago for Religion; what he had previously done for Certainty; what others before him had attempted for Happiness or the Sovereign Good, the Voix du Peuple proposes to undertake for Government.

After the belief in God, that which occupies the most prominent place in the general thought is the belief in Authority. Everywhere that there are men grouped in society, we encounter, with the rudiments of a religion, the rudiments of power, the embryo of a government. That fact is as basic, as universal, as indisputable as that of the religions.

But what is Power, and what is the best form of Government? for it is clear that if we manage to understand the essence and attributes of power, we will know at the same time the best form to give to it, what is, of all the constitutions, the most perfect. We would have, in this way, resolved one of the two great problems posed by the February Revolution: we would have resolved the political problem, principle, means and end, — we do not prejudge anything, — of economic reform.

Well! On Government, as on Religion, the controversy has endured since the origin of societies, and with as little success. It is for governments as for religions, for political theories as for systems of philosophy: that is to say, there is no solution. More than two thousand years before Montesquieu and Machiavelli, Aristotle gathered the

1849: What is Government? What is God?

various definitions of government, distinguishing them according to their forms: patriarchies, democracies, oligarchies, aristocracies, absolute monarchies, constitutional monarchies, theocracies, federative republics, etc. He declared, in short, that the problem was insoluble. Aristotle, with regard to government, as with regard to religion, was a skeptic. He had faith neither in God nor in the State.

And we who, in sixty years, have gone through seven or eight kinds of governments; who, hardly entered into the Republic, are already weary of our Constitution; we, for whom the exercise of power has only been, from the conquest of the Gauls by Julius Cesar until the ministry of the brothers Barrot, the practice of oppression and tyranny; we, finally, who witness in this moment the saturnalia of the governments of Europe, do we then have more faith than Aristotle? Isn't it time that we get out of this unhappy rut, and instead of exhausting ourselves any more in the search fort the best government, the best organization to make of the political idea, we should pose the question, no longer of the reality, but of the legitimacy of that idea?

Why do we believe in Government? From where, in human society, comes that idea of Authority, of Power; that fiction of a superior Person, called the State?

How is that fiction produced? How is it developed? What is its law of evolution, its economy?

Won't it be with Government as with God and the Absolute, which have so long and so fruitlessly occupied the philosophers? Would this not still be on of the first-born conceptions of our understanding, which we wrongly give the name of ideas, and that, without reality, without possibility of realization, expresses only something indefinite, which only has tyranny for its essence?

And then, relative to God and Religion, we have already found, by philosophical analysis, that beneath the allegories of its religious myths, Humanity pursues nothing other than its own ideal, could we still seek what we want beneath the allegory of its political myths? For in the end, the political institutions, so different, so contradictory, exist neither for themselves, nor by themselves; like the cults, they are not essential to society, they are hypothetical formulas or combinations, by means of which civilization maintains an appearance of order, or to put it better, seeks order. What then, once again, is the secret meaning of these institutions, the real reason why the political concept, the notion of government, comes to nothing?

In short, instead of seeing in government, with the absolutists, the organ and expression of society; with the doctrinaires, an instrument of order, or rather of policy; with the radicals, a means of revolution: let us try to see simply a phenomenon of the collective life, the external representation of our right, the education of some one of our faculties. Who knows if we could not discover then that all these governmental formulas, for which the Peoples and citizens have slit each others' throats for sixty centuries, are only a phantasmagoria of our mind, that the first duty of a free reason is to return to the museums and libraries?

1849: What is Government? What is God?

Such is the question posed and resolved in the Confessions of a Revolutionary, and of which the Voix du Peuple proposes, with the aid of facts furnished to it by the power and the parties who dispute it, to give daily commentary.

Just like Religion, Government is a manifestation of social spontaneity, a preparation of Humanity for a higher state.

What Humanity seeks in Religion, and calls God, is itself.

What the citizen seeks in Government and names King, Emperor or President, is also himself, it is Liberty.

Without Humanity, no God; the theological concept makes no sense: — Without Liberty, no Government; the political concept is without value.

The best form of Government, like the most perfect of religions, taken in the literal sense, is a contradictory idea. The problem is not to know how we will be governed best, but how we will be the most free. Liberty suitable and identical to order, that is all that power and politics really contain. How is that absolute liberty, synonym of ordered, constituted? that is what the analysis of the different formulas of authority will teach us. For all the rest, we do not accept the government of man by man, any more than the exploitation of man by man...

Thus, the march that we propose to follow, in treating the political question and in preparing the materials for a constitutional revision, will be the same that we have followed up to this day in treating the social question. La Voix du Peuple, in completing the work of the two journals that preceded it, will be faithful to their wanderings.

What should we say, in these two papers, fallen one after the other under the blows of the reaction and the state of siege?

We should not as, as our predecessors and associates have thus far:

What is the best system of community? the best organization of property? Or better still: Is property or community worth more? the theory of Saint-Simon or that of Fourier? the system of Louis Blanc or that of Cabet?

Following the example of Kant, who should pose the question in this way:

How does man possess? How does he acquire property? How is it lost? What is the law of its evolution and transformation? Where is it going? What does it want? What, finally, does it represent? For it appears sufficiently, by the indissoluble mixture of good and evil that accompanies it, by the tyranny that is its essence (jus utendi et abutendi) and which is the condition sine quâ non of its wholeness, that it is still, just like Religion and Government, only a hypothesis, or rather, a hypotyposis of Society, that is to say, an allegorical representation of a conception of our intelligence.

How, next, does man labor? How do we establish the comparison of products? How will circulation take place in society? On what conditions? According to what laws?

And the conclusion of all these monographs on property has been this:

Property indicates a function or allocation; community, reciprocity of action: usury, always decreasing, identity of labor and capital.

In order to bring about the disengagement and realization of all these terms, until now shrouded beneath the old proprietary symbols, what must we do? Let the workers guarantee work and outlets to one another; to that end, let them accept, as currency, their reciprocal obligations.

Well! today we say:

Political liberty will result for us, like industrial liberty, from our mutual guarantee. It is by guaranteeing liberty to one another, that we will pass from this government, whose purpose is to symbolize the republican motto: Liberty, Equality, Fraternity, leaving to our intelligence the care to find its realization. Now, what is the formula of that political and liberal guarantee? presently, universal suffrage, later, free contract...

Economic and social reform, by the mutual guarantee of credit;

Political reform, by the commerce of individual liberties;

Such is the program of the Voix du Peuple.

The Revolution advances, cried an absolutist paper yesterday, with regard to the message of Louis Bonaparte. Those people see the Revolution only in catastrophes and coups d'état. We say in our turn: Yes, the Revolution advance, for it has found interpreters. Our strength may fall short of the task; our devotion, never!

1850

Dilemma: Red or White

A captain of the line assures me—the papers friendly to the government will say tomorrow if the information is exact—that on the occasion of the next elections, the order has been given to prevent, by all possible means, the gentlemen of the military from attending the electoral gatherings. Any disobedience in this regard will be punished by eight days in jail.

The government is right. It is consistent with itself. It follows, imperturbably, like Mr. Cabet, its straight line. For sixty years, the French people, leading the rest of the world behind it, has descended the path of the Revolution; Mr. Louis Bonaparte has sworn to make us turn back up the path of the Revolution. That is why Mr. Louis Bonaparte has been made President of the Republic:—ask the legitimists; ask the doctrinaires or the Jesuits.

Now, whoever desires the ends desires the means; to make the army vote as a municipal guard and forbid it from political discussions: such is, with regard to the army, the means that the government proposes to use. And I repeat that the government, from its own point of view, has it right. Follow this reasoning, I beg you: it is as demonstrative as the history.

The Revolution of 89, by abolishing the old despotism and feudalism, led us to the Constitutional Monarchy.

The Constitutional Monarchy, after thirty years of parliamentary evolutions, led to the Republic.

The Republic established universal suffrage.

Universal suffrage make the soldiers eligible voters, make them, in fact, with the other citizens, arbiters of peace and war, judges of the politics of the government, inspector of the acts and opinions of their leaders—all things incompatible with the spirit of hierarchy and the feudal discipline of the army.

So there is an incompatibility between the current regime of the army, which costs us 400 million per year, and the exercise of political rights. And to conclude, either no republic or no army: that is the dilemma.

But what is true today of the army is true of all the rest. It is everywhere the same antagonism, the same incompatibilities. The government has seen it very well; by its propositions, its nominations, its communications, each day it reproduces the same alternative; and if we do not understand it, it is because we do not wish to hear it.

Red or *White*, it says to us,

Republican or *Cossack*,

Socialist or *Jesuit*,

Voltaire or *de Maistre*,

The *Revolution* or the *Holy Alliance*,

Labor or *Capital*,

Association or *Statute Labor*,

Free Credit or *Usury*,

The *Bank of the People* or *Malthus*,

The citizen army or the pretorian army.

There is no middle ground: it is necessary to choose. The question is precisely the same for the bourgeois, the peasant, the soldier, the philosopher and the statesman, for France and for Europe. Every other party is committed to the happy medium, to hypocrisy. Now, the experiment of the happy medium has been made, and the world does not want it. So it is a question of knowing if the people will be red or white, if the army will be for Christ or for Belial. We are happy to agree with the government, if not with regard to the goal, at least regarding the logic; and we support its dilemma with all our strength.

The government is white; we are red. It no longer wants the tricolor; neither do we. That is clear.

The Revolution of February was made by the red flag, which become from then on the symbol of the right to work and the beacon of Humanity. The tricolored flag has only ever been, despite all its glory, the flag of the happy medium, the flag of the doctrinaires. In 1804, not daring to restore the monarchy, it created an emperor. Forced in 1815 to hide itself, it returned in 1830 to give us

1850: Dilemma: Red or White

Louis-Philippe; after February, Mr. de Lamartine took it for the lightning-rod of socialism; and it is thanks to this that we had had, in a democratic Republic, along with the exclusion of the right to work, the presidency of a Bonaparte. Since then, the tricolored flag has no longer been anything but the flag of reaction and calumny. Moreover, it showed this very well in June when it bathed with so much delight in the blood of the workers. And we wrote from the mouth of March 1848, as if we could have foreseen those odious days.

"Red is the color of justice and sovereignty. And since all men love and seek the red, is not red the symbol of human fraternity?... Deny the red flag, dye the purple, but that is to eliminate the social question, the right to work. Every time that the people, defeated by suffering, has wanted to express, outside of that juridical legality that murders it, its wishes and complaints, it has marched under a red banner. The red flag, it is true, has still not made the tour of the world, like its fortunate rival, the tricolor. Justice has spoken very well; Mr. de Lamartine has not gone farther than the camp of Mars. It is so terrible, Justice, that one could not hide it too much. Poor red flag! Everyone abandons you! Well! I embrace you. I clutch you to my breast. Cheers to fraternity! The red flag is the sign of a revolution that will be the last. The red flag! It is the shroud of Christ, the federal standard of the human race."

Honest souls, who only see in the red flag the sign of vengeance, and for whom a bunch of peasants will suffice to make you afraid: do you want to abolish the scaffold once and for all? Plant a red flag atop it.

1850: Dilemma: Red or White

The red flag is the sign of the democratic reality, just as the white flag is the sign of the sign of feudal suzerainty. The tricolor is that of the politics of the seesaw and the presidency. Napoleon and Louise-Philippe, illegitimate monarchs, would adopt it. The reactionaries no longer want to, and you know why. No truck, they say, with the republican principle. And we respond, we socialists, no truck with the feudal principle!

As at all the times that the throne and altar have been united against liberty, the white flag is the banner of Catholicism in France as well as the monarchy: the red flag, on the contrary, is the symbol of the democratic and social philosophy. The Jansenists and Gallicans, false royalists and false Christians, ground around the tricolored flag.

That is why, from one side, the whites demand that the Church be richly endowed, and work with all their strength to render it its goods and its tithes; from the other, the reds want the clergy, like the laborers, subject to the law of free commerce and, as a consequence, only those who have need of the priest's services will pay him. The tricolors, who neither want to render the goods of the clergy nor abolish the parasitism of the Church, resist both; they have invented the budget of the cults and the salary of the priests, in order to declaim at once against the Socialist and against the Pope.

We do not want the Church to be salaried, say the whites. We do not want it to be endowed, respond the reds. And all shout at the same time: Down with the tricolors!

1850: Dilemma: Red or White

In the past, the magistracy was like property, hereditary and venal. Justice was given at a price in cash: that was the white justice. The judge lived on his spices, as the bailiff lives on his exploits. Under the general designation of *Parliaments*, the people of the courts and tribunals formed one caste. What we call the ministerial offices are a remnant of that old institution.

After 89, the venality of the offices should have been entirely abolished, and justice elective and free. This was the generalization of the just, the red justice. Instead of that, we have the salaried, tenured magistracy, a judicial order marching in connivance with the executive power. Part of the officers have, in addition, preserved their venal privileges. That is the system of the Héberts, the Dupins, the Lehons; the tricolored justice.

It is with the army as with justice, as with the Church, and with the government.

In the past, the grades higher than noncommissioned officer were reserved for the nobles, inaccessible to the commoners. Discipline by baton blows...

1851

Letter to A. M. Boutteville

Translated by Shawn P. Wilbur

Sainte-Pélagie, December 17, 1851.

A. M. BOUTTEVILLE

My dear Boutteville, the more I advance in my individual labors, the more I realize that the work that we make in common must be conceived and, as much as possible, written according the plan of mine, and in a manner so as to serve it as continuation and conclusion. The history of democracy is nothing other than the history of the emancipation of the human spirit in all spheres, and, and without counting the disadvantages for us to publish a book soon described as *demagogic*, it is clear that by taking the word *democracy* in a sense too close to that of jacobinism, we make quite uselessly the monograph of a hypothesis rejected for the moment, and perhaps for many years.

Thus, it is necessary to enlarge further our views and our plan, and to make ourselves more generalizing, more profound, by sacrificing something of the epic interest.

I have decided to give my book the title Kronos (or whatever you please), to match the *Cosmos* of A. de Humboldt.

It will include, from the origin of things, the creation, as they say, up to Luther, the moment where our history begins, and will be divided into sixteen periods.

From Luther's time until our own requires four others (twenty altogther), divided thus:

17th – From Luther to the Treaty of Westphalia (1517-1648)

18th – From the Treaty of Westphalia to the French Revolution (1648–1789)

19th – The French Revolution (1789–1848)

20th – Socialism (1848-****)

We will preserve that distribution; the last period will serve as the historic and prophetic *conclusion* of the nineteen preceding.

It is necessary then for you to attach to this summary all the facts relating to Christian-Muslim-European civilization, including America (excluding China, India, Mongolia, the Asiatic archipelago, the Burmas, Siam, Japan, etc., with the exception of that which concerns the affairs of Europe), and take for a superior principle of historical direction the movement of nations towards an order of things which must realize at once *liberty* (individual, locale, etc.) in its highest expression, and the *unity* of the human race.

Thus, *my* work and *yours* will form a continuous series, without crossed purposes or repetitions. By conserving more space in the treatment of my first sixteen periods, I could give more scope, interest and evidence to the demonstration of recent times, as also, in condensing more the manner of the first part of Bossuet's *Discours sur l'Histoire universelle*, and including only that table of facts, citations, reflections of major interests, we will have made a work of sound philosophy, instead of a masterpiece of literature.

It is understood that in the *Histoire de la Démocratie moderne*, the exposition in order of dates, as I employ it in *Kronos*, will not be followed; in this regard, the two works, though forming a continuous whole, will differ noticeably. It will be necessary to follow the method of Poinson, du Rozier and Des Michels in their very substantial, conscientious and exact, but insufficiently philosophical summaries of the Greek, Latin and Medieval history.

In a word, let us not loose sight of the fact that we must not aim to render useless the works made before us, or those that will be made after, but to make a treatise which throws light on the whole history of humanity and establishes its philosophy.

At our next meeting, I will speak at more length of all these things, and, in making you a part of my own work, I will convince you of the ease with which I group in a single narrative, a single idea, and single general evolution, all the history for example of the nineteenth and twentieth centuries, which includes as you know besides:

The empire of Charlemagne and all its divisions;

The Greek empire of the Orient;

The papacy and the schism of Photios;

The Angles, Saxons, Normans, Slavs, etc.

Islam, subdivided in three or four independent caliphates and in two great parties;

The war of Spain against the Moors, etc.

All of that, and it is the whole world (minus the Far East, the evolution of which separate, but always on the same plan and by virtue of the same laws), all that, I say, so complicated moments, can only be one, absolutely one, and it is as easy to recount that universal history, by stating at once all the contemporary facts, as it is to describe a session of the Convention.

So group, research, accumulate the facts, and limit yourself to giving them the most faithful expression; do not manage the dates and the facts. We must raise a monument which overshadows Catholicism and tyranny, and which is as precious and as accessible to the ignorant as to the wise.

My firm conviction is that we can do this if we wish to, and that this double labor must cast on the destinies of the species an as yet unknown and inextinguishable light.

The *Kronos* alone will form two large volumes, as much as the *Histoire de la Démocratie moderne*. By abridging from it the whole space of time that the other includes, I will give it more lucidity, firmness and scope, and make our labor more complete, easier to make and to understand, and more conclusive. It will always be the same work, published in two forms and by two different publishers.

I hope, my dear friend, that instead of becoming impatient with my reshufflings, you understand as I do that it is not possible to make a special history or any monograph without knowing as a basis universal history, and that you will be grateful to me for contributing thus, although indirectly, to the composition of a work which, without that contribution would, I warn you, have run the risk of being only a plea for the good of the cause.

Besides, you understand that the plan that I have marked for you has no need of modifications. The large divisions and the general sense I have indicated are already the consequence of my own studies; I ask of you only more generality still, more universality, conciseness and fullness.

The century has enough literature: let us give it facts and truths. One is always eloquent enough when one is Newton, Cuvier or Jussieu; let us try to be something like those gentlemen. If they are justly admired, they are not, after all, gods.

I extend my hand to you.

P.-J. Proudhon.

Letter to Langlois

To Mr. [Amédée Jérôme] LANGLOIS

My dear Langlois, all your criticisms are fair, and I would have to write ten volumes to clarify the points that appear obscure to me in your brochure, but they would still be so.

Society, it is infinite, and it is certain that there are *millions* of cases to resolve of which those who pose as reformers will never think. All that one can do, in the time of revolution, is to strongly deny the past, and, up to a certain point, the present, then to note the aim—an Ideal!—and to plant, in the direction of that *ideal*, some markers. The strongest of men will never do more than that, and barely that. Did Jesus Christ make Christianity? Though we worship him as its author, he did not know the hundredth part of it! Did Romulus or Numa make Rome? Was it Charlemagne who made feudalism? Was it Turgot, who only know what the men of 89 knew, who invented the constitutional system?...

A man never knows, can never express but a very small portion of the Truth. Truth, whether social or human, is a product of time...

Thus, in my last book, I made a critique; deduce from that critique the indication of an aim; I have posted some markers. Do not expect me to give you a system. My system is Progress, the necessity of working ceaselessly to discover the unknown, bit by bit, as the past is exhausted...

next year, that aspect, the most important of our work, will be brought to light in a manner to quickly seize minds; then one will understand that free credit and other formulas are for us only the first step out of the past; but that the future, in its fullness, evades us, and that it is hardly possible to imagine it except through a symbol, more or less mythical, that I call Anarchy, as others call it *Fraternity*. Then, also, one will see why and how sects and systems are nothing; why the true revolutionary only labors from day to day; why the destiny of man is a void, a gap placed before us. It is children that are amused by systematic perspectives. It is still the People, incapable of understanding that it must always go on, like the Wandering Jew, who love to rest with Cabet, Fourier, etc., under the shades of Community and Association. The People, like the reaction, would like to be done with it; now, I repeat, there is no end; and if history teaches us anything of the curve that we describe, we remain almost entirely ignorant of the future. Our forecast does not go beyond the antithesis that the present suggests to us.

That largely developed theory of Progress, a theory that posits the exclusion to all absolute notions, all the so-called definitive hypotheses, is that which, in my opinion, must furnish the solid, but always mobile basis of the future. It is that which shelters society from conservative idleness and from false revolutionary enterprises.

What does it matter, after that, that we are harassed every day by some new difficulty of details and application? Some difficulties? Can that one be regarded as a flat refusal when one exists in an *impossible* present? Would they hope to prevail against us, who cross their arms heroically and sleep soundly, awaiting the occasion of rushing forward to the rudder, without having the least knowledge of the Pole?...

You see, my dear friend, that far from concealing the objections that could be made, I am instead inclined to exacerbate them myself, but to refer them to those who propose them; for I don't know anyone who is not held to resolve them, unless they have decided, with the Jesuits and the big *rentiers*, that all is well.

I have written, in my latest work, five or six propositions that I regard as essential, and that is for the moment all that I wanted:

> 1. The government, at its highest point de perfection, is organized for the subjection and dispossession of the greatest number;

> 2. To the system of political powers, we have to substitute a system of economic forces;

> 3. Association, in the precise and legal sense of the word, is not an economic force; it is of the government;—nevertheless, there are cases where that modification of individual liberty appeared indispensable;

> 4. That system, or rather than equilibrium of economic forces, cannot be created by means of

authority; it must result from the tacit or expressed consent of the citizens, namely from *free contract*...

What I then add on the *liquidation*, the *organization of the economic forces*, the *dissolution of the political powers* are only general views, too condensed, I know, for the understanding of the details, still too rigorous *in its formulas* for the multiplicity of cases. I know all these things. But is it fair for me to object to them? In physics, are the most general laws anything but simple abstractions that, in individual cases, receive thousands of different modifications? Just so, the truest, most general laws of society are also only some abstract notions, which practice modifies infinitely. But we must have these notions, or else we can do nothing: we must post them, or perish on the road.

I believe, my dear friend, that these reflections, instead of leaving you idle and indifferent, under the pretext that I do not respond to everything, that [elements] remain unintelligible in my work, will urge you to seek yourself..., since, at this moment, I am nearly the only man who works seriously on these questions. What, in truth, do our fellows do? Each of them, convinced that they possess the key to the future, the formula of the absolute, remains tranquil and waits for the world to come and ask for its salvation. As for the need of *investigators* of the truth, we only find revelators. And I tell you that if we let ourselves go on in this way, we are lost.

P.-J. PROUDHON.

1852

The Extremes

Avoid the extremes, and seek the happy medium, says the Wisdom of the Nations.

That aphorism, of course, is very true: but it must be well understood.

It is up to philosophy to look into it and demonstrate it.

I say that every extreme, in itself, is false and implies a contradiction; but by extreme I mean the element constitutive of every synthesis, an element to which it does not [ ], which constitutes it [i.e. synthesis] that much better as it is found employed more energetically.

Thus, the proprietor is a constitutive element of the social order, necessary, indispensable.

To deny it implies a contradiction.

In the common language we say: Property must be curbed, not pushed to the extreme.

I will correct that language, which lacks scientific exactitude, and say: property, in itself, strong or weak, powerful or controlled, as you like, is exclusive, fraudulent, sinful, selfish, and wrong; it contains within it, theft.

However, that same property, such as it is, is indispensable to human order; and it is even because of this that it is necessary. Remove that individualist character, and [ ] you render it powerless....

It is not the extreme, [ ] property, that is to be avoided: that extreme always exists, since it is the very principle....

Here, all the happy mediums in the world are lies, pure arbitrariness.

It is necessary to balance property with a contrary principle, which is, as you prefer, collectivity or community.

(There is no moderate community: community in itself is as bad as property.... It calls, not for a corrective, shears, a gardener to fight it, a [ ] to geld it: it needs a balance.

The two principles must be joined, married, mutually penetrating, in a manner to form a [ ].... *Thus*:

Theory: *Everything that can be appropriated must be appropriated; everything that can be grouped, even among the things appropriated, must be grouped.*

(Similarly with *Competition, Credit, Government*, etc.; division of labor, collectivity.)

Other antinomies are subject to a different law, for example, that of *Dead weight—live weight*. It is certain that we tend, and will constantly tend, to reduce one and increase the other: that is the law of Progress. Cf. [ ] *Dead weight, live weight,* pages 11–12.

The Social Revolution Demonstrated by the Coup d'Etat of December 2, 1851

Translated by Shawn P. Wilbur

Note by Shawn P. Wilbur

One of the things that ought to be clear from recent developments here is that sometimes the most interesting, and also the most unexpected, insights into Proudhon's work come from double-checking those things that "everyone knows" about his work. It was, after all, in the context of tracking down how close he came to saying "anarchy is order" that I ran across the dubious translations in *The General Idea of the Revolution*, and that has led to a general scouring of his work for discussions of "anarchy" and "anarchism," which keeps raising interesting points about the early uses of that term.

When I started working through what I was finding, I was reminded that some of Proudhon's discussion of anarchy occurred in a work which has, in fact, been partially translated, but which is very seldom consulted, probably because of its unsavory reputation. Proudhon's 1852 work, *The Social Revolution Demonstrated by the Coup d'Etat of December 2, 1851* was partially published in a 1972 book, *December 2, 1851*, edited by John Halstead, collecting contemporary writings on the *coup*. The collection is a bit scarce now, and often not cheap if you can find a copy, but given the very small number of Proudhon translations available, its obscurity is fairly remarkable. It does not

1852: The Social Revolution Demonstrated by the Coup d'Etat of December 2, 1851

appear to be, as it might be under other circumstances, one of the "grails" of the literature. Much of the reason for that is undoubtedly that the work has been treated as one of the great missteps of Proudhon's career, with the common claim being that it was written in support of Louis Napoleon's coup and regime. That's probably a fairly poor reading.

I think the simplest way to approach the work is to think about what Proudhon had already said about the nature of "the Revolution" and the workings of historical change, and to compare the common understanding of this work, which was addressed *in some sense* to the Emperor, with the widespread enthusiasm for *The General Idea of the Revolution*, which called upon the *bourgeoisie* to continue their own revolution. I'm sure for some, these questions of address are sufficient to banish both works, but nobody will be surprised if I'm not convinced. And those who find inspiration in the work that gave us the famous and beloved "to be governed" rant might perhaps find reasons to take a look at the more audacious later work.

The Social Revolution develops as I think a careful reader of Proudhon might expect. He had been predicting something very much like the coup for some time, and had ended up in prison precisely because he had missed very few chances to oppose Louis Napoleon. For him to argue then that the events of December 1851 had as much to do with broader historical movements than they did with the newly minted Emperor might be easily taken as a new affront, rather than any sort of support. In *The General Idea of the Revolution* he had spoken of the indifference of the people to governmental forms, so long as their interests were served, and he had called that indifference revolutionary, even while he was attempting to infuse "the Revolution in the 19th century" with an idea (*justice*, ultimately) which would both serve the interests of the people and avoid the pitfalls of false solutions like the coup. The more familiar you are with Proudhon's conception of progress the fewer surprises there are in the work, I think, but I suspect that for many readers the conclusion, "Anarchy or Caesarism," would come as a pleasant surprise, as he addressed in it, quite directly, whether or not he was, as is sometimes claimed, "rallying" to the new regime. I'm posting here the conclusion of that concluding chapter, which shows off some of Proudhon's infamous "patriotism" (in, I think, a not terribly unpleasant light) but also clarifies not just his posture towards Louis Napoleon, but to government and rulers in general.

The Social Revolution Demonstrated by the Coup d'Etat of December 2, 1851

Do you believe, I am asked at this moment, by an indiscreet, perhaps malicious curiosity, that the December 2 accepts the revolutionary role in which you confine it, as in the circle of Popilius? Would you have faith in its liberal inclinations? And based on this inevitability, so well demonstrated by you, of the mandate of Louis-Napoléon, would you rally to his government, as to the best or least worst of transitions? That is what we want to know, and where we await you!...

— I will respond to that question, which is a bit suggestive, with another:

1852: The Social Revolution Demonstrated by the Coup d'Etat of December 2, 1851

Do I have a right to suppose, when the ideas that I have defended for four years have obtained so little success, that the head of the new government will adopt them straightaway and make them his own! Have the taken on, in the eyes of opinion, that character of impersonality, reality, and universality, which would impose them on the State? And if these ideas, all still young, are still hardly anything but the ideas of one man, from whence would come the hope that the December 2, who is also a man, will prefer them to his own ideas!...

I write so that others will reflect in their turn and, if there is cause, so they will contradict me. I write so that truth being manifested, and elaborated by opinion, the revolution, with the government, with the government, or even against government, can be accomplished. As for men, I readily believe their good intentions, but even more in the misfortune of their judgment. It is said in the book of Psalms: *Put not your trust in prince, or in the children of Adam*, that is to say in those who thought is subjective, *because salvation is not in them*! So I believe, and unfortunately for us all, that the revolutionary idea, ill defined in the minds of the masses, poorly served by its popularizers, still leaves to the government the full choice of its politics; I believe that power is surrounded with impossibilities that it does not see, contradictions that it does not known, traps that the universal ignorance conceals from it; I believe that any government can endure, if it wishes, by affirming its historical reasons, and placing itself under the direction of the interests that it is called to serve, but I also believe that men change little, and that if Louis XVI, after having launched the revolution, had wanted to withdraw it, if the Emperor, or if Charles X and Louis-Philippe had preferred to be lost [doom it?] than to continue it, it is improbable that those who succeeded them would have made themselves straightaway, and spontaneously, its promoters.

That is why I hold myself apart from government, more inclined to pity it that to make war against it, devoted solely to the homeland, and I join myself body and soul with that elite of workers, head of the proletariat and middle class, the party of labor and progress, of liberty and the idea, which, understanding that authority is nothing, that popular spontaneity is of no use; that liberty which does not act is lost, and that the interests that need to put themselves in relation with an intermediary which represents them are interests sacrificed, accepts for its goal and motto *the Education of the People*.

O homeland, French homeland, homeland of the bards of the eternal revolution! homeland of liberty, for, despite all your servitudes, in no place on the earth, neither in Europe, nor in America, is the mind, which is all of man, so free as it is with you! homeland that I love with that accumulated love that the growing son bears for his mother, that the father feels grow along with his children! I will see you suffer for a long time yet, suffer not for yourself alone, but for the world which rewards you with its envy and its insults; to suffer innocent, only because you do not know yourself?... It seems to me at every instant that you are at your last ordeal! Awaken, mother: neither can your princes, your barons and your counts do anything for your salvation, nor can your prelates no how to comfort you with their benedictions. Guard, if you wish, the memory of those who have done well, and go sometimes to pray at their monuments: but do not seek their successors. They are finished! Commence your new life, O first of immortals; show yourself in your beauty, Venus Urania; spread your perfumes, flower of humanity!

And humanity will be rejuvenated, and its unity will be created by you: for the unity of the human race is the unity of my homeland, as the spirit of the human race is nothing but the spirit of my homeland.

Unanimity: Universal Consent

There are things, in the moral order, about which the human race is unanimous; there are even many of them.

So isn't it possible that all the questions of politics, economics and morals could be simplified or clarified in such a way that the response to them would be unanimous?

In this way, the *direct* government of the people would be possible.

It is according to that idea, confirmed by the testimony of the sciences, that [Pierre-Napoléon] Domenjarie [1852] has written his pamphlet, *La loi morale, loi d'unanimité*, which we have read in prison.

That philosophical thesis [reveals] the ignorance of the author, but it is nonetheless useful to clarify it.

The things about which there can be unanimity (it is not a question of *facts/deeds*) are all *definite* abstractions, whatever order of ideas they may belong to.

Thus, *is it not permitted to kill a man*: Non occides.

But the disagreements begin when it is a question of *practical* cases:

Is it permitted to kill in legitimate defense?

Is it permitted to kill in war?

Is it permitted to kill judicially?

Is it permitted to kill deserters?

Is it permitted to kill a man or woman caught in flagrante delicto in the act of adultery?

Is it permitted to kill a tyrant?

Is it permitted to kill the abductor of a minor child? etc.

Now, on the practical cases, there is necessary flexibility, and as the circumstances alone make the *law* or *non-law*, it follows that one cannot posit an absolute principle, and that unanimity is impossible.

Thus, on a principle of abstract mathematics, there will be *unanimity*.—But if it is a question of assessing the results of a business, of an enterprise, of an experiment, etc., opinions can vary infinitely.

Similarly, in the moral realm, there is unanimity on principles, because the principle expresses an ideality, an abstraction. Only do to others what you would like others to do to you: everyone is unanimous on this precept, which we find expressed spontaneously everywhere.

It is an abstract, ideal formula.

But what should I want for myself? What can I demand? What is my right? That is where unanimity ceases to exist, and it is necessarily replaced by free debate, which ends in the transaction or the Contract.

The value of a product is a common example: it summarizes all cases.

--

Now, Reason asks itself:

Is there a science for undefinable things, on which unanimity will never practically exist, as there is one for definite things?...

It is this question to which the economic science responds.

--

From this previous explanation, it is easy to deduce and *a priori* judgment that declares void the so-called science of Fourier, which aspires to [resolve] everything, *mathematically*, that is to say abstractly, and by means of definitions.

From this as well, the elimination of the Communist thought, which, supposing unanimity, suppresses debate, competition, contract; the very principle of conventional right!....

It is time to open the eyes of the public in that regard and especially to repress the [ ] presumption of these poor

Devils who believe they have found the secret of the world when they have produced a [ ] gross naïveté.

What then is the science of indefinable things, of things on which there remains unnecessary doubt, and where unanimity is impossible?

It is the science that teaches us to know the [causes], the reason, the *laws* that rule this very variability: and how bye judicious and equitable convention, we arrest that variability, and convert into something definite a thing that is not of that nature.

Sic Notion of dead weight [*poids mort*];—variable.

Notion of maximum load [*poids utile*];—variable.

Relation between one and the other;—variable.

What are the causes of these *variations*?—How do they come about?—What is their mode, their character?—What utility [can we] draw from them for the conduct of life? etc., etc. How to behave with them? etc.

1855

New Propositions Demonstrated in the Practice of Revolutions

1. The interests established by society are mobile, subject to a constant and fundamentally unstable shifting.

2. Fixity, permanence or perpetuity in the relations of interests is a chimera.

3. That mobility of interests is the primary source of revolutions.

4. An interest, however unjust it may be, can only be abolished on the condition of being replaced by another, which itself could appear every bit as unjust later.

5. The human mind has a horror of the void; it does not accept pure negation, even if it is the negation of the greatest of crimes.

6. Nations do nothing from pure love or pure justice; there is always a self-serving motive for every reform.

7. The worship of truth for its own sake is pure nonsense in revolution.

8. All religion, every political institution, all the economy of society are successive modifications of cannibalism.

9. The ideas that govern society, with the interests, are mobile like those interests themselves, liable to increase

and decrease, subject by nature to conflict and contradiction, perpetually changed.

10. Consistency in ideas is the opposite of the social Mind; the immutability of symbols and professions of faith, in Society, is a chimera.

11. That fundamental oscillation of ideas is the second cause of revolutions.

12. An idea, however absurd it may be, can never be entirely abolished, except when it is replaced by another, which could appear as absurd later.

13. The mobility of ideas and interests is not sufficient to explain Revolutions.

14. Human Nature remains the same, with regard to worthiness and unworthiness;—well-being increases, the sum of knowledge is multiplied: the quantity of virtue remains the same.

15. *Evil, vice, selfishness* and *sadness* are essential elements of humanity.

16. The antagonism of powers creates all of our life: the status quo, bread, the absolute, happiness, sanctity, perfection is nothingness, death.

17. The intimate knowledge of that truth is the principle of resistance to revolutions.

18. The feeling of the beautiful and the sublime, the fascination with the absolute, is the cause that tips the balance and incites revolutions.

19. The beautiful, the sublime, the absolute, the perfect, the true and the ideal are the infinite in thought.

20. This feeling produces the marvelous in Humanity; it is the supreme cause, the *ultima ratio* of revolutions.

21. The idea of God is not the conception of a *Supreme Being*, but of a *Supreme Ideal*.

22. The supreme ideal is without reality: *there is no God*.

23. A society cannot exist without a transcendent ideal: without religion, modern society is in danger of dying.

24. Every ideal has a real and intelligible basis: every reality and every idea is susceptible to idealization.

25. The mind inevitably tend to realize its ideal, in nature, in labor, in person, in government, in religion: that is why it decides to make a revolution.

26. Society needing an ideal, and that ideal needing to belong to a real being, we must seek a supplement to the idea of God.

27. Truth, as well as Justice, is essentially mobile and historical; there is nothing absolute or eternal about it.

28. Only the laws of movement are absolutely and eternally true.

29. The state of revolution is the normal state of societies.

30. Every manifestation supposes a subject: thus, the series of revolutions leads us to suppose a revolutionary subject.

31. *Revolutions* are the *Transitions* [Passages] of Humanity

32. There have been some presentiments of that idea; the Peoples, the Poets, the Writers have had an intuition of it.

33. The phenomena of revolution can only be explained and understood with the aid of this hypothesis

34. The hypothesis of a revolutionary subject is as rational and more legitimate than that of God and that of Providence.

35. A being is not a simple thing, but a group.

36. All beings, living and unorganized, are groups.

37. Everything that forms a group is a reality or has the power of realization.

38. The old ontology went astray which it defined the *Being* as a simple substance.

39. Simple substance, *mind* or *matter*, is a chimera.

40. A man is an organized group, in which the mind arises from the organization.

41. The People are an organized group: thus, the People are a real being, endowed with Life, Personality, Will, Intelligence and prescience.

42. The definition of man by Bonald is the same, at base, as that of Cabanis:—a simple transposition of terms has made all the difference.

43. The family, the familial group, is a *Complex Being*, which has its Self, like the People and the Individual.

44. The old ontology, in its materialist form, leads to this proposition: Matter does not exist.

45. In its spiritualist form it leads to this other proposition: Mind does not exist.

46. To set aside the notion of *substance* and *Cause*, and move onto the terrain of *Phenomena* and *Law*, or of the Group.

Propositions: To Leave Behind Abstractions, Utopias, Systems, Doctrines, Theories and Empiricisms of the Parties Schools and Sects

I

1. There exists between men a tendency or attraction that pushes them to group and act for their greatest interests and the most complete scope of their liberty, collectively and en masse.

2. From that tendency in the group results, for the human mass, a new and incalculable power, which can be considered as the proper and unique force of Society, commonly known as the Sovereignty of the People.

3. That force is manifested in all the labors that demand an energy out of proportion with the means of the individual; in the large workshops and factories, in the armies, but especially in the political organization of Government.

4. The importance of that force is such that we can affirm boldly, without fear of being refuted, as the most distinguished fact of the history of the nations, that there is no civilization for the people, no progress, not morality for individuals, no liberty or well being, apart from the legitimate exercise and the rational application of that force.

1855: Propositions: To Leave Behind Abstractions, Utopias, Systems, Doctrines, Theories and Empiricisms of the Parties Schools and Sects

5. Royalty is the symbolization of the social force: the socialist utopias are its mythology.

6. The social force is the property of all: it tends to divide it equally in all.

7. The guarantees of liberty and well-being, the stability of States, the order of nations are on account of the number of Rulers, of the of those sharing the social force.

8. The social order will be perfect, equilibrium unassailable and stability absolute if all those who contribute to the formation of the collective force are, at the same time and in proportion to their faculties, sharers in the social force, constituent parts of the sovereigns.

9. Now, governmental practice is far from having reached that degree of perfection: we have never even seen an example where the number of the governors was only half plus one of the individuals contributing to the collective force: that proposition has even appeared absurd to all the publicists.

10. The social force has been constantly usurped from the profit of a small number against the majority, delivered to the whims of one party and more often still of one individual.

11. That alienation of the collective power constitutes, ipso facto, the political organism called monarchic; it gives rise to dynasties, aristocracies, nobilities, patriciates, bourgeoisies and, on the other hand, serfs, slaves, helots, pariahs and proletarians.

1855: Propositions: To Leave Behind Abstractions, Utopias, Systems, Doctrines, Theories and Empiricisms of the Parties Schools and Sects

12. Democracy is the protest of the oppressed people against the alienation of the social force. Powerlessness of that protest, caused by the ignorance of the facts, by political ideology and verbiage.

The powerlessness of the democracy comes from the fact that it has always wanted to make the governmental organism, as tyranny had created it, serve the emancipation of the people, but it has not has been able to create itself a property in it.

The true cause of the alienation of the social force is the poverty, original or [ ] organic or fortuitous, of the majority of the people.

II

1. In fact, if we study history, we see that in general, when all differences are deducted, the enjoyment of the benefits created by the social force is, for each individual, in direct proportion to their fortune.

2. As a result, the poverty, first cause of that alienation, is aggravated and by it, and that here the two terms Alienation of the social force and Poverty are reciprocally Cause and effect of one another.

3. Analogy and correlation between Property and Government. For the exercise and enjoyment of the collective force to be without reproach, the public power to which all contribute must be possessed by all, like the soul, industry, commerce and knowledge.

1855: Propositions: To Leave Behind Abstractions, Utopias, Systems, Doctrines, Theories and Empiricisms of the Parties Schools and Sects

4. Thus the problem of the Emancipation of the people is double:

> To create in the disinherited masses a real patrimony, effective, useful, susceptible to appropriation and yet inalienable.

> To give to the people, to each citizen, their effective, complete, inalienable sovereignty, susceptible to distribution and yet sheltered from all usurpation.

III

1. Again—In order to do that, to study asceticism, absolutist organism, and instead of wanting to employ it in the service of the people, to disorganize it and create one that will be the counterweight of the first.

2. The Sovereignty that is exercised only by mandate is fictive and vain.

3. Sovereignty is reciprocal.

4. The Sovereignty in each locality and each individuals is proportional to the interests that the individual or locality represent.

5. Sovereignty increases by its exercise, as Wealth increases by Labor.

6. Government is identical in all times and places

1855: Propositions: To Leave Behind Abstractions, Utopias, Systems, Doctrines, Theories and Empiricisms of the Parties Schools and Sects

7. Paris, seat of the French government. Its predominance deduced from the order of things.

8. Assembly of the sections.

   Government Commission.

   Government Committee.

   Functions.

9. Renewal of the representatives. Sovereignty is mobile: it cannot be exercised by all, to the same degree, at the same moment.

10. Relation of the Commune of Paris with the Communes of France. The Commune, original, natural, traditional, imperishable seat of Government.

11. National assembly. Its functions.

12. The national assembly oversees and verifies the acts of the Government Commission and Committee.

13. Case of conflict. Solution.

14. The tyranny of a million men is impossible, when the sovereignty is not long the patrimony of one party or one caste. The [ ] of Paris gives meaning to that of Charles X, Louise-Philippe or Napoleon III.

15. Revolutionary operations.

1855: Propositions: To Leave Behind Abstractions, Utopias, Systems, Doctrines, Theories and Empiricisms of the Parties Schools and Sects

Formation of the patrimony of the people.

IV

1. Bis. Distribution of the social force by groups and sub-groups: autonomous. It is not enough to raise the wages of the worker, to reduce the hours; he must be made master of the thing.

2. Demolition of tyranny: elimination of parasitism.

3. Commonplace, organic affaires, etc... All of that remains the same.

4. Revolutionary justice.

5. How the social force, or sovereignty of the people, is found divided. Each enjoys two things that they did not have previously:

> A complete individual liberty.

> Something that surpasses the scope of individual activity: that something is the portion of sovereignty. Participation in all deliberations, elections, jurisdictions; certainty of being heard in all their demands; all things that engender glory, security, wealth, consideration and virtue in the individual.

6. The functionary, in this system, truly becomes a civil servant; he is no longer a master. Illusion of the ambitions in this regard soon set straight.

1855: Propositions: To Leave Behind Abstractions, Utopias, Systems, Doctrines, Theories and Empiricisms of the Parties Schools and Sects

7. End of controversies: pointless, interminable, innumerable disputes brought to naught.

8. Immediate application in the overthrowing of tyranny:

Form sections.

Insure propaganda.

Establish the authority of the Commission and the Committee.

See the right of Justice bestowed.

Organize the vindicte of the people.

Gather in the face of the power.

Strike the tyranny [in a preemptive manner]

Finally, proceed against the [ ]. their henchmen, dictators and satellites by all means of extermination.

1857

Letter to Villiaumé

Translated by Shawn P. Wilbur

My dear Villiaumé, it is too warm for me to venture, with my sick head, all the way to Rue Marsollier. I am thinking instead of fleeing for ten or twelve days to some hole in Franche-Comté, where the devil may perhaps not come to torment me with his pomps and work.

But you, who are spry, come some evening after your dinner and we will have a mug at the local cabaret, which will do you as much good as an ample banquet. Friendship, and understanding as well, is surely found in a modest *to your health*.

I regret to learn of the illness of Béranger, whom I have not seen.

I had intended to pay tribute to him this year with a copy of my next book: it is an honor that will be denied me.

It occurs to me that I have known hardly any of the distinguished men of the century: Châteaubriant, P.-L. Courier, Jouffroy, Cousin, Nodier, E. Burnouf, Guizot, Thiers, Barrot, Royer-Collard, Lamartine, A. de Musset, A. de Vigny, Béranger. Lamennais, Arago, etc., etc.

With those few that I have encountered, I have had to do battle: P. Leroux, L. Blanc, V. Considérant; there will be others.

Am I not the excommunicated of the era!

Of course I will have no one at my burial. There is a proverb that says: *Væ soli!*... Woe to the loner!... thinking of it, I ask myself if I do not drag along the chains of some great culprit condemned in a former existence, as J. Reynaud teaches?

I begin to be very weary of life and seek only to speak my piece before I die. That done, I say: *To hell with me and the human race!* Regards.

P.-J. Proudhon

1861

Relation of the State and Liberty, According to Modern Right

Translated by Shawn P. Wilbur

Modern right, by introducing itself in the place of the ancient right, has done one new thing: it has put in the presence of one another, on the same line, two powers which until now had been in a relation of subordination. These two powers are the *State* and the *Individual*, in other words *Government* and *Liberty*.

The Revolution, indeed, has not suppressed that occult, mystical presence, that one called the sovereign, and that we name more willingly the State; it has not reduced society to lone individuals, compromising, contracting between them, and of their free transaction making for themselves a common law, as the Social Contract of J.-J. Rousseau gave us to understand.

No, Government, Power, State, as on wishes to call it, is found again, under the ruins of the *ancien régime*, complete, perfectly intact, and stronger than before. What is new since the Revolution, is Liberty, I mean the condition made of Liberty, its civil and political state.

Let us note, besides, that the State, as the Revolution conceived it, is not a purely abstract thing, as some, Rousseau among others, have supposed, a sort of legal fiction; it is a reality as positive as society itself, as the individual even. The State is the power of collectivity which results, in every agglomeration of human beings, from their mutual relations, from the solidarity of their interests, from their community of action, from the practice of their opinions and passions. The State does not exist without the citizens, doubtless; it is not prior nor superior to them; but it exists for the very reason that they exist, distinguishing itself from each and all by special faculties and attributes. And liberty is no longer a fictive power, consisting of a simple faculty to choose between doing and not doing: it is a positive faculty, *sui generis*, which is to the individual, assemblage of diverse passions and faculties, what the State is to the collectivity of citizens, the highest power of conception and of creation of being.[25]

---

[25] Liberty and the State. — The antithesis of the State and of Liberty, presented here as the foundation and principle of modern society, by replacement of the supremacy of the State and the subordination of Liberty, which made the base of ancient society, that antithesis, eminently organic, will not be admitted by the publicists and partisans of the principle of authority, of the eminent domain of the State, of governmental initiative and of the subordination of the citizen or rather subject; it will not be understood by those who, formed by the lessons of the old scholasticism, are accustomed to see in the State and free will only abstractions. Those, just like the old partisans of divine right, are born enemies of self-government, invariable adversaries of true democracy, and condemned to the eternal arbitrariness of the reason of State and of taxation. For them the State is a mystical entity, before which every individuality must bow; Liberty is not a power, and taxation is not an exchange; principles are fictions of which the man of State makes what he wants, justice a convention and politics a bascule. These doctrinaires, as they are called, the skepticism and misanthropy of which today governs Europe, are as far beneath the ancient monarchists and feudalists, as arbitrary will is beneath faith, Machiavelli beneath the Bible. Europe owes to this school of pestilence the confusion of ideas

This is why the reason of the State is not the same thing as individual reason; why the interest of the State is not the same as private interest, even if that was identical in the majority or the totality of citizens; why the acts of government are of a different nature than the acts of the simple individual. The faculties, attributes, interests, differ between the citizen and the State as the individual and the collective differ between them: we have seen a beautiful example of it, when we have posed that principle that the law of exchange is not the same for the individual and for the State.

Under the regime of divine right, the reason of State being confused with the dynastic, aristocratic or clerical reason, could not always be in conformity with justice; that is what has cause the banishment, by modern right, of the abusive principle of the reason of State. Just so, the interest of the State, being confused with the interest of dynasty or of caste, was not in complete conformity with Justice; and it is that which makes every society transformed by the Revolution tend to republican government.

Under the new regime, on the contrary, the reason of State must in complete conformity with Justice, the true

---

and the dissolution of morals by which it is beset: the slack maxims Jesuits could produce nothing comparable.

This is not the place to open a discussion of the actuality of the State and of Liberty: I will content myself with referring provisionally to my work *Justice in the Revolution and in the Church*, Fourth and Eighth Studies of the Belgian edition.

expression of right, reason essentially general and synthetic, distinct consequently from the reason of the citizen, always more or less specialized and individual.[26] Similarly, the interest of the State is purged of all aristocratic and dynastic pretension; the interest of the State is above all an interest of noble right, which implies that its nature is other than that of individual interest.

The author of the Social Contract a claimed, and those who follow him have repeated after him, that the true sovereign is the citizen; that the prince, organ of the State, is only the agent of the citizen; consequently that the State is the chose of the citizen: all that would be bon à dire while it was a question of claiming the rights of man and of the citizen and of inaugurating liberty against despotism. Presently the Revolution no longer encounters obstacles, at least from the side of the *ancien régime*: it is a question of rightly knowing its thought and of putting it into execution. From this point of view the language of Rousseau has become incorrect, I would even say that it is false and dangerous.

Determination of the functions, attributes and prerogatives of the State, according to modern right

The State, a power of collectivity, having its own and specific reason, its eminent interest, its outstanding functions, the State, as such, has *rights* too, rights that it is impossible to misunderstand without putting

---

[26] Opposition of collective and individual reason. See, on this curious subject, the work indicated in the preceding note, Sixth Study of the Belgian edition.

immediately in peril the right, the fortune and the liberty of the citizens themselves.

The State is the protector of the liberty and property of the citizens, not only of those who are born, but of those who are to be born. Its guardianship embraces the present and future, and extends to the future generations: thus the State has rights proportionate to its obligations; without that, what would its foresight serve?

The state oversees the execution of the laws; it is the guardian of the public faith and the guarantor of the observation of contracts. These attributions imply new rights in the State, as much over persons as things, that one could not deny it without destroying it, without breaking the social bond.

The State is the justice-bringer par excellence; it alone is charged with the execution of judgments. On this account as well, the State has its rights, without which its own guarantee, its justice, would become null.

All of that, you say, existed before in the State. The principle then and its corollaries, the theory and the application remain at base the same, nothing has changed? The Revolution has been a useless work.

This has changed between the ancient and the new regime, the in the past the State was incarnated in a man: *"L'Ètat c'est moi;"* while today it finds its reality in itself, as a power of collectivity; — that in the past, that State made man, that State-King was absolute, while now it is subject to justice, and subject as a consequence to the control of the citizens; — that in the past the reason of the State was infected by aristocratic and princely reason, while today, exposed to all the critiques, to all the protests, it has strength only from Right and Truth; — that in the past, the interest of the State was confused with the interest of the princes, which distorted the administration and caused justice to stumble, which today a similar confusion of interests establishes the crime of misappropriation and prevarication; — that finally, in the past, the subject only appeared on its knees before it sovereign, as we saw it in the Estates General, while since the Revolution the citizen deals with the State as equal to equal, which is precisely what allows us to define tax as an exchange, and to consider the State, in the administration of the public funds, as a simple trader.

The State has preserved its power, its strength, which alone renders it respectable, constitutes its credit, creates awards and prerogatives for it, but it has lost its *authority*. It no longer has anything but Rights, guaranteed by the rights and interests of the citizens themselves. It is itself, if we can put it this way, a species of citizen; it is a civil person, like families, commercial societies, corporations, and communes. Just as it is not sovereign, neither is it a servant. As has already been said, that would be to remake the tyrant: it is the first among his peers.

Thus liberty, which counts for nothing in the State, subordinated, absorbed was it was by the good pleasure of the sovereign, liberty has become a power equal in dignity to the State. Its definition with regard to the State is the same as with regard to the citizens: *Liberty, in the man, is the power to create, innovate, reform, modify, in a word to do everything that exceeds the power of nature and that of the State, and which does no harm to the rights of others,* whether that other is a simple citizen or the State. It is according to this principle that the State must abstain from everything that does not absolutely require its initiative, in order to leave a vaster field to individual liberty.

Ancient society, established on absolutism, thus tended to concentration and immobility.

The new society, established on the dualism of liberty and the State, tends to decentralization and movement. The idea of human perfectibility, or progress, has revealed itself in humanity at the same time as the new right.

The Theory of Taxation

Translated by Shawn P. Wilbur

Relation of the State and Liberty, according to modern right

Modern right, by introducing itself in the place of the ancient right, has done one new thing: it has put in the presence of one another, on the same line, two powers which until now had been in a relation of subordination. These two powers are the *State* and the *Individual*, in other words *Government* and *Liberty*.

The Revolution, indeed, has not suppressed that occult, mystical presence, that one called the sovereign, and that we name more willingly the State; it has not reduced society to lone individuals, compromising, contracting between them, and of their free transaction making for themselves a common law, as the *Social Contract* of J.-J. Rousseau gave us to understand.

No, Government, Power, State, as on wishes to call it, is found again, under the ruins of the *ancien régime*, complete, perfectly intact, and stronger than before. What is new since the Revolution, is Liberty, I mean the condition made of Liberty, its civil and political state.

Let us note, besides, that the State, as the Revolution conceived it, is not a purely abstract thing, as some, Rousseau among others, have supposed, a sort of legal fiction; it is a reality as positive as society itself, as the individual even. The State is the power of collectivity which results, in every agglomeration of human beings, from their mutual relations, from the solidarity of their interests, from their community of action, from the practice of their opinions and passions. The State does not exist without the citizens, doubtless; it is not prior nor superior to them; but it exists for the very reason that they exist, distinguishing itself from each and all by special faculties and attributes. And liberty is no longer a fictive power, consisting of a simple faculty to choose between doing and not doing: it is a positive faculty, *sui generis*, which is to the individual, assemblage of diverse passions and faculties, what the State is to the collectivity of citizens, the highest power of conception and of creation of being (D).

This is why the reason of the State is not the same thing as individual reason; why the interest of the State is not the same as private interest, even if that was identical in the majority or the totality of citizens; why the acts of government are of a different nature than the acts of the simple individual. The faculties, attributes, interests, differ between the citizen and the State as the individual and the collective differ between them: we have seen a beautiful example of it, when we have posed that principle that the law of exchange is not the same for the individual and for the State.

Under the regime of divine right, the reason of State being confused with the dynastic, aristocratic or clerical reason, could not always be in conformity with justice; that is what has cause the banishment, by modern right, of the abusive principle of the reason of State. Just so, the interest of the State, being confused with the interest of dynasty or of caste, was not in complete conformity with Justice; and it is that which makes every society transformed by the Revolution tend to republican government.

Under the new regime, on the contrary, the reason of State must in complete conformity with Justice, the true expression of right, reason essentially general and synthetic, distinct consequently from the reason of the citizen, always more or less specialized and individual (E). Similarly, the interest of the State is purged of all aristocratic and dynastic pretension; the interest of the State is above all an interest of noble right, which implies that its nature is other than that of individual interest.

The author of the *Social Contract* a claimed, and those who follow him have repeated after him, that the true sovereign is the citizen; that the prince, organ of the State, is only the agent of the citizen; consequently that the State is the chose of the citizen: all that would be bon à dire while it was a question of claiming the rights of man and of the citizen and of inaugurating liberty against despotism. Presently the Revolution no longer encounters obstacles, at least from the side of the *ancien régime*: it is a question of rightly knowing its thought and of putting it into execution. From this point of view the language of Rousseau has become incorrect, I would even say that it is false and dangerous.

Determination of the functions, attributes and prerogatives of the State, according to modern right

1861: The Theory of Taxation

The State, a power of collectivity, having its own and specific reason, its eminent interest, its outstanding functions, the State, as such, has *rights* too, rights that it is impossible to misunderstand without putting immediately in peril the right, the fortune and the liberty of the citizens themselves.

The State is the protector of the liberty and property of the citizens, not only of those who are born, but of those who are to be born. Its guardianship embraces the present and future, and extends to the future generations: thus the State has rights proportionate to its obligations; without that, what would its foresight serve?

The state oversees the execution of the laws; it is the guardian of the public faith and the guarantor of the observation of contracts. These attributions imply new rights in the State, as much over persons as things, that one could not deny it without destroying it, without breaking the social bond.

The State is the justice-bringer par excellence; it alone is charged with the execution of judgments. De ce chef encore, the State has its rights, without which its own guarantee, its justice, would become null.

All of that, you say, existed before in the State. The principle then and its corollaries, the theory and the application remain at base the same, nothing has changed? The Revolution has been a useless work.

This has changed between the ancient and the new regime, the in the past the State was incarnated in a man: *"L'État c'est moi;"* while today it finds its reality in itself, as a power of collectivity; — that in the past, that State made man, that State-King was absolute, while now it is subject to justice, and subject as a consequence to the control of the citizens; — that in the past the reason of the State was infected by aristocratic and princely reason, while today, exposed to all the critiques, to all the protests, it has strength only from Right and Truth; — that in the past, the interest of the State was confused with the interest of the princes, which distorted the administration and caused justice to stumble, which today a similar confusion of interests establishes the crime of misappropriation and prevarication; — that finally, in the past, the subject only appeared on its knees before it sovereign, as we saw it in the Estates General, while since the Revolution the citizen deals with the State as equal to equal, which is precisely what allows us to define tax as an exchange, and to consider the State, in the administration of the public funds, as a simple trader.

The State has preserved its power, its strength, which alone renders it respectable, constitutes its credit, creates awards and prerogatives for it, but it has lost its *authority*. It no longer has anything but Rights, guaranteed by the rights and interests of the citizens themselves. It is itself, if we can put it this way, a species of citizen; it is a civil person, like families, commercial societies, corporations, and communes. Just as there is no sovereign, there is no longer a servant, as it has been said, that would be to remake the tyrant: he is the first among his peers.

Thus liberty, which counts for nothing in the State, subordinated, absorbed was it was by the good pleasure of the sovereign, liberty has become a power equal in dignity to the State. Its definition with regard to the State is the same as with regard to the citizens: *Liberty, in the man, is the power to create, innovate, reform, modify, in a word to do everything that exceeds the power of nature and that of the State, and which does no harm to the rights of others*, whether that other is a simple citizen or the State. It is according to this principle that the State must abstain from everything that does not absolutely require its initiative, in order to leave a vaster field to individual liberty.

Ancient society, established on absolutism, thus tended to concentration and immobility.

The new society, established on the dualism of liberty and the State, tends to decentralization and movement. The idea of human perfectibility, or progress, has revealed itself in humanity at the same time as the new right.

Note D, Page 65

Liberty and the State. — The antithesis of the State and of Liberty, presented here as the foundation and principle of modern society, by replacement of the supremacy of the State and the subordination of Liberty, which made the base of ancient society, that antithesis, eminently organic, will not be admitted by the publicists and partisans of the principle of authority, of the eminent domain of the State, of governmental initiative and of the subordination of the citizen or rather subject; it will not be understood by those who, formed by the lessons of the old scholasticism, are accustomed to see in the State and free will only abstractions. Those, just like the old partisans of divine right, are born enemies of *self-government*, invariable adversaries of true democracy, and condemned to the eternal arbitrariness of the reason of State and of taxation. For them the State is a mystical entity, before which every individuality must bow; Liberty is not a power, and taxation is not an exchange; principles are fictions of which the man of State makes what he wants, justice a convention and politics a bascule. These *doctrinaires*, as they are called, the skepticism and misanthropy of which today governs Europe, are as far beneath the ancient monarchists and feudalists, as arbitrary will is beneath faith, Machiavelli beneath the Bible. Europe owes to this school of pestilence the confusion of ideas and the dissolution of morals by which it is beset: the slack maxims Jesuits could produce nothing comparable.

This is not the place to open a discussion of the actuality of the State and of Liberty: I will content myself with referring provisionally to my work *Justice in the Revolution and in the Church*, Fourth and Eighth Studies of the Belgian edition.

Note E, Page 66

Opposition of collective and individual reason. See, on this curious subject, the work indicated in the preceding note, Sixth Study of the Belgian edition.

10. General Summary

1861: The Theory of Taxation

Such is the ensemble of ideas resulting from my study of the question raised by the State Council of the canton of Vaud. To first free these ideas from the mass of facts, from the chaos of empiricism, and then explain them with advantage, demanded a profound critique of the fiscal institutions, a critique that I could have made much more voluminous, for no cost but the citations, but that, such as it is, appears to me sufficient for enlightened minds or administrators versed in practice.

A complete theory of taxation, of its principles, its rules, its nature, its object, its anomalies, and its function in the economic system of nations, has never, as far as I know, been given: thanks to the appeal of the honorable councilors of the State of Vaud, it will at least have been sketched, and for the first time.

What is that theory?

Here is no preconceived system, no utopian tendency, nothing that could appear foreign to even the most old-fashioned sorts, nothing that the most routine tax system could by right find paradoxical. We have taken hold of the facts and we have analyzed them; we have isolated their principle and put their spirit in relief. In a rapid review, we have outlined the history of taxation, in ancient as well as modern society; we have determined its aim and clarified its contradictions, which means its laws.

Then, with the aid of reductions, transformations, displacements, applying proportionality here and progression there; sometimes striking the question of consumption, sometimes production and circulation, and making the system pivot on land rent, we have ended—or at least such is my hope—with a rational, harmonious ensemble, all the parts of which suppose one another, like the members of an animal; we have produced an organic whole, a function of a still larger organism, which is society and the State.

Let the more experienced rework, now, the plan for reforms that we have just presented in rough form, taking the French budget for their topic; let others, applying it to the various States of Europe, subject it to all the modifications demanded by local customs and habits; let them change the proportions proposed in this report; it will matter little.

Whoever concerns themselves with taxation and seeks, for any country or society, its normal constitution, must take into account, above all, the facts and propositions that we have demonstrated, which can be considered as so many axioms. These facts and propositions are:

That taxation, according to ancient law, was first a *tribute*;

But that, according to modern law and economic science, it is nothing other than an exchange;

That this transformation of taxation, from ancient society to the new society, is the corollary of the transformation undergone by the State, once sovereign, but now balanced by a rival power, *Liberty*;

That from that fundamental notion, namely, that taxation is an exchange, its whole theory is deduced;

That thus, unlike other traders, the State owes its services at *cost price*;

That it does not *impose* them, but waits for the nation to demand them;

That as a consequence of that *free* demand of the citizens, the tax quota could not increase in an indefinite manner, but must on the contrary decrease endlessly, from which arises the necessity of assigning *maximum* to taxation;

That the centralization of government in a large country is incompatible with that unlimited reduction of the general costs of the State, and consequently with the regularity of the budget;

That, in a normal state of thing, the sum of the contributions would appear to have to be one *twentieth* of the total product of the country, and can be reduced to *thirtieth*;

That, in modern societies, all the citizens being equal before the law, the expenses of the State must be settled without distinction by all and in *proportion* to their abilities;

That all taxation, whatever its form and its base, is ultimately collected on the collective *product*;

That as a consequence all tax fees are reduced to a tax on consumption;

That, through the movement of values and the rule that presides over the formation of prices, that tax on consumption finds itself settled, in a very large part, not individually as it seems from the rates of contribution, but by the masses;

That as a result of this taxation, taken in its general case, is reduced, but for minor details, to a *capitation*;

That, with regard to the inequality of fortunes, that capitation constitutes a true *progressive tax* in inverse proportion to fortune and direct proportion to indigence;

That, under the influence of these two causes, the incessant movement of values and the inequality of fortunes, the problem of the *balancing of taxation* is insoluble, and that all that we can obtain in this regard is reduced to an *approximation*;

That in order to return to Justice in taxation, the true method, the single and unique means is thus to work toward the *equalization of fortunes* themselves, something that does not depend on the initiative of the State, but solely on the intelligence and will of the citizens who consent to the tax;

That every attempt made in another direction in order to arrive at the equalization of taxation, either by a *progressive tax*, or by a *tax on capital*, or by a *tax on rent or income*, leads to absurdity and brings about enormous perturbations for public economy;

1861: The Theory of Taxation

That a single tax, invariably resulting in the concentration in one single instance of all the fiscal iniquities divided in a multitude de taxes, would be the most crushing of taxes and the worst of systems;

That the true march to follow being, in the final account, to submit to the law, or, to put it more correctly, to the egalitarian tendency, the whole difficulty consists in turning taxation in that direction and organizing it in that spirit;

That the first thing to do in order to arrive at that end is to constitute an allowance to the State;

That this allowance should be established on the rent of lands appropriated and in a good state for cultivation [exploitation];

That on top of that allowance, on which the whole system of taxation must pivot, the State should establish two categories of taxes, one on *public services*, directly reproductive, credit, means of transport, mines, docks, waters and forests, etc.; the other consisting of a series of *facultative* contributions, on all the objects of consumption and use, on transactions, etc.;

That for these various contributions, the State will apply, according to the circumstances, progression to some, proportionality to others, in such as way as to promote the egalitarian movement, the initiative, direction and acceleration of which will be up to the nation alone.

All of that, I dare say, is simple, clear, natural, logical, and, for whoever rallies to the new right, conclusive. The practice finds its explanation there, the historical movement its justification, the utopia itself its reason. The transitions can be handled as slowly as you wish.

Now, that legislation of taxation, where we see the ancient iniquity converted little by little into an instrument of Justice, is not our invention, and it is that which makes its triumph. We have deduced it from principles and facts above all arbitrariness; we have freed it, in short, from the movements of history and the contradiction of ideas; we have grasped its vestiges and indicated the organizing and liberal tendency even in the inventions of the most tyrannical tax system. So that if our democratic civilization, victorious over foolish resistances, ever manages to determine its aspirations and to constitute itself on a true basis, it would find its most decisive argument, and its consolidation, in the theory of taxation.

The progressive, indefinite reduction of the costs of the State;

Some taxes combined in such a way that they serve at once to pay for the public services, to moderate the economic movement, to discipline the market, and to promote the emancipation of the working classes;

The balance of properties;

The inviolability of inheritances;

Thee leveling of fortunes;

Society advancing with an even step in justice, liberty and wealth:

That is what we mean from now on by this word, odious and curse for so many centuries, Taxation.

1864

Letter to Several Workers in Paris and Rouen

Translated by Mitch Abidor

Citizens and friends:

This work was inspired by you and belongs to you.

Ten months ago you asked me what I thought of the electoral manifesto published by sixty workers from the Seine. You especially wanted to know if, after having pronounced yourselves at the elections of 1863 with a negative vote, you should persist in this line or if, because of the circumstances, you were permitted to support with your vote and your influence the candidacy of a comrade worthy of our sympathy.

There can be no doubt concerning my opinion on the thoughts expressed in your manifesto, and I frankly expressed it when I received it. To be sure, I was pleased by this reawakening of socialism: who in France had more right to be pleased than I? And I was in agreement with you and the Sixty that the working class isn't represented and that it has the right to be so; how could I possibly feel otherwise? If such were possible, would not working class representation be today, as it was in 1848, the official affirmation of socialism from the political and economic points of view?

But between this and the participation in elections, which would commit, along with democratic consciousness, its principles and its future, there is an abyss that I did not hide from you, citizens. And I can add that these reservations, welcomed by you, have since then been confirmed by experience.

What then is French democracy up to, once so proud and pure, and which, on the word of a few ambitious ones, imagined that through use of a false oath it could go from victory to victory? What conquests have we gained? Through what new and powerful idea has our policies been revealed? In the last eighteen months what successes have been signaled by the energy of our advocates or have repaid their glibness? Have we not been the witnesses of their perpetual defeats and failures? Duped by their parliamentarianism, haven't we seen them beaten on almost all questions by the government's orators? And when they were taken into court for the crime of having formed associations or met without authorization, when they had to explain themselves before the country and those in power, were they not confounded by that legality they vaunted and whose interpreters they posed as? What pitiful intrigues! And what a pitiful defense! I leave you to judge... After so many noisy debates can we deny that deep down our representatives have no other ideas, tendencies, or policies than the policies, tendencies, and ideas of the government?

Thanks to them it is now the case for young democracy what was once the case for old liberalism, two schools which an effort is being made to pair off: the world is beginning to back away from them. It is said that the truth,

1864: Letter to Several Workers in Paris and Rouen

right, and freedom are no longer any more on this side than on the other.

It is thus a matter of revealing to the world, through authentic testimony, the ideas, the true ideas of modern people, to legitimize its reformist aspirations and its right to sovereignty. Is universal suffrage truth or is it fiction? It is once again a question of restricting it, and it is certain that aside from labor very few take it seriously.

It's a matter of demonstrating to working class democracy what happens when a party enters political life when it lacks sufficient consciousness of itself and its ideas, and has given its votes to names that don't represent it. How when the superior class loses the direction of a movement it is up to the inferior one to take it. And how a people, incapable of regenerating itself through this regular succession, is condemned to perish. Do I dare to say that it's a matter of making French plebeians understand that if in 1869 it takes it into its head to yet again win a battle for the benefit of its bosses as it did in 1863-64, its emancipation could be put off for a half-century?

Have no doubt, my friends, that protest via the blank ballot, so little understood, so poorly received... that this absolute declaration of incompatibility between an outdated system and our dearest aspirations, this stoical veto, cast by us against presumptuous candidacies, is nothing less than the announcement of a new order of things, our becoming aware that we are the party of right and of freedom, the solemn act of our entry into political life and, I daresay, the signaling to the old world of its oncoming and inevitable fall...

Index

absolutism, 198, 217, 219, 258, 271, 273, 274, 373, 379

army, 31, 53, 146, 147, 300, 320, 321, 322, 325

association, 24, 52, 122, 152, 159, 218, 234, 264, 265, 302, 390

authority, 13, 26, 36, 57, 67, 87, 91, 96, 173, 188, 205, 208, 212, 213, 215, 216, 258, 267, 272, 273, 274, 277, 278, 280, 281, 284, 285, 287, 288, 290, 299, 304, 306, 315, 335, 344, 362, 372, 378, 379

bourgeoisie, 147, 213, 215, 219, 222, 223, 278, 341, 357

capital, 46, 48, 64, 84, 114, 144, 145, 162, 165, 166, 169, 178, 182, 183, 208, 212, 213, 214, 215, 216, 219, 220, 221, 224, 225, 226, 227, 228, 229, 230, 231, 232, 234, 235, 236, 237, 238, 239, 240, 241, 242, 243, 244, 245, 246, 247, 248, 249, 250, 251, 252, 253, 254, 255, 258, 262, 265, 268, 277, 282, 284, 292, 298, 299, 304, 307, 317, 384

Church, 5, 147, 162, 166, 173, 199, 225, 226, 261, 299, 324, 325, 380

class, 4, 10, 17, 33, 35, 46, 63, 75, 88, 98, 107, 112, 132, 143, 146, 168, 171, 181, 212, 215, 217, 219, 220, 222, 229, 231, 237, 247, 248, 253, 282, 286, 287, 344, 386, 389, 391

commune, 32, 129, 372, 378

community, 2, 14, 24, 51, 125, 153, 159, 257, 316, 317, 338, 368, 375

contract, 46, 174, 245, 317, 335, 348, 367, 371, 374, 377

corporation, 74, 141, 372, 378

Council, 134, 381

economic, 15, 90, 104, 120, 124, 129, 131, 136, 141, 142, 147, 148, 151, 152, 168, 169, 177, 182, 185, 212, 214, 215, 217, 221, 226, 228, 230, 231, 236, 253, 254, 258, 260, 262, 265, 282, 283, 289, 291, 292, 293, 299, 307, 312, 334, 335, 346, 348, 381, 382, 386, 389

economy, 8, 35, 79, 103, 108, 112, 113, 116, 117, 120, 129, 138, 148, 162, 163, 182, 199, 207, 219, 224, 225, 228, 231, 232, 233, 236, 239, 251, 252, 253, 255, 260, 282, 301, 313, 351, 384

freedom, 132, 176, 178, 213, 214, 216, 218, 221, 262, 272, 274, 276, 277, 391

French, IV, 90, 115, 128, 129, 130, 155, 194, 247, 287, 295, 320, 328, 344, 360, 382, 390, 391

justice, 22, 35, 44, 49, 51, 77, 92, 105, 127, 141, 171, 173, 174, 181, 190, 192, 202, 207, 225, 231, 246, 255, 268, 270, 298, 300, 307, 311, 323, 325, 342, 351, 361, 369, 371, 375, 377, 378, 380, 387

labor, 3, 8, 9, 16, 17, 24, 25, 26, 29, 35, 38, 39, 40, 41, 42, 44, 46, 47, 48, 50, 60, 62, 65, 68, 69, 70, 74, 79, 83, 85, 90, 92, 97, 99, 103, 108, 109, 110, 111, 112, 113, 114, 115, 116, 118, 121, 123, 129, 130, 131, 132, 142, 148, 159, 160, 161, 162, 163, 165, 166, 168, 169, 170, 177, 178, 182, 183, 199, 204, 212, 214, 215, 221, 222, 226, 227, 228, 231, 236, 237, 238, 239, 243, 244, 245, 246, 247, 248, 251, 253, 254, 258, 259, 260, 262, 263, 264, 268, 271,

282, 284, 292, 297, 299, 300, 304, 307, 309, 317, 324, 327, 330, 331, 333, 338, 343, 344, 353, 356, 391

liberalism, 217, 219, 390

liberty, 16, 19, 26, 48, 51, 52, 53, 77, 81, 88, 96, 97, 103, 130, 131, 132, 146, 148, 151, 153, 159, 173, 174, 175, 176, 181, 189, 190, 192, 194, 195, 197, 199, 200, 201, 206, 207, 214, 233, 244, 248, 250, 255, 262, 272, 284, 286, 290, 293, 295, 297, 301, 304, 305, 306, 307, 315, 317, 324, 328, 334, 344, 356, 357, 361, 368, 370, 371, 372, 373, 375, 376, 377, 379, 387

mass, 17, 21, 37, 39, 40, 46, 73, 74, 80, 99, 122, 127, 141, 143, 147, 248, 267, 270, 276, 277, 281, 283, 289, 290, 293, 294, 343, 356, 359, 381, 384

Monarchy, 320, 321

Parliament, II, 267, 325

participation, 35, 45, 198, 390

political, 5, 15, 16, 18, 20, 26, 33, 37, 38, 79, 82, 92, 103, 107, 108, 112, 113, 116, 120, 121, 122, 123, 135, 138, 141, 146, 147, 148, 156, 162, 163, 172, 174, 177, 178, 198, 212, 213, 214, 217, 219, 221, 224, 225, 228, 232, 233, 239, 253, 255, 258, 260, 262, 269, 273, 274, 280, 281, 282, 283, 284, 287, 290, 293, 299, 307, 308, 312, 313, 314, 315, 317, 320, 321, 334, 335, 351, 356, 357, 358, 367, 374, 389, 391

power, 10, 15, 27, 30, 33, 48, 55, 58, 59, 67, 74, 79, 81, 88, 92, 93, 94, 95, 96, 98, 103, 120, 121, 122, 124, 126, 130, 138, 139, 143, 179, 180, 182, 183, 184, 192, 196, 197, 200, 215, 228, 237, 241, 245, 246,

249, 265, 267, 268, 272, 274, 276, 277, 278, 279, 280, 284, 286, 287, 288, 289, 291, 293, 295, 296, 297, 298, 301, 303, 304, 306, 307, 310, 312, 313, 315, 325, 334, 335, 337, 338, 343, 352, 354, 356, 357, 358, 362, 367, 370, 371, 372, 374, 375, 377, 378, 379, 380, 382, 390

property/properties, 14, 41, 43, 55, 66, 84, 90, 91, 96, 107, 108, 114, 116, 117, 118, 119, 120, 121, 122, 123, 125, 126, 128, 131, 134, 137, 145, 146, 147, 158, 162, 163, 166, 167, 169, 171, 182, 183, 191, 217, 219, 220, 231, 240, 243, 245, 257, 260, 263, 264, 268, 282, 283, 298, 316, 317, 325, 337, 338, 357, 371, 377

regime, 46, 249, 321, 341, 342, 369, 371, 375, 376, 377

Religion, 22, 26, 109, 255, 298, 310, 311, 312, 314, 315, 316

Revolution, I, II, 144, 145, 159, 163, 170, 171, 176, 177, 178, 183, 184, 212, 213, 214, 215, 217, 222, 223, 260, 262, 265, 266, 282, 283, 286, 290, 292, 293, 294, 305, 312, 315, 318, 320, 321, 322, 328, 340, 341, 342, 351, 352, 354, 360, 361, 367, 369, 370, 371, 372, 374, 376, 377, 378, 380

Rousseau, 18, 23, 43, 188, 198, 199, 200, 367, 370, 374, 376

socialism, 166, 178, 191, 194, 197, 201, 208, 218, 219, 257, 261, 263, 273, 302, 323, 389

Society, I, 112, 123, 124, 141, 142, 144, 245, 260, 268, 311, 316, 332, 352, 353, 356, 387 sovereignty, 120, 121, 123, 174, 213, 216, 288, 323, 359, 360, 361, 391

State, I, II, 34, 52, 53, 85, 114, 115, 120, 134, 145, 163, 168, 169, 211, 212, 215, 216, 217, 218, 219, 220, 221, 239, 258, 259, 260, 263, 264, 265, 272, 277, 278, 282, 283, 284, 285, 286, 288, 289, 290, 291, 292, 293, 294, 295, 297, 299, 300, 301, 302, 303, 304, 305, 306, 307, 313, 343, 357, 367, 369, 370, 371, 372, 373, 374, 375, 376, 377, 378, 379, 380, 381, 382, 383, 384, 385, 386

suffrage, 10, 148, 212, 213, 214, 290, 291, 293, 307, 317, 321, 391

tax, 50, 115, 121, 131, 141, 142, 145, 147, 166, 183, 212, 229, 230, 232, 235, 251, 255, 265, 282, 283, 285, 292, 300, 307, 372, 378, 380, 381, 382, 383, 384, 385, 386

utopian, 216, 277, 381

worker, 6, 7, 32, 37, 48, 50, 97, 109, 110, 111, 112, 115, 116, 118, 130, 132, 143, 165, 166, 168, 178, 189, 206, 212, 213, 221, 264, 265, 274, 276, 317, 323, 344, 361, 389

working class, 10, 17, 46, 287, 386, 389, 391

[This page intentionally left blank.]